THE URBAN EXPERIENCE AND FOLK TRADITION

Publications of the American Folklore Society
Bibliographical and Special Series
General Editor, Wm. Hugh Jansen
Volume 22 · 1971

THE URBAN EXPERIENCE
and
Folk Tradition

edited by
AMÉRICO PAREDES
and ELLEN J. STEKERT

PUBLISHED FOR THE AMERICAN FOLKLORE SOCIETY BY
THE UNIVERSITY OF TEXAS PRESS · AUSTIN AND LONDON

International Standard Book Number 0–292–70122–5
Library of Congress Catalog Card Number 72–157253
Copyright © 1971 by the American Folklore Society

Composition and presswork by
The University of Texas Printing Division, Austin
Bound by Universal Bookbinders, Inc., San Antonio

CONTENTS

A PREFATORY NOTE

THIS VOLUME is essentially, of course, a reissue of the special issue, number 328, of the *Journal of American Folklore*. The decision to publish was arrived at in the usual way, through the polling of a jury of readers—nameless heroes who give selflessly of their time in order to support their discipline. It is, I gratefully acknowledge, due to the wise counsel of these readers that the order of materials has been rearranged for this volume and that a bibliography and an index have been added in order, we hope, to make the volume most effective and useful.

Although tradition frowns on immodest editors, I still confess that I feel this an important book, a pioneer book. Certainly no folklorist or any other scholar is so parochial as to suppose that his discipline discovered poverty or urban disease. But every folklorist should know that his discipline includes analytical techniques and perspectives that should assist all those concerned with urban problems. And in that way, this volume strikes a blow for ecumenical rapport among several scholarly fields.

It is a book that should incite pride in a number of people: Dr. Stekert, who conceived the original symposium; the Wayne State University Alumni Association, which sponsored that symposium; Dr. Paredes, who, with Dr. Stekert, labored to hammer the reports of the symposium into a unified special issue of the *Journal of American Folklore*; and the three anonymous readers who, while making the already-cited suggestions, unanimously accepted the work.

I am happy about it, too.

W. H. J.

FOREWORD

THE ARTICLES in this issue of the JOURNAL OF AMERICAN FOLKLORE are the result of a symposium on "The Urban Experience and Folk Tradition" held at Wayne State University, May 20–21, 1968, attended by a number of scholars interested in the ways the urban experience affects folk tradition and in avenues through which folklore studies might contribute to the understanding and solution of urban problems. My concerns in planning the symposium were twofold: to devote an entire series of papers to folklore in the urban environment and to bring together folklorists and scholars from other disciplines in an exchange of views.

Only a short while ago urban folklore seemed a strange, almost contradictory concept. What little folklore was collected in the cities usually was classified according to the rural area of the informant's origin or given other group or genre distinctions that avoided the idea of "urban." The most widely collected urban groups were the immigrant groups and the Negro migrant to the cities, undoubtedly because most of these people derived from "peasant" or rural communities. We have come a long way in accepting the fact that folklore exists in the city. Yet we should not pride ourselves too much, for the concept of urban folklore still needs definition. The idea poses basic questions ranging from "What is urban?" to "What is folklore?" And among other problems confronting us is the task of defining and developing methods of working with fads and mass media—cultural products that influence much of the urban dweller's world.

The papers that follow represent both old and new approaches to the study of urban traditions. Their approach is old in that they focus on traditions brought to the city and acted upon by the metropolis. Traditions that have originated and developed in the urban milieu are explored only fleetingly. The papers also reflect past approaches to urban tradition in that they treat the lore of groups low on the socioeconomic ladder. There is no direct treatment, for example, of traditions held by the white Anglo-Saxon, Protestant middle class, a group that has been called, for better or worse, the "dominant culture." But the papers and the discussions following them do offer new and important approaches to the study of tradition in the urban environment. They illustrate how an accurate knowledge of the traditions of different groups helps explain the currents of urban life. Folklorists who work in metropolitan areas are faced with networks of tradition far more complex than those encountered in less heterogeneous communities. The urban center is the scene of complex interaction between many groups with widely differing traditions. In some cases a new synthesis has developed, in others there has been minor change, while often the proximity of groups in the urban environment has bred conflict, fed by misunderstanding or ignorance of traditions and traditional behavior.

What follows is not an exact reproduction of what took place at the symposium. Some of the papers have been extensively revised; many of the discussants' comments also have been rewritten. Persons who presented papers were given the opportunity to reply in written statements to the revised comments on the revised papers. What appears here is the result of this convoluted give-and-take, accompanied by an edited version of the floor discussion. Hopefully, some of the energetic exchange of ideas that took place during the meetings has found its way into these pages.

Wayne State University
Detroit, Michigan

ELLEN J. STEKERT

INTRODUCTION

THE JOURNAL OF AMERICAN FOLKLORE is indebted to Ellen Stekert, organizer of the symposium "The Urban Experience and Folk Tradition," and to the participants in the symposium for their thorough discussion of a subject that still excites controversy. These papers are, without a doubt, a contribution to our discipline; but if the reader expects to find in them ready answers to the problems of urban lore, he will be disappointed. The symposium raised questions rather than answered them; its major conclusions are signposts along the roads that research in urban folklore must follow.

One thing made clear is that when the folklorist moves his field of operations from the country to the city he must reassess his theoretical and methodological equipment. This involves more than the usual, "Is there really such a thing as a folklore of the cities?" though such a question still is pertinent. It is raised by Linda Dégh in her prepared comments to Richard Dorson's paper, and one must admit that it is a question not completely settled for many folklorists, though the concept of urban folklore has gained much ground in recent decades.

If one goes by what people do rather than by what people say, one could use the papers presented here as an argument for Dégh's point of view. As Stekert herself admits in the Foreword, two of the four main papers deal almost exclusively with rural survivals in the city. Stekert's own paper is concerned with folk medicine developed among rural, "peasant" folk of European background over the centuries and what happens to it when it is transferred to an urban environment, where it no longer can perform all its old functions. Wilgus deals with the history of country music and its transformation into "citybilly" (to borrow his own term), once it comes to town. The papers by Abrahams and Dorson, though they range more widely, also touch upon the persistence of rural folkloric elements in the city. It is these elements, precisely, that Dégh singles out in her comments on Dorson's paper as what, in her opinion, may truly be called urban folklore.

In other words, urban folklore brings up again the question of survivals, conveniently laid to rest a generation or so ago. When anyone mentions survivals today, he is reminded that what appears to be a survival is merely a cultural item that has changed function. Yet, most antisurvivalists believe in the so-called dysfunctional principle in culture, what Ruth Benedict more than forty years ago called the "mammoth load of useless lumber" that weighs down most cultures—man-sized fishhooks, incest taboos that threaten tribal extinction, folk beliefs that result in cruelty, deprivation, or death for members of the group.[1] One could argue, of course, that there is no such thing as a dysfunctional cultural item, everything depending on the point of view. If a group of college students burn the dean's office, the act is quite dysfunctional from the viewpoint of the college as an entity, whether we view that entity as a Malinowskian organism or not. But burning the dean's office may be extremely functional from the viewpoint of the motivations of the students. Most of us can agree, however, that some things are more functional than others.

A common error has been the assumption that the survivalists of the nineteenth century saw no function at all in the materials they studied. But a reading of what they wrote shows that they were aware of such things, including some of the psychological functions of folklore. What distinguished the survivalist viewpoint was not the denial that folklore had a social and contemporary value (some survivalists, in fact, were believers in applied folklore). The distinguishing feature was the belief that the most important thing about folklore was its historical significance. Malinowskian functionalism, on the other hand, has an antihistorical bias, and a bias against geography as well—so that the whole cosmos may be apprehended in a Trobriand village.

The Malinowskian approach has been applied by folklorists to good advantage. In the collecting of folksong in rural areas, for example, it allowed us in the Americas to turn from an exclusive interest in old European ballads to contemporary folksong. But it often has blinded us to a difference between our living, creative traditions of songmaking and what I would call the "preserved" folksong traditions, valued by the folk group chiefly because they are old—in other words a difference between the active, viable folkloric item and the bit of history that still breathes. If this distinction has been blurred in rural areas, where it is a matter of the old versus the new, such is not the case in the cities, where the difference is brought into sharp focus. This was a point raised by Elli Kaija Köngäs a decade ago, apropos of immigrant folklore.[2] The student of urban folklore cannot help being aware of the difference between the living traditions of the city and the rural lore brought to town and adapted to the urban scene—given new forms and functions (as with Wilgus' country-western music) or surviving as "cultural lumber" (as with some of Stekert's items of rural folk medicine transported to the city).

The papers by Abrahams and Dorson include more of the living urban traditions, but they still are interested in the fortunes of rural lore in the city. Dorson's paper—as one would expect of a folklorist who also is a historian—has a strong historical tone. Abrahams alone focuses strongly on the living urban traditions, but even he becomes involved in historical matters, so that he feels it necessary to state that origins and dissemination of stereotypes are not after all his primary concern. They seem to be of primary concern, however, to some of those commenting on his paper. I would not say that the study of urban lore is going to make survivalists of us all, but it is worthwhile to take a second look at concepts we have thrown aside. They may have new uses for us, even if we must give them new labels.

[1] "The Science of Custom," *The Century Magazine,* 117 (1929), 641–649; reprinted in Alan Dundes, *Every Man His Way* (Englewood Cliffs, N.J., 1968), 180–188.

[2] "Immigrant Folklore: Survival or Living Tradition?" *Midwest Folklore,* 10 (Fall 1960), 117–123.

If the study of folklore in the city brings up theoretical problems, simply by reviving old questions, it also points up in dramatic fashion new problems in methodology. Collecting, analysis, and presentation of urban lore involve problems different from those faced by the folklorist working with "peasant" or "primitive" materials. In preparing his materials for publication, the worker in urban lore must develop the uncomfortable but necessary feeling that the people he is studying are looking over his shoulder as he writes. His informants can and do read, and they are becoming increasingly interested in what people from the universities say about them. What the folklorist publishes will in all probability be read, if not by the informants themselves at least by their friends and relatives, who will be more than glad to point out to the informants any inaccuracies or misrepresentations they think are there.

Some unpleasant experiences may befall the folklorist who undertakes work in the city with the same methodology he has applied to rural and primitive groups. He may—as is so often the case—take the approach of the nineteenth-century explorer returning from the wilds of Borneo or darkest Africa, eager to tell all about the fascinating savages he has met, painting colorful vignettes of his informants, describing their private lives in minute detail, humorously exhibiting the skeletons in their family closets as revealed to him in confidence, vividly describing their personal idiosyncrasies and giving names, genealogies, and all other identifying data. Then our urban folklorist may be extremely surprised to find himself facing a lawsuit. This very practical problem is one the folklorist in the city cannot ignore. He has to present his data as completely as possible if he is going to do a scholarly job; yet, there is much he cannot reveal. Where to draw the line, what to say and what to leave unsaid, becomes a problem. If the folklorist is too reticent, he may be accused by his colleagues of concealing information; if he is too revealing, he may draw the ire of his informants. The problem is familiar to other social scientists, sociologists for example, but it is pretty new to folklorists; and it is an especially difficult problem for us because we are interested in the kind of personal information that may give offense to the informant if published in its entirety.

In other words, the scholar working with urban folklore quickly discovers that the subjects of his research are able to talk back at him. One of the most interesting results of the Detroit symposium was the way the main speakers were challenged by the discussants and by participants from the floor. Some of these challenges were of the type one would expect in any scholarly meeting, made by colleagues who disagreed on points of theory or method. Such indeed were many of Marion Pearsall's comments on Stekert's paper and those by Linda Dégh and Leonard Moss on the paper by Dorson. But the remarkable thing was the number of speakers (some scholars and some not) who rose to challenge the learned doctors as spokesmen for their ethnic group, questioning not points of theory and method but the whole view of the subject under research, and at times questioning even the right of the scholar to do studies outside his own ethnic group.

In one instance this led to an addition to the materials of the symposium. Morton Leeds' paper was delivered as an after-dinner talk, with no formal commentary scheduled. But Lawrence E. Gary—a social scientist and articulate black intellectual—challenged Leeds so vigorously from the floor that he was invited to write

THE URBAN EXPERIENCE AND FOLK TRADITION

RICHARD M. DORSON

Is There a Folk in the City?

NORTH UIST LIES AMONG THE OUTER HEBRIDES in the Atlantic coastal sea, a Scottish outpost on the western edge of Europe. When the plane from Inverness swoops down toward the airport at Benbecula, the isle looks like a lonely crater of the moon, pockmarked with hollows and lifeless lakes, striated with mountainous ridges, coated with vapor. A nearer view is no more encouraging. There are no hotels, no villages, nothing but solitary crofters' stone cottages scattered at long intervals over the empty moors. A driving rain and wind blow across the moors, stinging the face and dampening the clothes. Trousers do not keep a press long in the Hebrides. Roads are primitive, and cars when they meet must jockey to find a "passing place," a widened shoulder of the road located at intervals, because the roads are all one way, whichever way you are going. Gaelic is the tongue everyone speaks from birth, and English is the second language.

This is the country and here are the folk known to folklorists. No richer tradition in the western world has been uncovered than the Gaelic treasure found in the Hebrides. John Francis Campbell of Islay gathered his classic four-volume *Popular Tales of the West of Scotland* (Edinburgh, 1860–1862) from the Hebrides and Highlands. Alexander Carmichael amassed five volumes of folk blessings, hymns, charms, and incantations from the same area in his *Carmina Gadelica* (Edinburgh and London, 1928–1953). At the present time John Lorne Campbell, laird of the Isle of Canna, continues to mine the isles, with book-length collections from single narrators on Barra and South Uist, while his wife, Margaret Fay Shaw, has brought forth a substantial sheaf of folksongs from South Uist. Even the hoard of Campbell of Islay and his collectors is still being tapped in the twentieth century, with two posthumous volumes of folktales and the impressive cache of local historical traditions titled *The Dewar Manuscripts* (Glasgow, 1964).

North Uist and the Hebrides are the case I offer as a classic illustration of the terrain of the folklorist and the concept of the folk. I was there the end of August 1967, accompanying a collector from the School of Scottish Studies in the University of Edinburgh, John MacInnes, himself island born and raised. Although the Hebrides have been so amply collected, and although only some two thousand souls remain on North Uist, John says there are layers upon layers of tradition still to be peeled, a lifetime of work. The people of North Uist are all one; their names begin with Mac, they appear all at some point to be interrelated; they have inhabited this isle for ten clear centuries. In common they speak Gaelic, farm the land, cut peat, and tend the sheep; and they visit each other in sociable *ceilidhs* in which they recall marvelous events of yore occurring on the isle. The name of almost every locality and landmark involves a tradition. Only in faith are they divided between Catholics and Protestants.

If the remote countryside, symbolized by North Uist, has provided the questing ground of the folklorist, what business has he in the city? On ready answer is that the folklorist deals with people, and the people have left the country and flocked to the cities. While North Uist has dwindled to a couple of thousand crofters, Gary in northwest Indiana has risen from empty sand dunes in 1906 to become a metropolis of 200,000, peopled by over fifty nationalities. To Gary and its neighbor East Chicago, one-third its size, I went in February 1968, to live under field conditions. Knowing no one, I sought to form contacts and interview representatives of the dominant ethnic groups. Gary received nation-wide publicity when it elected a Negro mayor, Richard G. Hatcher, on November 7, 1967, an election reflecting the rise in the city's colored population to over 50 percent. The other major groups in Gary are the Serbian, Croatian, Greek, and "Latin," a term that includes Mexicans and Puerto Ricans. Throughout Lake County as a whole the Poles predominate. East Chicago has proportionately a smaller Negro and a larger Latin element, with its mayor, John B. Nicosia, representing an earlier, now established Italian colony. When speaking of East Chicago the commentator must include Indiana Harbor, a community within the city; before they were combined, East Chicago and Indiana Harbor were known as the twin cities. They are still physically separated by a forest of giant oil drums and installations lined along Route 20. Close connections bind the two—or three—cities, for they are all part of the steel kingdom that has sucked into its fiery vortex the manpower of many peoples. Inland and Youngstown in East Chicago and U.S. Steel and Bethlehem in Gary are the regal plants that must be fed twenty-four hours a day, seven days a week, with iron ore and coal and tended by men and women. The need for laborers in the mills is never sated. First it was met by East Europeans from every Balkan country, then by southern Negroes, then by Mexicans and Puerto Ricans brought up in truckloads and planeloads concurrently with southern whites, who streamed north from Kentucky and southern Illinois, Virginia and Tennessee, Alabama and Louisiana. "Eighty-five percent of them around here is from the South," one Kentuckian observed airily.

Such a complex of ethnic and regional groups is bound to attract the folklorist, especially when the groups involved derive from the peasant-farmer and laboring classes. Linda Dégh and her husband Andrew Vaszonyi first penetrated Indiana Harbor in the winter of 1964–1965 and again in the summer of 1967, speaking with the sizable body of emigrants from their native Hungary. They had soon realized that one ethic group led into another, and my mission was to explore in a preliminary way these other groups. Born and schooled in New York City, living in London for three stretches totaling two years, and in Tokyo for ten months, I had experienced the world's largest cities, but never as a collector of folklore. My folklore field trips had taken me to the country towns. My present purposes were threefold: to ascertain if the folklorist could ply his trade in the city; to contrast the vitality of the traditions among the various ethnic and racial groups; and to observe the effect of life in an urban, industrial center upon these imported cultures.

Obviously a stay of twenty-three days can only begin to probe these questions. But experiences in the field can be intense and concentrated, they may yield intimate revelations into lives, experiences, hatreds, fears, and cherished symbols that one may never encounter in years of routine living. By "the field" I mean an area in which the folklorist lives completely divorced from his own usual schedule, occupation, and residence—a period in which he devotes all of his waking moments to making contacts, interviewing, recording, listening to and observing the people with whom he is concerned. In this sense I lived in the field in Gary, staying downtown in the environs of the Negro ghetto, in the recently bankrupt Hotel Gary, an integrated, gloomy structure no longer patronized by middle-class travelers.

Gary lies in northwest Indiana hard by Lake Michigan, a city created overnight on flat dunes in 1906 to house steelworkers and now grown to over 200,000 souls who live off steel. The reputation of Gary matches the sullen glow of the ever-lit furnaces in the mills, for, thanks in good part to a *Time* article, Gary symbolizes the urban jungle, crime-ridden, race-wracked, and cultureless. One's first impression driving into Gary along the endless central avenue of Broadway bisecting the city confirms the worst—particularly if the day (February 2, 1968) is rainy and drear, the surrounding countryside brown and muddy, and the roadsides deep in water. Broadway is lined with one-story joints, bars, liquor stores and increasingly crummy shops as one gets further down town into the Negro ghetto. A movie marquee reads "Greek movies on Saturday, Spanish on Sunday." Polluted air envelops the city, dust and grime cover the buildings, litter fills the alleys. Gloom, ugliness, and apprehension set the tone of Gary. Armed guards stand on the ready in every bank, and the buses cease running in the early evening because of knifings of waiting passengers. Drivers lock their car doors and sweat out the red lights. "We were held up here last month on payday at noon by four Negro gunmen, when the guard stepped out for a coffee break," a welfare agency director told me my first day in Gary. "I'm hoping to move the office away from here [16th and Broadway] soon; we're right in the midst of the pimps, queers, dope pushers, and whores. Even while I've been talking to you someone has been observing the layout." And he nervously wiped his white brow and looked at the sea of black faces.

One of the quests of this trip was to see if and how a folklorist could operate in a strange city among a number of ethnic and racial groups. To make contacts I visited Negro Baptist churches on four successive Sundays; called on Harold Malone, father of a Negro student of mine in Bloomington; dropped in on the International Institute of Gary, where a Serbian, a Greek, and a young black woman all introduced me to people; made the acquaintance of William Passmore, head of the Job Corps office in East Chicago, who kindly offered me a wealth of leads; looked up likely informants from student folklore collections turned in to a folklore course at the Northwest Campus in Gary; hung around the dilapidated Baltimore Hotel opposite the Inland Steel plant; followed suggestions from a trustee of Indiana University living in Gary, Robert Lucas. It was the old story of developing contacts through all likely means, chasing around town, calling people up to make appointments, trying to explain my mission. But I found persons in every group hospitable and friendly and often anxious to talk of their experiences and of life in the "Region," as this pocket of northwest Indiana is locally called. The following pages, some extracted from my field diary, attempt to convey a sense of the cultural pluralism in urban folklore.

The Negro

My few weeks in Gary and East Chicago did not uncover a master folk narrator, although one may well be there. In no group indeed did I encounter a narrator of this type, though I did meet excellent talkers. Let me consider Negro tradition under the heads of proverbs, tales, voodoo, and the folk church.

On two occasions I heard northern-born, educated Negroes—who had looked blankly at me when I asked about Old Marster and Brother Buzzard—employ patently Negro proverbs to crystallize an idea and drive home a thought in the course of a tense discussion. The first situation developed in the Job Corps office on Columbus Avenue in East Chicago, where I met Willie P., both of whose legs had been amputated while he was in his teens because of a spinal disease. His mother, Laura, 73, a snowy-haired fragile old lady born in Alabama, granddaughter of a slave, related to me with quavering voice and perfect command of dates the series of long hospital sieges and near-fatal operations that Willie had endured patiently and even cheerfully. The Déghs had put me in touch with Willie, who knew all the civic leaders in East Chicago and gave me every assistance. This morning Willie—boyish, studious-looking and gentle, who at times had double-dated with Mayor Hatcher—was giving a little moralizing talk to three Negro boys of fourteen and fifteen, dropouts and potential delinquents. The boys squirmed and twisted uneasily as Willie lectured them from his wheelchair behind his desk. Willie had lapsed into the soft, slurred tones that colored people frequently use with each other. He reiterated the need for them to stay in school, to train themselves for their future jobs, to learn discipline. "A hard head makes a hard bed," he said climactically.

No proverb could have been more appropriate. "Hard head" is a phrase current among southern Negroes, who use it in jocular ghost tales about revenants that return in answer to a relative's prayer but outstay their welcome; hence the comment, "Brother, that's how come you dead now, you so hard-headed." The teller explains parenthetically, "Head hard or head long means you go looking for trouble."[1] Willie summarized and capped his message with this pithy saw.

Another day I was in the Children's Public Library of East Chicago talking with Mrs. Edna W., college-educated, precise in speech, decorous in manner, a world away from Old Marster. She began speaking about the conditions of the Negro and the election of Mayor Hatcher, but in a note rarely reported. This was a note of mistrust of Negro aggressiveness, a fear of consequences stemming from Hatcher's election, distress at the stridency of Negro youths no longer respectful of their elders. "There are one-third of us who feel this way, but our

---

[1] See Richard M. Dorson, *American Negro Folktales* (New York, 1967), 328.

voice won't be heard. I won't be heard in Washington." She was telling me more than she had ever told anyone. Mrs. W. was opposed to open housing. Let the whites and the blacks each live by themselves; people are not comfortable in surroundings they are not used to. "I don't want to be a fly in the buttermilk," she said. And so, to dramatize her opposition to the open-housing ordinance, so strong an article of faith to Negro militants and white liberals, the librarian had recourse to a Negro proverb with apt color imagery.

The tales that seemed to me so much a touchstone of Negro folk tradition were slow in coming. At first I was the carrier and the teller. But in the course of two evenings (one in the home of the Reverend H. J., pastor of a store-front church, with an evangelist preacher and a deacon present, the other in the home of the Reverend B. G., pastor of a Baptist church, along with his deacon L. T., southerners all and steelworkers all) tales came to the surface, one triggering another. They were old favorites: "The Coon in the Box," "Dividing Soul," "Poll Parrot and Biscuits," "Why the Fox Has a Short Tail." But as I was going out the door, the Reverend H. J. thought of one entirely new to me, "The Train Going Uphill and Downhill," employing slow, drawn-out phrases for the uphill climb, and fast, chug-chug phrases for the descent.[2] Charles K. of the Gary Human Relations Commission told me a number of civil-rights stories with which he and his companions had whiled away the time during his six jail confinements for demonstrating. One was a television variant of the old Negro down South who hollers "Help!" on the radio when urged by southern governors to tell how well he is treated.[3] Another was a Negro variant of a Jewish joke about the would-be radio announcer with a dreadful stutter who claims he is the victim of bias. Civil-rights stories (the phrase is the informant's) are one segment of the southern Negro repertory which thrives and expands in northern cities.

One interview disclosed a displacement of tale tradition by book tradition, albeit not a learned book tradition. Todd R., 70, who had come from Alabama to Gary in 1922 and worked for forty years in the steel mills before retiring, remembered nostalgically the South and "country living" as the best in the world. But he told only one tale, "The Race" (Type 1074), in the shortest version I ever heard: "The rabbit and the turtle had a race; the rabbit stopped to pick berries and the turtle won." He stirred briefly to the legend of the snake and the child and said he had heard in Alabama that the girl died when her father killed her pet snake. Todd's real interest lay in reciting names, dates, and facts about Negro Americans, garnered from two battered and tattered booklets he showed me: *Afro-American World Almanac*, and *A Tribute to Achievement* issued by the Pfeiffer Brewing Company.

Voodoo or cunjer seemed at first as invisible as folktales. Harold M. took me calling on a family friend, Mrs. Katie S., a school matron born in Memphis, friendly, poised, and proper. The only element of tradition she displayed dealt with cuisine, "soul food," the Negro diet of turnip greens, chitterlings, corn bread, cabbage, sweet potatoes, which kept together bodies and souls of colored folk in the South. The cheaper cuts and leavings of the hog and cow—neckbone, pig feet, pot licker—were nutritious. Old Marster gave them to the slaves, and

---

[2] Compare "The Mean Boss," Ibid., 156–157.
[3] See "The Governor's Convention," Ibid., 319–320.

the slaves throve, while the white people fell prey to rare diseases. To my question whether she liked the food of other groups in Gary, Mrs. S. replied that she enjoyer *tacos* until she heard that the Mexicans were cutting up cats for the meat. When we left her house I asked Harold Malone about her husband. Andrew S. had been born in Coldwater, Mississippi, had come to Gary in 1943, and was now laid up in the hospital, claiming he had been voodooed by his son, who had given him canned corn that turned to worms.

Another voodoo case was headlined in the Chicago *Daily Defender*, the only American Negro daily, on February 20, the day I drove into its office with Bill Passmore, who wrote a weekly column for them on East Chicago news. The city editor, Thomas Picou, a severe young intellectual, talked to be about his paper's philosophy of cohesion and adequate news coverage for the Negro. He did not have much to say about the banner headline of the day, "Possessed by 'Voodoo': Mother Charged in Triple Slaying," blazoned on the front page. The news story appeared on page three and is reproduced below.

MOTHER OF FOUR CHARGED IN 'VOODOO' SLAYING

Husband, Two Aunts
Killed at Reception

By Donald Mosby
(Daily Defender Staff Writer)

A 27-year-old mother of four, who thinks she is possessed by "a voodoo lizard," was charged yesterday with killing her husband and his two aunts at a suburban wedding reception.

Held without bond is Mrs. Ruby Luckett, 107 Riverview Ave., Lockport, whom, one wedding guest said, "looked is if she were in a daze," moments before she reputedly shot the trio Sunday night. Mrs. Luckett is accused of killing her husband, Peter, 29, a laborer, and his aunts, Mrs. Sadie Porter, 62, of 404 E. 72d St., and Mrs. Lisa Harper, 43, of 118 Oak Ave., of Lockport. Luckett died yesterday in St. Francis Hospital.

According to Dixmoor Ptl. John North, the shooting deaths grew out of an argument between Mrs. Luckett and her husband in the basement of 14337 S. Honore, Dixmoor, where a wedding reception for Luckett's sister was in progress. The home belongs to Sullivan Wright, brother of the groom.

North said Mrs. Luckett shot her husband during the height of an argument and repeated the attack upstairs when she saw Luckett's aunts—Mrs. Harper and Mrs. Porter—sitting on a couch.

Luckett was shot in the chest, Mrs. Harper, in the chest and Mrs. Porter in the head.

According to the suburban policeman, Mrs. Luckett feared her relatives were practicing some kind of "voodoo power" against her.

Mrs. Luckett was driven to Dixmoor police headquarters by some departing wedding guests, who were apparently unaware of what had happened inside the home.

According to police, Mrs. Luckett admitted shooting the trio, and handed over to police a .38 calibre revolver, believed to be the death weapon.

In court yesterday, she told a judge her relatives had put a lizard in her stomach as part of a voodoo spell and that she had to keep salt and water under her bed to satisfy the voodoo curse. Mrs. Luckett is scheduled to appear in Midlothian Court March 21.

The *Daily Defender* story called to the mind of one of my companions, Larry J., an account he had heard of a girl who voodooed the man of her desire. This man was paying her no heed, so on the advice of a girl friend she obtained two pairs of his pants and hung them up in her closet, and now the couple were living together.

For the core of Negro traditional expression, behavior, and belief we must turn to the church. Gary possesses over two hundred Negro churches. On successive Sundays I visited the First Baptist, the Calvary Baptist, and the St. John Primitive Baptist churches; these represented, in descending order, the scale of affluence, status, prestige, and denial of southern Negro culture. The First Baptist Church building was brand new, facing a pleasant park, cathedral-like in its dimensions, upper-class white in its service. Professional people attended this church—doctors, lawyers, teachers. The women vied with each other in the loftiness and dazzling colors of their hats. All was decorous and efficient; the congregation sang from hymnbooks, the minister preached with dignity, and only the faintest responses of "Amen" and "That's the truth" echoed his words. But with the Calvary Baptist Church—also in a new but much less pretentious building— the institutions of southern Negro folk religion came into view. Here was a highly personal, joking, exhorting, chanting pastor, F. Brannam Jackson, recalling the days when he was a little old barefoot boy on the bayou, and mosquitoes were so large they were called gallinippers, and when they stung you, you felt as if you had lockjaw. Here was a swaying, throbbing choir, singing without hymnbooks, reinforced by pianist and organist and the responsive congregation, spurred on by ecstatic soloists, who would interrupt their songs to cry "Shout out." In the front row sat a uniformed nurse, who sprang into action when a heavy woman a few rows back "got happy" and with some others fanned her vigorously back into normalcy.

A new item in the Gary *Post Tribune* had caught my eye, "Negro Plight is Theme," announcing the "annual Homecoming Day" at the Calvary Baptist Church in honor of Negro history week, with a full program of service, chicken dinner, panel speakers, and a slave-time play, in honor of Negro History week. The three speakers were each in his own way highly articulate and impressive. Twenty-four-year-old Bill Joiner, first Negro manager of a branch of the Gary National Bank, was modest and quiet-spoken; Mrs. Nancy Brundige, an urban sociologist for the city of Chicago, was positive and direct; and Charles H. King, director of the Gary Human Relations Commission, was a performer of shattering eloquence. These were Negro intellectuals telling the Negro folk about business opportunities, historical achievements, and spiritual strengths of their race with a conviction and force deeply admired by the one white auditor. The whole day was indeed a testimonial to the facility of Negro oral expression in singing and speaking. As King said, Negroes were the greatest singers in the world because church singing was their one permitted mode of utterance. He rocked the audience with illustrations of phrases from spirituals taken in their innocuous literal sense by the slavemasters, but intended in quite specific and material ways by the singers (a matter often debated by white scholars). King made a number of effective points: that segregation began after, not during, slavery, for the slave could attend the same church as his master, even though he had to sit in the gallery (hence Lincoln's Emancipation Proclamation was the biggest lie in American history); that the church was the center of Negro fellowship and community life, for it was the Negro's only social organization ("The Negro stays in church all day, while the white man comes for an hour and leaves; isn't that so, Professor?"); that the Baptist church was most available to the Negro, for it required no superstructure of outside authorities.

After these speeches and a comment I was called on to make, the chairs were rearranged, and an informal playlet presented, "De Lawd, the Negroes' Hope in a New Home." The scene was ostensibly laid on a slave plantation, and the appearance of members of the congregation in cotton dresses and sun bonnets, idly stroking a butter churn and a wash board, sent the spectators into spasms of laughter. Most of the action was confined to a chorus singing such spirituals as "Climbing Jacob's Ladder," "Deep River," and "There'll be a Great Day When We All Gather Home." At the conclusion the attractive young wife of the pastor made a statement on the zeal of the performers (one had canceled a trip to New Orleans in order to be present) and the historical relevance of the drama. "I would rather be the persecuted than the persecutors." Negro church songs were often hard to follow. I asked a Negro friend about this, and he said he himself could not be sure of the words, since the singers picked up words listening to each other.

The Primitive Baptist Church represented still another aspect of Negro worship, the extended family unit with aspirations for autonomy. A dozen adults and a dozen children were present the two Sundays I attended, and the obese woman who led the choir of five—and supplied one daughter to the choir and five to the Sunday school—was the pastor's sister-in-law. Yet the group met in a neat, fresh-painted room in their own small building, acquired four months before for five thousand dollars. Previously they had held services in a dingy store-front up the block. Elder George M. had carpentered and plastered the new church himself. He had worked in the steel mills for eleven years and made thirty-seven dollars a day instructing crane operators, although he could neither read nor write. When I expressed surprise he called his wife, "Tell this guy how I can't read." He had been born in Arkansas and educated at Muncie Central on a football scholarship, apparently doing well in classes in spite of his handicap. He received special instruction from a white teacher at Ball State University. He had possessed the gift of preaching since he was five, being ordained by the Lord.

Handsome, athletic, still young, he preached with fervor and intensity, dipping his knees, holding a handkerchief or book to his right cheek, intoning phrases in a rising cadence with closed eyes, sometimes opening out and shaking his palms. The Primitive Baptists believed in "making a joyful noise unto the Lord" and in footwashing, which they practiced one Sunday in the month. Elder M. gave me permission to record the service the following Sunday, and asked me to play it back in church. Listening intently, he remarked, "That sounds just like country singing." Any listener would marvel at how so small a group could fill the room with song, chant, and response in swelling harmony. The elder had served as minister for five years and commented about himself, "I'm the most unlearned pastor they had, and carried them the furthest." He obtained historical references from a book his wife read to him, which he showed me, *World's Great Men of Color, 3000 B.C. to 1946 A.D.* by J. A. Rogers, published at 37 Morningside Avenue in New York.

Negro folk religion or traditional worship, as characterized in these observations, is directly connected with civil rights and urban politics. This point was ingeniously made by Charles H. King when I recorded a talk with him in his basement office in the Gary Municipal Building. King was forty-two, dark and mottled in complexion, burly in physique. His mother had been born in Boston, his father in Atlanta, and he himself in Albany. A regular contributor to *Negro Digest* with perceptive articles on the Negro church, King had shown me an autobiographical chapter of an unpublished manuscript in which he described the attempt of his father, a preacher in Harrisburg, Pennsylvania, to have young Charles "get religion" through exposure to a visiting revivalist. Charles was not converted and was painfully embarrassed. He ended the chapter by saying he later experienced religion in his own way. When I asked him how, he related an experience that had befallen him when he was eighteen as a sailor in the United States Navy on shore leave. Two shore patrolmen, southern whites, ordered him, "Boy, straighten your cap," and when he reacted too slowly, poked him in the ribs and called him nigger. King slugged one, and they dragged him off to the guardhouse and lashed him two hundred times with a belt, the buckle leaving permanent scars on his back. At his trial, the ship's captain mocked him publicly, saying, "So they called you nigger. Well what did you expect them to call you?"

After that episode King felt a need for faith, but he developed his own concept of social relevance in his ministry, employing the techniques of the southern Baptist preacher while rejecting the escapism into heavenly hopes. King pointed out that Negro civil rights leaders—and he named a string, beginning with Martin Luther King—were all former ministers. He too belonged to this sequence, having pastored for three years at Clarksville, Tennessee, and for ten years at Evansville, Indiana. Negro civil rights agitators used the same devices on the platform they had employed on the altar—the incantatory repetition (Jees-us, Jees-us), the encouragement of shouting, the emotional singing—but now it was all channeled into the specific goals of earthly recognition for the Negro. King cleverly illustrated the mincing, polite singing of an all-white church at Miller whose choir had practiced a spiritual in his honor the day he came as guest preacher, and his own booming, leather-lunged rendition he demonstrated to them as a corrective. "When I was finished, there were at least eight people with wet eyes." Such expertly manipulated sounds induced in the Negro congregations the mass hypnotism or cataleptic trances popularly known as "getting happy," and now Negro social reformers and politicians were arousing their audiences with these traditional means. King himself decried unbridled emotionalism for either theological or extremist ends, and gave me an article he had just written, "The Specter of Black Power," describing a Black Power symposium he had attended, and sharply criticized, at Howard University.[4]

An extraordinary opportunity to see a concrete illustration of King's thesis came the evening of February 14, when I found myself in a crowded basement room where the Political Alliance Club of Northwest Indiana was meeting. This was an organization for minority groups, but the members were all Negro save for one or two Puerto Ricans. A tense, chunky white woman, obviously under con-

---

[4] *Sign: National Catholic Magazine* (February 1968), 13–17.

siderable strain, sat in the speaker's chair. This was Marion Tokarsky, now a celebrity for revealing the vote fraud attempted against Mayor Hatcher.[5] That very day she was on the front page of the Gary *Post Tribune*, in a garbled story saying the prosecutor was dropping charges against her—her punishment by the machine for her public revelations—in return for her turning state's evidence. The only white person present besides myself was a policeman, appointed by Hatcher as part of her twenty-four-hour protection. Mrs. Tokarsky spoke a rough and sloppy English, not the clumsy English of the immigrant but the street English of the little-schooled American. She delivered her recital of the attempted vote fraud, and her decision to break with the Democratic Party machine and support Hatcher, in the form of a divine revelation.

"I am no saint," she began, "just an instrument of the Lord," and she repeated this thought at intervals. Her tale was a melodrama which would make Hollywood thrillers seem plausible. She had been a staunch Democratic committee-woman for twelve years in Glen Park, the residential center of the anti-Negro east Europeans. The machine turned against Hatcher, not because he was a Negro but because he would not do their bidding. Last July they had given her a sample voting machine with instructions on how to split the ticket and vote against Hatcher. She smuggled a sample voting machine in her shopping bag to show Hatcher, who had a picture taken of it. Democrats and Republicans alike were working to defeat Hatcher; some 5,280 names were removed from the voting rolls. Marion Tokarsky went through a period of doubt and confusion, at one time questioning Hatcher's loyalty. "I prayed as I never prayed before." The federal government flew in, and assured her she would not be involved or have to go to court.

Then one day the subpoena came. She turned over the matter all day Saturday, and at twelve o'clock Mass the Sunday before election she prayed directly to God. She explained to her Baptist audience that as a Catholic she had always before prayed to Saint Anthony or the Blessed Virgin, who could get the ear of the Lord in her behalf. But now she prayed directly. " 'God, please just give me the courage to go to court tomorrow. If I find just a few words in this missal I'll have courage.' And it was as if He had come right down from heaven." She opened the missal, and right before her eyes, in the Book of Psalms, was the word she had requested: " 'In the midst of the Assembly he opened his mouth. . . . The mark of the just man tells wisdom and his tongue tells what is right.' And I thanked God. Now I asked God to show me that Hatcher would win. 'Cause I knew I was crucified if he didn't."

Again the Lord answered her with an apt quotation.

And the next day when I went to court I didn't have to think, the words came right out of my mouth. And the defense lawyers asked me questions that I gave answers to, made them look like jackasses. So it was someone bigger than me doing it. They asked, "Mrs. Tokarsky, will you testify that a Democratic official asked you to do something illegal?" "Yes," I said, "if you'll name them one by one." "Why won't you name them, don't you know them?" "Yes," I answered, "but I don't know if you do." At that they reddened and asked two names, to which I said yes, and then they stopped. I called the mayor Sunday evening and said, "Dick, this is Marion. You know, you're going to win the election." And I read to

[5] *Time*, November 17, 1967, p. 26.

him out of the missal. He said to me, "Ever since the primary I knew I was going to win. But this is the most glorious thing that has happened to me."

There was a good deal more in this vein. Mrs. Tokarsky was fired from her job, arrested and jailed, her children spat on, her husband, who had just renovated his gas station, threatened. But the Lord sustained her throughout. "The day that I was arrested and they put me in jail, I didn't feel one ounce of sorrow or regret. I felt elated." This was on December 29, and on New Year's Eve, alone with her children, she asked God for another message and found it in Psalms 19:13, "O Lord, you heard His voice cry to you from the temple . . . devising a plot and they will fall into it themselves."

Throughout the narration, the listeners interjected the customary responses of Baptist congregations, especially when Mrs. Tokarsky underlined her points with such precepts as "Faith can really move a mountain" and "God helps those who help themselves." At the end of her talk an elderly gentleman in the front row cried out, "That's the gospel. It should be heard all over the world." Defying all the rules, the representative of the Slavic groups in Glen Park had made common cause with the ghetto Negroes. Their medium of communication was the political revival meeting, and together they saw Mayor Hatcher as blessed by the Lord in the battle against the forces of evil. Marion Tokarsky was the prophet through whom God has spoken. In recompense for her sacrifice, the Negro community is heavily patronizing her husband's gas station.

Serbians

"The Serbians live on tradition and heritage," observed one of my new Serbian friends. More than any other ethnic group in Gary and East Chicago, the Serbians do indeed cherish and abide by their Old World inheritance, an inheritance vivid and sorrowful in their minds, from the battle of Kossovo in 1389, when they sank heroically in defeat before the Turks, down to the Chetnik battles against Nazi Croatians and Tito's Communists. This is not book history but live and remembered history, as Americans rarely remember and identify with their own. Several Gary Serbs explained that orally recited history kept alive the Serbian spirit during five centuries of Turkish oppression and darkness. When the Turks blinded the learned clergy, the priests sang from memory heroic recitations of the Serbs, accompanying themselves on the one-stringed fiddle, the *gusle,* which they improvised from a stick and a strand of horsehair after the Turks confiscated their musical instruments. All the Serbs I met were proud and sad. Eighty-year-old George R., still erect and twinkling, recited emotionally a *gusle* song he had learned over seventy years before in Serbia. Thirty-one-year-old Walter T. has been in the States only since 1956, with his wife Milly (Miholjka), whom he brought over in 1963 from his native village, making sure she wasn't "brainwashed." Red-haired Milane S., a fiery Montenegrin with an LL.D., rushed at me when I came into her boss's office carrying a tape recorder and asked if I was a Communist spy; but I ended by taping her experience as a Chetnik fighter who escaped through Communist lines. Dragich B. ("Blaz"), an ex-waiter and former Chetnik, thrust his story upon me in the Chetnik-run Europa cafe. Rade R., the oak-chested leader of the mother church group in East Chicago, wept three times while recounting atrocities committed against his people in the second World War.

These and other Serbs showed the effect of a common tradition. They shuddered at the crimes of the hated Ustashis, who allegedly had butchered two million Serbs during the last war. Walter T. gave me a booklet, *The Crime of Genocide*, published by the Serbian National Defense Council of America (Chicago, 1951), that contained shocking pictures of mutilated women and children and a decapitated priest's head held by grinning Ustashis as well as an introductory anecdote about Ante Pavelich, the Croatian Ustashi leader, exhibiting on his desk a wicker basket filled with forty pounds of human eyes. Rade R. gave me a copy of the book *Genocide in Satellite Croatia, 1941–1945* (Chicago, n.d.) by Edmond Paris, translated from the French, and documenting these horrors. I recorded eye-witness atrocities related by Walter T. and his godfather; by Milos R., who had lost fifteen members of his family during the war; and by Rade R. and his wife, Mira, born in Novi Sad. Rade, as a Belgrade policeman, had been called to pick up the bodies of eight children floating down the Sava river with the head of their mother nailed to a board, under a sign reading, "A present from the Ustashis." Mira had seen the Hungarian troops bomb the Danube ice and push Serbian and Jewish families into the water underneath. Overwhelming bitterness against the Croatians, the Nazis, and the Communists filled their talk. The Communists especially aroused their passion, and they saw signs of communism and communist propaganda everywhere in America—among the Negroes, the hippies, the clergy.

A great split rent the solidarity of American Serbs in 1963, over the so-called mother church issue. One wing rejected the authority of the mother church in Belgrade and its edict redistricting the American diocese, whose seat was in Libertyville, Illinois. They called the opposing faction communists, and were in turn labeled schismatics. The issue resulted in bitter litigation, still in progress, and divided the Gary and East Chicago Serbs into two churches in each city. Rade represented the mother church faction in East Chicago, and he minimized the differences between Serbs and Croats, saying both fought equally with the Chetniks and Partisans. He himself had been born in Croatian Bosnia but belonged to the Serbian church. He told of Ustashis so hungry they ordered the camp cooks to fry livers of young boys. Both factions presented their case vigorously to me, and the only sure conclusion one could draw was that the most cohesive of all the ethnic groups in Steeltown had fallen into civil war.

National and folk traditions blend in the lives of the Serbian steelworkers. *Gusle* singers perform in Gary at saint's day family parties and recite the old heroic lays. Draža Mihajlovich, the Chetnik leader whom the Serbs feel was betrayed by Roosevelt and Churchill at Yalta, is the most recent of the venerated heroes extending back to Marko Kraljevich and Miloš Obilich. The analogy between oppression under the Turks and under the Communists is often drawn. Historical plays presented in Saint Sava Church so excited emotions that members of the audience pelted the Turks, played by their own friends. George R. recited for me in Serbian the "Gusle Song" describing a renegade Serbian who joined the Turks. One day finding a *gusle*, he attempted to play it but could not, because "the *gusle* does not lie." He bent tearfully over the instrument, imploring forgiveness, and a Turk whacked off his head. In the basement of Saint Sava Church I observed a program of Serbian songs, dances, and speeches with not a word of English used. After the stage program young and old joined hands in the traditional *cola* dance to the accompaniment of two thumping accordion players.

The most striking example of Serbian cultural nationalism in Gary is the story of Bishop Varnava Nastich. He was born in Gary on January 31, 1914, the son of an immigrant barber, and was baptized Voislav in the Saint Sava Serbian Orthodox Church. As a child he excelled at *gusle* performances, and clippings refer to him as a youthful prodigy in reciting Serbian folklore and old ballads, even being taken on tour to Serbian communities in other cities. He also served as altar boy in Saint Sava Church. At the age of nine, in 1923, he left Gary with his parents, brother, and sister for Yugoslavia. His father operated the popular "American Restaurant" on King Alexander Avenue in Sarajevo. Within three or four years after their return, Voislav had won the gold medal awarded by King Alexander to the best boy *guslar*. At eighteen he undertook theological studies and graduated from the theological faculty of the University of Belgrade in 1937. Three years later he took monastic vows in the monastery at Mileshevo and changed his name to Varnava. During the war years, 1941–1945, Varnava refused a bishopric in the so-called Croatian Orthodox Church of the Nazi puppet state under Ante Pavelich. In 1945 he was ordained a priest, and in August 1947 he was consecrated a bishop. Within a year he was arrested and brought to trial by Tito's government, actually for speaking against communism, ostensibly for collaborating with the Ustashi, an infamous charge. There followed eleven years of imprisonment, harassment, surveillance, brutality, and death by poisoning, according to half a dozen informants, including Saint Sava's priest, Father Peter Bankerovich, who with others tape-recorded for me a statement about Varnava. Father Peter recalled how a telegram announcing the death of Bishop Varnava was delivered in the midst of the high celebration in church on the fiftieth anniversary of the founding of Saint Sava, November 14, 1964. He gave me a copy of the 368-page commemoration book printed in Gary in both Serbian and English, and concluded his taped remarks by reading from the communication sent by Bishop Varnava from Monastery Beocin on September 3, 1964. One paragraph reads:

"I rejoice, because your Feast is my personal feast also, for I was among the first of your Altar-boys and I was the first one after the formation of your Church congregation to whom was given the rank of 'Chtec'—Reader—under the arch of your Church. Under the blessed heaven of your Church Community, my first formation of my physical and graceful-spirited life sprouted."[6]

A play was written and produced in Gary in January 1965 about Bishop Varnava, "Martyr to Communism," acted in the Saint Sava Church auditorium by children, to acquaint them with his heroic life and death. I read the typescript of the play in the home of its author, Daisy Wuletich, Gary-born, who had visited the Bishop in 1961 in Beocin Monastery with her mother, born in Montenegro.

[6] *St. Sava Serbian Orthodox Church Fiftieth Anniversary: Our Religious Heritage in America, 1914–1964; November 14–15, 1964.* (Gary, n.d.)

Daisy had drawn from personal letters of the Bishop, from an account of the trial in the booklet *Our Spiritual Hero,* and from her personal observations. The play itself was simple fare, a first act depicting the trial, in which the bishop defied the communist judges to the cheers of the crowd, and a second act set in the hospital showing him in familiar scenes before receiving a fatal injection. Thus he talks with his uncle about the car "pesho," a Peugeot given him by the Gary church so that he could travel around the country. He writes in a letter to his Gary friends, "I realize that at any time my car can turn into a Cross for me. This is its Cross-aspect of this Cross-aspect, too, is one and not the least of the reasons for my loving it so." The car became a symbol of his persecution, for it was exorbitantly taxed by the Communists. In the play this diagogue takes place:

Uncle: How sentimental you are about the car! You take better care of it than some people do of their own children.
Bishop: My little Pesho is important to me.
Marko: How fervently you speak of your car!
Bishop: I do speak of it fervently and I love it fervently! One reason being, of course, the American-red blood in me.

In another place in the play Bishop Varnava alludes to a visit he made to the shrine of Saint Basil (Vasilije) at Ostrog in Montenegro to pray for his sick mother. Daisy and her mother, Cveta, had also visited Ostrog, and Cveta, a sickly old woman, now told in Serbian, and Daisy translated, a miracle she had heard in Trebinje, the town where she was born in 1893.

A Turkish girl in Trebinje was all doubled up. No doctor could help her. So her parents finally took her to the shrine of Saint Basil in a basket up the mountain. They left the basket there all night. And when they came in the morning she was perfectly well and straight and walked down the mountain. The basket was placed at the foot of the coffin. The girl left a necklace of gold ducats in the chapel as her gift.

Then the people asked her what kind of a doctor is this Vlasha (a derogatory term used by the Turks against the Serbs). She answered, "No doctor, just a stiffened Vlasha." And that night when she went to bed, her body was deformed again. In the morning she found the ducats under her pillow.

She went back two or three times again but was never cured.

The Wuletichs showed me pictures of the monastery of St. Basil carved out of the mountainside, and Cveta graphically illustrated, with sudden animation and sweeping gestures along the wall, how the Nazis had bombed all around the shrine without every effecting a direct hit. So the modern legend of Bishop Nastich has formed a link with the historic legend of Saint Basil. There is also a connection with Saint Sava, the patron saint of children, since the play was performed by children on January 31, the birthday of Bishop Nastich and the nearest Sunday in 1965 to January 27, the death day of Saint Sava.

Another evening found me in the home of Mrs. Emily B., a first cousin of the bishop, who had in her possession boxes full of letters, photographs, clippings and memorabilia of Varnava's career. Her father had come to Gary in 1906 from a town in Montenegro near that of Vanava's father and helped lay tracks for the streetcar. Her husband Djordje had fought with the Chetniks alongside Milande Spadijer. Emily, a sad, dark-haired woman of fifty-six with a slight hunchback, confided to me that Montenegro was the cradle of Serbian culture, language, and songs. Her mother was the sister of Varnava's father, who founded the Saint Sava Church in Gary, and Emily herself had taken care of the boy, a few years her junior. It was clear that the bishop's tragedy was her obsession. She showed me a photograph of Varnava—ascetic, bespectacled, talking to another bishop, with a dim figure from the Udba, Tito's secret police, in the background beside an automobile—and another of his funeral (sent her by her uncle), his body resting in a plain open casket, while the patriarch-german can be seen in white cap instead of black, an obvious mark of disrespect. Emily told of the cruel "accident" planned by the Communists in 1949 when Varnava was being taken from the prison of Sjenica to that at Srem. The guards placed the prisoners in a car on a siding, and at about 1:00 A.M. the engine rammed into it at full steam. All but eleven were killed. Varnava was thrown out of the window with both legs and one arm broken. A witness immediately telephoned his brother. However the militia put a guard at the scene of the accident, and the Udba prevented medication being given or the insertion of metal pins in his heels. Varnava was placed in an army train without mattresses or covers and taken to a hospital in Srem.

Emily and her fellow Serbs in Gary had worked ceaselessly to obtain the release and return of the bishop, through pressure on the State Department and the Indiana senators. The Saint Sava group hoped that Varnava might even succeed Dionisije as the American bishop at Libertyville. After the 1963 edict of the mother church creating three North American bishops, Varnava entered the controversy with letters supporting the anti-Communist stand of the Serbian Free Church. Emily showed me some of his letters, written in mixed Serbian and English; the English prose was eloquent and idiomatic. Varnava never lost his American spirit, Emily said; when he first went to Yugoslavia he wrote how he missed his movie idols Tom Mix and William S. Hart, chewing gum, the funny papers, and electric light switches.

Had a *gusle* song been written about the Bishop? I asked Emily. She produced a three-and-a-half-page typescript, running fifty-seven lines a page, titled *Smrt Vladike Varnave*, "The Death of Bishop Varnava," composed by Milisav Maksimovich, of Cincinnati, Ohio, and dated April 3, 1965.

The mother church group with whom I met at Rade Z.'s house in East Chicago promptly deflated Varnava, saying the Gary people had made a legendary figure out of hot air. It was a myth that the Communists beat him up; actually he had jumped off a train. He was not a true diocesan bishop but an assistant vicar bishop. The fact was that by his fruitless outcries he had proved an embarrassment to the Serbian Church.

In the life story of Bishop Varnava Nastich, all the elements of Serbian-American tradition fuse. He was born in Gary and died in Beocin, reversing the usual immigrant process. Letters and visitors kept his memory green in Gary. He recited *gusle* legendary songs as a youthful singer, and after his death he became the subject of a *guslar* bard. A play was produced in Gary about his martyrdom. His life and death struggle against the Communist oppressor reenact the heroic tragedies of earlier Serbians against the Turkish tyrants. He has become a potent symbol in the fateful church issue now splitting friends and families in Gary and East Chicago.

Croatians (from diary)

My next appointment was with Nick E., seventy-eight, retired, a great-grand-father. He lived out in the Glen Park section beyond the Northwest Campus. Nick was in the center of organized Croatian activities; he had been president of the Croatian Fraternal Union for a dozen years and was still honorary president. Although Nick called the Serbs Oriental and the Croats Western, he had an Oriental look about him, with a large oval face. He did not speak or volunteer readily but seemed content to answer questions. Finally he remembered a ghost story he had heard on one of his five visits to Croatia. The spark ignited when I asked him about the Serbs. Now he uttered all the counter-charges to refute Wal-ter T.'s venom of the day before, and I got this on tape. The Serbs had assassinated Stepan Radich, leader of the Peasant Party for an independent Croatia, in Con-gress House in Belgrade. Serbia was trying to dominate Croatia, which had for-merly held Bosnia-Hercegovina and Dalmatia, within the second Yugoslavia. The Serbs were taking over the Croatian language. Serbia took the money from Croa-tian factories to rebuild Belgrade at the expense of Zagreb. Croatians pay twice as much tax as the Serbians, and in Yugoslavia a friend had denied this publicly but told him privately it was true. Nick would not associate with Serbians in Gary. They were fanatic royalists for Peter, the son of King Alexander now living in Paris. Alexander was assassinated in Marseille by Croats in revenge for Radich. Serbia had taken the rich Vojvodina from Croatia. Nick showed me the "Croatian Voice," *Hrvatski Glas*, published in Winnipeg. An issue of February 10, 1968, had an article about a Croatian priest, Professor Draganovich, being kidnapped by the Serbs from Rome and taken to Belgrade, and another entitled "Separation of Croatia from Yugoslavia," all in Croatian.

As I was getting ready to leave, Nick put on records of sweet *tamburitza* music he had purchased in Zagreb, brought out two *tamburs* he had ordered from Kos Slavko, near Zagreb, and showed me large color photographs of the *tamburitzan* groups he directed, about thirty young people. They would take part in a na-tional festival in Des Plaines, Illinois, on July 7. He rehearsed them every Friday night in the Croatian Hall and also gave lessons in Croatian. A man in Gary, Milan Opacich, made *tamburs*, but Nick could get one from Yugoslavia for $50 instead of paying $175 for one here. The name of one song on the record was "Three Days She Was Picking the Corn," and Nick said most were folksongs.

A phone call came and Nick said he had to witness the signature of the will of an old friend of eighty-two, Zlatko K., who would be dead of cancer within three months. He insisted on taking me to the house nearby. Zlatko was tooth-pick thin, his skin tight; he was gaunt, hollow, emaciated, hairless, but spry of mind and ready to be interviewed. He began telling of his immigrant experiences, being fired the first day on his job in a sausage factory in Chicago for stepping on a lever that sent the meat flying all over the room. An attorney showed up to draw up the will, and after the business advised me to leave, but with the un-derstanding that if Zlatko felt in the mood I could return. Two middle-aged tear-ful daughters were present. (*end diary*)

Croatian tradition proved a good deal thinner than Serbian. One Croatian told me that he had married a Lithuanian and that his children were ethnic mongrels; but the Serbs remained clannish and tended to marry among themselves. The comic experience recounted by Zlatko K. belongs not to Croatian but to general immigrant lore about mishaps on first landing in America. Bessie M., of Serbian descent, related how her father ate a banana, skin and all, his first day in New York and exclaimed he had never tasted anything so horrible. A Romanian restaurant owner, John N., recounted an involved saga of his arriving in Detroit in the middle of the night with forty dollars strapped around his waist, not a word of English at his command, and waiting for the cab driver to locate a Romanian speaker. These comparable incidents, at once ludicrous and pathetic, in totality comprise one large chapter of immigrant folk history.

Greeks

At the International Institute I met the staff members who dealt with Greek families, Mrs. Stella D., a short, matronly, worried-looking woman born in Chicago but raised in Gary and active in Greek organizations there. Her father had been born in Athens and her mother in Smyrna. As president of the local Ahepa chapter, Stella had gone to Athens for the international congress in 1964. She enumerated a long list of Greek societies and clubs in town, saying they were often organized according to the regions or islands from which people came. I asked her about the evil eye, and she responded excitedly, saying she had learned the prayer to overcome its effects from her grandmother, but indirectly, by overhearing, since the prayer could only pass from man to woman and woman to man. It was necessary to burn three cloves and repeat the prayer; when the clove sparked, the spell was broken.[7]

"I've tried it on my daughters," Mrs. D. continued.

When I was young my grandmother did it to me often. I was sick and I'd perk up right away. Grandmother told me that a horse had fallen down on the street in Smyrna because someone had put the evil eye on it, without meaning to; she said the prayer and the horse got up. In Chicago a doctor friend used to come when he was feeling low and say, "Stella, tell me the prayer," and after it was said he'd feel better right away. Three cloves should be burned and placed in a little wine glass of water. Then say the prayer, bless the water with the sign of the cross and sprinkle it around. The prayer is repeated three times, with a count, 5–10–15–20–25 and so on. She could not utter the prayer.

On another occasion Stella introduced me to a client of hers, Emmanuel V., a friendly, clean-featured newcomer of thirty-eight who had been in Gary only four years, joining his father who had come from the isle of Kalymnos in the eastern Aegean in 1923. Emmanuel sold sponges and worked part time in the steel mills. In halting English, with the aid of Stella, he related an event that had caused a great stir on Kalymnos.

It happened in 1908 or 1909. There was a diver named Latare, he has a big rock in his hand weighing over thirty pounds, to weight him down, and no clothes. They drop him over the side of the ship, and he goes straight down about 175 feet. And a big shark was lying on its side, and its mouth was open. Latare went right through the mouth and the rock hit the stomach. And the shark threw the man out. The man on top pulls up the rope, so Latare came up, with marks all over his back. They had a big picture of him and the fish in the city hall. The king went to see him. People paid one Italian lira to look at him. Jim Z.,

---

[7] See Richard M. Dorson, *American Folklore* (New York, 1959), 163, for a similar account.

who came here six years ago from Kalymnos, when he was 27, saw the picture. It was a miracle, the only time it ever happened.

Emmanuel invited me to the East Side Coffee House off 7th Avenue that evening, where Greek men met to play cards, talk, and have light refreshment. When I arrived, he had stepped out, and I sat conspicuously alone, eyeing and being eyed by the groups of dark-haired, dark-complexioned men sitting around tables reading Greek newspapers, conversing in Greek, and eating a sweet Greek pastry called *galakton baurike*. The men were all ages, in working-class clothes; women were not permitted, and one came to the door, but no further, to signal her husband. After a while the owner, Denos K., heavy-set and serious of mien, sat at my table and began conversing in passable English. Denos had been born in 1918 in Tarpon Springs, Florida, the transplanted community of Greek sponge fishermen, but lived in Kalymnos from 1921 to 1933, when he returned to Tarpon Springs and became captain of a sponge fishing boat. He moved to Gary with his brother in 1947, when some chemical killed off the sponge beds.

While we talked, Emmanuel entered and joined us. Then others crowded around, and suddenly our table was the center of excited conversation about Kalymnos, about Latare the lucky diver, about Saint Nicholas, patron saint of fishermen. A pleasant young barber, the Jim Z. who had seen the picture of Latare, counted twenty men from Kalymnos around the room. One was a famous diver, now converted into a railroad switchman, a cousin of Emmanuel, burly and impassive, and out of the conversation because he had no English. Over the mantel rested an elegant ship model called the *Kalymnos*. From somewhere in the room Jim brought a couple of prize sponges, one long and tufted and shaped like a helmet. Now Denos produced a treasured book with a torn blue paper cover showing a suited diver holding a large sponge in one hand and a claw-like instrument in the other. It was titled *Strangers at Ithaca, The Story of the Spongers of Tarpon Springs*, written by George Th. Frantzis and published by the Great Outdoors Publishing Company in St. Petersburg, Florida, in 1962. He looked through it lovingly, the others clustering around, as he pointed to persons he knew in the photographs. One was of his mother, "Eleni Georgious K., one of the first Greek beauties to come to Tarpon Springs," showing just her head. She was strikingly beautiful, with madonna-like features framed in black hair. In an emotional gesture Denos gave me the book, along with a postcard picturing a rugged peak and sheltered bay of Kalymnos.

In my notebook Denos drew a rough map of the inland coast of Florida to illustrate how in 1935 the hurricane had hit every city from Palmyra to Pensacola save Tarpon Springs.

The sponge fishermen in Kalymnos give the sponges they get on their last day to Saint Nicholas. In Tarpon Springs they say Saint Nicholas saved them from the hurricane. In 1935 my uncle, who was in the Bahamas as a sponge buyer, came to visit us in Tarpon Springs. The radio announced the hurricane coming. My uncle had had experience with the hurricane every year in the Bahamas. He called my father, "Get up and get prepared." And my father said, "Don't worry, Saint Nicholas is going to take care of that. Go back to bed." And the hurricane hit all the other cities, went out to sea about a hundred and fifty miles and came back and hit Pensacola, below Tarpon Springs.

These Gary Greeks no longer knew the *paramythia*, the old folktales with which they used to while away evenings on the sponge boats. But traditions enveloped the East Side Coffee House, conveyed in the pictures of Kalymnos, the ship model, the sponges, the true tale of Latare, and the faith in Saint Nicholas.

Mexicans (from diary)

I was introduced to Victor L., a young, positive fellow with pockmarked skin, who promptly invited me to his Adult Citizens English class at Riley School that evening. Then I was off to William M., who had invited me to a Mexican meal when I called at 4:00 P.M. His wife, Tilly, was an attractive dark-haired girl about thirty years of age, with boys of two and four. Bill was sturdy, full-faced, serious, darker than she. Tilly did not look Mexican, except for a slight olive complexion. They were second generation but filled with tradition, or aware of it. Tilly was one of thirteen children. Her dad had come from Mexico at twenty-six, fifty-three years before, from Yuriria, Guanajauto, which she had visited, and was thankful she had been born in the States. Her mother came from Jalisco, and recalled being helped off a train by Pancho Villa. Tilly had once dated a Greek boy of means, but with the understanding that both their parents would arrange their marriages. Tilly and Bill began telling me various Mexican folklore matters: about the *mariachi*, popular singing groups with stringed instruments bringing seventy-five to one hundred dollars an hour in the area; how Thomas Alva Edison was really Mexican; an account of La Llorona mixed with the female ghost of Cline Avenue, actually seen by Tilly's brother, a cab driver, who was interviewed on TV; the potato water cure of Tilly's mother to preserve her black hair and save that of her brother-in-law, which was coming out in patches. "She advised him to use water from boiled potatoes for three months." I recorded them.

Dinner was a regular Mexican meal of stew beef, yellow rice, and beans. Tilly and Bill told me that *enchiladas* and *tacos* were only used on special occasions. Everything they said I found of interest. Their church, "Our Lady of Guadalupe," in the Harbor was having trouble keeping its parishioners, though it was the only Mexican church in town. The priests were Irish (Father Flanagan) or English (Father Meade), and when Tilly's family sponsored Father Frias from Mexico, well-spoken and handsome, the people flocked to hear him. A substantial sum was raised to send to Mexico, for a church or hospital, whereupon Father Flanagan got mad and refused to let Father Frias speak again. Tilly said that at the *mariachi* dances the "Mexican would come out" even in Americans, in the *grito*, a protracted yell. The church was losing parishioners because the younger people —and older ones—were moving out, and the Texans planned only to stay ten years and then return. Her family kept going to the old church for sentimental reasons, although they were closer to St. Mary's. Tilly remarked that the Mexicans did not stick together, as did the Serbians. Two rivals had lost out in the election for state representative to a non-Mexican, by one hundred votes. She and Bill had had to leave their Ivy Street apartment because the Serbian landlord was renting to Serbs. Pride and stubbornness were downfall traits of the Mexicans. Tilly mentioned a University of California book, *Mexican-Americans in a Mid-*

west Metropolis, that was so inflammatory—it described Mexican laborers being loaded into boxcars—that it could not be sold locally.[8]

After dinner I followed Bill across town to his foster mother's, around the corner from the old church in Indiana Harbor. Mrs. Tomasita G., a tiny, wrinkled, Indian-featured old lady, had been born in 1893 in Doctor Arroyo, south of Monterrey, and had come to East Chicago in 1917. Later Bill told me that she took a raw egg with garlic every morning, washed her eyes with lemon juice, had all her teeth, and had begun to wear glasses only two years before. She was a *curandera*, and her cures were based on faith. "She must be a devout Catholic," I observed tritely. "No, she's a Mormon," said Bill. "She goes to Highland to services there twice on Sunday, morning and afternoon." And not to the Catholic church next door, that Bill and Tilly drove across town to attend.

Mrs. G. had raised Bill and his three siblings, Texas-born, by herself, since he was three. When he entered her miniature apartment, he kissed her respectfully on the hand and cheek. We sat in a tiny dressing area in front of her four-poster bed, and she related cures for *susto* in Spanish, which Bill then translated. He volunteered a cure she had done for him when he was eight ("I was leery of it until then"); she had bathed him in a raw egg at night, which was cooked in the morning, and the fever gone. Another charm, involving a prayer written on paper strips and placed on four corners of the bed, drove away cockroaches. We only had a little time before the 7:00 P.M. class, which by coincidence the old lady was attending. A friend came in, a funny old gal with expressive gestures, Elisa D., from Michoacan, Mexico, and she told a comical *cuento* into the tape, a noodle tale, which Bill translated. Then we all drove off to Riley School. It turned out that Victor L. and Bill M. had gone to school and worked in the mill together. Victor pulled out of the class a grizzled Mexican, and found a classroom for us to talk in. He was Ray A. of East Chicago, born in La Barca, Jalisco, in 1901; he came to Arizona in 1921 and to East Chicago the next year. His English was fair, but he preferred Spanish. After some questioning I struck responses with La Llorona, *susto brujería*, and Pancho Villa. His mother had given him a cure for *biles*, a virulent kind of *susto* causing throwing up and eventually death. A main ingredient was sour tamarind. After he left, Bill M., who had been translating, spoke of his difficulty in following the Spanish; he was just too much out of practice, although he sometimes used it at the mill or with the old folks. But in Mexico he felt at a loss. Puerto Ricans spoke very rapidly when they first came. He mentioned hybrid words, English with Spanish endings, like *watcheli*. He had learned to read Spanish by reading the Bible three times in Spanish.

Now Victor L. joined us and spoke in a very interesting and informed way about the language business and Puerto Rican-Mexican conflicts. He was the son of old Mexicans; and his sister, two years old, had had a terrible time learning English in school until her teacher told her father to speak English to her. Victor then had no trouble. He had kept up his Spanish with his parents later, in the store and in the mill. He had an A.B. and an M.A. in Education from Indiana University. His wife of four years was Puerto Rican, of a high-rank family. He

---

[8] Julian Samora and Richard A. Lamanna, *Mexican-Americans in a Midwest Metropolis; A Study of East Chicago* (Los Angeles, 1967).

had flown at Christmas time to San Juan to get parental consent, while his brothers-in-law on the island had been afraid to approach the father. A couple of aunts, who were around her constantly, were from Spain. Victor attacked a number of stereotypes: that the Puerto Ricans all had Negro blood (his wife was a redhead, and there were plenty of blondes), that they didn't practice discrimination (there were ghettos in Puerto Rico), that they spoke so rapidly. Every other Spanish-speaking group was supposed to talk rapidly. He agreed with Bill M. that Harbor Spanish was a thing unto itself (citing a master's thesis by a Freddie Maraville), and he gave examples. He would use *autobús* in San Juan and be corrected to *huahua* and then be laughed at back home. He spoke of the warmth and hospitality of the Puerto Ricans, and also of the Mexicans. He had never expected to marry a Puerto Rican girl. Mexicans felt they could look down on Puerto Ricans because of their Negro blood. All Latins loved their mother and their country. Pride was one reason for their not learning English, and another was housing discrimination forcing them into Mexican ghettos. Two-thirds of the Puerto Ricans put their country first; they were the nationalists and territorialists. Mexicans were good workers and could take the heat in Open Hearth #2 at Inland. (*end diary*)

Puerto Ricans (from diary)

In Gary I had an appointment with A. M. in the National Bank Building. I arrived before he did in his plush office on the 9th floor—one of the few such offices I had encountered. He turned out to be youngish, yellow-skinned, square-faced, deliberate, and slow-speaking. He was an upper-class Puerto Rican, with French and Spanish blood, he said. He had an A.B. from Northwest Campus of Indiana University and his law degree from Valparaiso University, with other education in Europe. Our conversation was halting; I asked questions and he gave slow answers. He did not see much difference between Puerto Ricans and Mexicans; the food was pretty much the same. (But Mrs. Carmen R., a Puerto Rican married to a doctor from the Dominican Republic, had given me a long list of typical Puerto Rican dishes.) Puerto Ricans were not used to cold weather when they came to Gary. Most came from the small towns, not San Juan, and had been agriculturists, but since the 1940s, under Operation Bootstrap, 185 new industries had opened in Puerto Rico. Mexicans were nationalistic; they think they will make money and return home. I began cautiously to ask him about *brujería*, and finally drew a spark. "I had a client the other day that said her husband's girl friend was trying to destroy her with the *brujería*, and that she had heard voices. They stick pins in a doll, with the person's name on it. I tried to talk her out of it." He knew of the *botánica* shop that sold herbs, seeds, candles, and *escapularios* of cotton with the Virgin or a saint on them, to use against the *brujería*, and gave me the name of a former owner, Mrs. Pilar F., who was herself accused of being a *bruja*. I asked about *susto*, and he did not know of any connection with *brujería* but called out to his secretary, a pretty young Mexican, if she knew of such a connection and was surprised to hear her say yes. He gave me a note of introduction to take to Mrs. F.

On the way out I asked the secretary, Carmen M., about *susto*. Her mother had a recipe: suspend the egg over the sick person, then place it in a glass of water, and drop in crosses made of broom straws or toothpicks, which will float. In the morning the egg may be cooked, depending on the sickness. But she had not tried it. "I don't want to get involved."

Now I decided to try Pilar F., who lived in the Brunswick section of Gary, a quiet neighborhood with small homes and plots of ground between them. An enormously fat, blubbery dark woman, slightly Oriental in aspect and somewhat sinister looking, was carrying a bundle of clothing out the door. She called Pilar when I showed her my letter. Pilar was a half-sister to this one, lighter, fat but not so fat, with more regular features, open and pleasant, and with good English. She took me right inside and after reading A. M.'s note answered everything I asked, while trying to silence an unquenchable two-year-old, an adopted son, Carlito. She gave me an LP record of Puerto Rican music, containing traditional *plena* songs (like calypsos), and said that a local orchestra played such songs at the Puerto Rico Demo Club at birthday parties—piano, trumpet, guitar, saxophone, soloist. Yes, they made up local *plenas*. Now I questioned Pilar about her life history. She was born in 1932 in Santurce del Barrio, in a very poor section called Tras Talleres, the only child of parents who had each been married before, giving her stepbrothers and stepsisters. In 1949 she went to live with her half-brother in New York, and attended P.S. 101, at 111th between Lexington and Madison. Pilar retraced her career in close detail: a return to Puerto Rico to attend her sick mother, a course in New York in practical nurse's training, while living with her half-brother, who was a cook's helper for twenty-five years in the Hotel Vanderbilt; a decision to move to Washington, because of unspecified trouble in her brother's family; her failure to get a nurse's poistion in Walter Reed Hospital because she arrived ten minutes late for the test, not knowing the Pentagon was across the Washington, D.C., boundary in Virginia; her loneliness in Washington, where there were only twenty to thirty Puerto Ricans; her job in charge of linen at the Shoreham Hotel—she was ever after soured against nursing; the return to New York, and her decision, because of the noise, to find another place where she could live with Puerto Ricans; the move to Gary in 1957, as a result of a letter from a home-town friend living there; her first income from using her fifteen-dollar jalopy to drive Puerto Ricans and colored people daily to a clinic at Michigan City, making fifteen dollars a day by charging each $3; a move to East Chicago and a job there as typist with the city; a year in Chicago at Oak Forest Hospital; a return to East Chicago to work in politics for Mayor Nicosia on behalf of the Puerto Ricans; laborer in Inland Steel, in the tin mill; marriage in 1963; present job as jail matron, which she enjoyed. Her husband Lorenzo had worked in Youngstown seventeen years, knew no English, and even spoke Spanish poorly, but he had made $11,000 the past year as second helper in the blast furnace, where only he could speak Spanish. When it was necessary to communicate in English, he wrote messages. While we were talking, he came in, a slender, sallow man with a small mustache and a furtive look, but he offered me a cup of coffee in friendly fashion.

In all this Pilar had not mentioned the *botánica*, so I brought it up, and she looked a little surprised but giggled and spoke most openly about the whole business. So I brought in the tape recorder, and she told all her secrets to it. A. M.

said I should not mention *brujería* but let Pilar bring it up, but she showed no hesitation at all in talking about the matter. "The Spanish people believe in voodoo, and they come buy herbs and take a bath in it and say it will bring good luck." There were about twenty-five *botánicas* in Chicago, and many in New York. Her own, run by her sister in East Chicago, had had to close as a result of the criticism of the churches, Catholic and Protestant. The Catholics imposed a course called *curcillistra* [*cursillo*], which cost $37 to $40 for three days, and which even her half-sister took. Pilar regarded the *botánica* as a drugstore, to sell supplies to people affected with *brujería*. While we were talking she brought out charcoal, incense, and seeds and burned them in a little dish, describing the procedure for the tape-recorder. Usually she did this Fridays at midnight, and she always stayed home Fridays (hence I had come on the right day). She said giggling—and she giggled all the way through—that her husband told her the incense was to make him stay at home. Pilar had learned about voodoo—she fumbled for the word on the tape—from a spiritual meeting she had attended as a young girl in Puerto Rico, which she described graphically. At the end she mentioned a fly from Spain, *moscas cantareas*, black and blue, which made a z-z-z-sound, and was considered very lucky. Well, she and other *botánicas* would sell substitute flies, or substitute incense, when they couldn't get the real articles, and this led to a crackdown by the government. These articles were used to bring good luck in the numbers game; even snakes were sold, and she mentioned one good-luck snake that would curl up on the sofa. She said all this frankly into the tape. On leaving I offered to pay Pilar for the record, but she refused any money. (*end diary*)

Conclusions

A field trip of twenty-three days cannot of course answer the theoretical questions framed at the outset of this inquiry. Still from the numerous interviews and the data obtained in notebooks and on tape and in the form of donated publications and other materials, plus of course the strong impressions derived from personal observation, I put forward the following concepts of modern urban folklore. How well they will stand up after further work in the Gary-East Chicago area and to what extent they may apply in other metropolitan localities remains to be seen, but I advance them with some conviction.

1. PAUCITY OF CONVENTIONAL FOLKLORE. The old familiar genres of folklore, particularly the tale and song, do not seem abundant in the city. Even jokes, the modern folktale, are forbidden in the steel mills for fear their ethnic slurs may arouse hostility. One can of course find storytellers and folksingers in the city, and in the country village not every soul is an active tradition carrier by a long shot. But genre folklore has become increasingly displaced by other kinds of oral tradition, which deserve the attention of collectors. A good example was my evening in the Greek coffee-house, that might as well have been on the Aeagean isle of Kalymnos, which indeed most of the men present claimed as their birthplace. They were eager to tell me all they knew of Greek life and lore, and other people had told me no group was so clannish as the Greeks. None could tell *paramythia*, the popular fictions with which the sponge fishermen had regaled each other in the old days and in the Old Country; yet traditions of other

kinds retained a powerful hold upon them. Among the Negroes and other ethnic groups I encountered a generally similar response. My closest Negro friend, Harold M., Mississippi born and bred, was exceedingly articulate but not on matters of southern lore. The steelworkers' union of which he was an official dominated his thoughts and conversation. He finally did tell me two anecdotes; one was a civil-rights joke and the other dealt with an eccentric millworker. When tales and songs are collected, as in the Polish folksongs recorded by Pawlowska and the Armenian folktales recorded by Hoogasian-Villa in Detroit, they may belong to an inactive memory culture rather than to a vigorous living growth.[9]

2. RICHNESS OF CULTURAL TRADITIONS AND PERSONAL HISTORIES. If the conventional genres are hard to come by, folklore, or perhaps better folk culture, is nevertheless present and pervasive. American folklorists—and this certainly includes myself—have sought for texts and largely overlooked other kinds and forms of cultural traditions less easy to report. Among the Negroes, the Baptist church is in most of its manifestations a folk institution transplanted from the South. I was told there were over two hundred such churches in Gary. The ethnomusicologist and student of folk music can have a field day analyzing the combination of choral and instrumental, country and city, gospel and rhythm elements in these church performances. For the Serbians, calendar feast days play a pivotal role in their lives, both the saints' day celebrations associated with each family and the great church holy days. In a number of ethnic societies, choral and dance groups perform regularly, such as the Croatian *tamburitzan* club. On my last evening in Gary I attended a Serbian entertainment in Saint Sava Hall, the basement auditorium of the church, and saw local girl dancers, a singer, and two flailing accordionists; and finally, with the chairs cleared, a circular *cola* dance with adults and children all joining hands. The whole program was in Serbian, and one could see before one's eyes youngsters absorbing Serbian traditional song, music, and dance. To the religious and social occasions should be added the celebration of national holidays, like the Mexican one on September 16, a festal pageant with floats and a proud team of *charros*, the costumed horsemen.

Ethnic cuisine is still another flourishing form of tradition among every sizable group: the southern whites, the southern Negroes, the east Europeans, the Latin. A truck driver for Inland Steel from Kentucky discoursed rhapsodically in Mrs. Green's hotel about the heaping platters of farm fare back home. As noted above, one Negro middle-class lady from Memphis said that soul food kept the colored people from getting the rare diseases of the whites. A Puerto Rican housewife indignantly denied that Puerto Ricans had no dishes of their own to compare with those nationally publicized by the Mexicans, and she reeled off a string of recipes. The best restaurant in Gary, now enveloped by the Negro ghetto, was Greek. Ethnic restaurants tended to take on the character of social clubs. From southern hillbilly to Romanian, the people of Steel City cherished their foods.

Another dimension of folk culture to be fathomed is personal history. There are thousands of sagas created from life experiences that deserve, indeed cry for, recording. The folklorist need not worry about their relation to the oral genres.

[9] Harriet M. Pawlowska, *Merrily We Sing: 105 Polish Folksongs* (Dertoit, 1961); Susie Hoogasian-Villa, *One Hundred American Folktales* (Detroit, 1966).

Here are precious oral narratives dealing with a series of great folk movements—from the southern states, from Mexico and Puerto Rico, from eastern Europe—and this migration should be described in terms of humanity as well as of mass statistics. No discipline other than folklore looks in this direction. Oral history is concerned with the elite, anthropology with underdeveloped countries, sociology with social organization. The personal history may well be a genre of its own, honed and structured through periodic retellings. It is at any rate a fluent oral form on the lips of a number of tellers. Several memorable life stories came to my ears with virtually no prompting. The relation by seventy-three-year-old Laura P., the frail mother of a double amputee, Bill, about the long travail and cheerful endurance of her son, fits into no known formula. It was a heart-rending account of hospitalization and surgery, despair and grief, but without particular overtones of prejudice or poverty. On reflection the history seems to belong with what Charles Keil has called the role of the Negro in America as one long sacrificial ritual. Victor L., who had come from Mexico in 1906; Edward B., who had been born in the Guiana forest; Zlatko K. from Croatia, dying of cancer at eighty-two—all launched promptly into detailed life histories. Certain incidents are clearly traditional, such as the comic misadventures of the newly arrived immigrant.

3. THE ROLE OF THE SPOKEN WORD. The culture of Gary-East Chicago is largely an oral culture, in the sense that talk flows freely. Television has not displaced conversation; the Book-of-the-Month Club pretensions of the middle class are little in evidence. Especially is this true for the Negro, bearing out the claims of Abrahams and Keil that the black ghetto is an auditory and tactile as opposed to a visual and literate culture, with the man of words as the culture hero. In the immigrant groups the potential man of words is often hampered by his inadequacy with English, although the desire to communicate will not be denied. I think of the long evening with Walter and Milly T. in which they conveyed all kinds of information through a limited English vocabulary. The Negro man of words appeared as preacher-entertainer, gospel singer turned preacher plus steelworker, athlete turned preacher plus steelworker, and preacher turned civil rights leader. The three superb speeches given in the Calvary Baptist Church during Negro history week, by a young bank manager, a lady sociologist, and a city official stand out in my mind in contrast to the suffocatingly dull seminar on Gary's Model City project held at Bloomington, at which professional educators mouthed their irrelevant jargon.

4. THE ROLE OF THE BOOK. If this is not a highly literate society, nevertheless it is a society that greatly values special book publications for their symbolic value. In one group after another I encountered references to, demonstration of, and sometimes even the bestowal of a cherished tome. These books shared two common factors: they were far off the main stream of American publishing, often being issued with obscure imprints, and they served to reinforce cherished elements of the folk inheritance. When Chetniks spoke of their sufferings at the hands of the hated Ustashis and recorded on tape examples of atrocities they had personally beheld, they regularly alluded to and produced printed evidence to substantiate their statements, such as the pamphlet Walter T. gave me, *The Crime of Genocide*, and the book, *Genocide in Satellite Croatia*, men-

tioned previously. My last evening in Gary I saw Walter at the dance entertainment in St. Sava Hall, again distributing paperback books in Serbian. They were by Lazo Kostich, now living in Switzerland, and author of over fifty books documenting the atrocities that had taken the lives of two million Serbs in World War II. "He is defending my blood," said Walter simply. In the Greek coffeehouse, owner Denos K. proudly brought forth a history of the Greek settlement of sponge fishermen at Tarpon Springs, Florida, *Strangers at Ithaca.*

Another kind of book reinforcement supported ethnic pride in historical achievements customarily ignored in majority group histories. An eloquent Polish patriot in Gary with his own Polish-Language radio program, T. Stan Dubiak, told me that there were 127 Polish-American organizations in Lake County. He complained about the Poles being left out of American history and triumphantly produced a volume, *Jamestown Pioneers from Poland 1608–1958*, documenting the presence of Polish colonists at Jamestown. In my interview with seventy-year-old Todd R., a retired Negro steelworker born in Alabama, I was astonished at his ability to produce little-known facts, names, and dates of Negro history, coupled with his dearth of folklore. Eventually he showed me two battered booklets, an *Afro-American World Almanac* and *A Tribute to Achievement.* Similarly Elder George M. in his preaching at the Primitive Baptist Church, although he could not read, relied for his impressive citations of Negro accomplishments on a book his wife read to him, *World's Great Men of Color 3000 B.C. to 1946 A.D.*

Books could be feared as well as cherished. The study by Samora and Lamanna, *Mexican-Americans in a Midwest Metropolis: A Study of East Chicago,* is a case in point. The fury it aroused in the Mexican community made the sale of the work impossible. The concept of the book in these instances is wholly different from the attitude toward books of casual bookbuyers and book readers. These books have a talismanic character, and they are unique, not simply titles in a library.

5. OTHER ARTIFACTS OF TRADITION. If a symbolic book serves as an artifact tangibly reinforcing the traditional culture, it can be joined by many other artifacts of more than sentimental worth. These physical objects decorate the home or clubroom and fill the closets and drawers, and the ethnofolklorist should seek to inventory them. They may take the form of old country costumes for ceremonial occasions, portraits of national heroes like Draža Mihajlovich, musical instruments like the *gusle* and tambour, or recordings obtained from the old country. Walter T. played for me a tape recording he had made in Belgrade of a record of a Serbian folksong being played on a local radio station. In the Greek coffeehouse a ship model named *Kalymnos* and two giant sponges refreshed club members' memories of their island birthplace and occupation. As the folklorist today is enlarging his vision to include folklife, so in dealing with nationality groups he should play special heed to the transported and imported items of material culture that help to bridge the chasm between the Old World and the New.

6. REINFORCEMENT. The two preceding points lead into a related matter, the idea of reinforcement of the parent culture through continuous contacts. This concept, which I earlier suggested in *American Folklore*, contradicts the stereotype of the immigrant, northern Negro, Appalachian white, urban Puerto Rican, or Mexican as cut off abruptly and irrevocably from his traditions in an

alien and hostile environment.[10] In one instance after another, in every one of these groups, the evidence accumulates as to the continuing links with the *heimat*, through visits—by the American-born as well as the foreign-born or northern-born—correspondence, bringing of relatives or mates to the metropolis, and subscription to foreign-language periodicals and newspapers. The case of Bishop Varnava Nastich is a classic example of the linkage between Europe and America, reversing the immigration pattern as the Gray-born Serb returned to Yugoslavia to become the first American bishop in the Serbian Orthodox Church and a rallying figure for Gary anti-Communists. The bishop's cousin in Gary, Emily B., possesses extensive files on Nastich—reams of eloquent letters, half in English, half in Serbian; photographs; and clippings from American newspapers and Serbian publications. Daisy Wuletich and her mother described to me in close detail their visit with the bishop in the monastery in Beocin. The Nastich episode of course involves high drama, but in the regular course of events the dwellers in Gary and East Chicago scheduled trips to their places of birth or those of their parents.

The effect of this intermittent but consistent reinforcement needs to be measured. Once Harold M. told me that the pastor at his church, Trinity Baptist, had noticeably reverted to southern-style preaching after a vacation in Arkansas. Further inquiry can lead to subdivisions within the transplanted cultures. The Gary Greeks meet in separate coffeehouses according to their islands or mainland communities of origin; the Negroes join churches whose pastors come from their own southern states; the Croats in northwest Indiana address each other by nicknames designating the valleys and hillsides of their youth. Presumably reinforcement from these distinguishable backgrounds will show different shadings, just as dialects vary between regions.

7. CULTURAL PLURALISM. The generalizations offered under the preceding headings must be countered by another generalization, that each cultural group is unique in terms of its folklore retentions and pattern of assimilation and acculturation. Negroes may look upon all white people as "Whitey," northerners may lump Mexicans and Puerto Ricans together as Latins, WASPs may speak in the aggregate of eastern Europeans, city dwellers may call all southern migrants hillbillies, and these terms themselves are revealing of cultural attitudes and stereotypes. One does not need to spend much time in the field to appreciate the considerable differences that exist between ethnic and racial groups in their degree of folk-cultural tenacity.

The Serbs and the Croats provide a good illustration, since they are usually conjoined in the minds of outsiders, and their language, although written in different alphabets, is called Serbo-Croatian. But the Serbs are much more tradition-oriented than the Croats. One reason is the Church and another is the State. The Serbian Orthodox Church unites the American Serbs—or disunites them into two warring fractions in the present ecclesiastical dispute—but it at least keeps aflame their national conscience. The Croats are swallowed up in the Roman Catholic Church and will mingle more with other Catholic ethnic groups such as the Poles and Italians. Serbia has its history as an independent state and a subjugated

---

[10] *American Folklore*, 156.

nation under the Turks to inspire her expatriates with heroes, legends, and tragic epics; but Croatia was a province submerged in the Austro-Hungarian empire, with little historical tradition to call its own. As John Sertich put it, the Croats were tribal rather than national, never having had their own king. The legend of Bishop Varnava Nastich grew out of the Gary Serbian community and could never have developed among the Gary Croatians. This is not to deny the American Croats their ties to old country and their interest in folk music and costume, as in the *tamburitzan* ensembles. The question here is one of degree and density of cultural conservatism.

Similar contrasts came to the surface after some inquiries about differences between Mexicans and Puerto Ricans. The latter fitted more easily into Gary-East Chicago because they had already lived under the American flag. The former supposedly worked better in the steel mills because they were accustomed to heat. Mexicans wed Indians and Puerto Ricans wed Negroes. In terms of tradition, the Mexican seemed much stronger, again because of a national history as a frame of reference. Mexican ethnic cuisine has become part of the national restaurant business, while Puerto Rican dishes are unknown.

One factor in assessing cultural pluralism and its effect on folklore is the dilution that occurs, or may occur, through intermarriage. A Croat who had remarried to a Lithuanian said that his children had no tradition. A young Mexican woman related she had once dated a Greek boy, but with the understanding that they would never marry, for the Greeks always stayed together. Marty G., the son of a Mexican father and a southern Appalachian mother whom I recorded for a long pleasant hour, called himself a "Mexican hillbilly," but his inheritance appeared to be all on the hillbilly side. He spoke with intimate knowledge, sympathy, and wit about the "stumpjumpers," "ridgerunners," and "crackers" of the South. My own judgment, until other evidence appears, is that ethnic traditions do not blend in a mixed marriage but either cancel each other out or result in one triumphing.

8. ETHNIC SEPARATISM. The present urban field experience supports my previous findings in rural areas that the strong force of what I call ethnic separatism keeps the in-group folklores apart; they cannot cross into each other's zones. It is the individual who must cross into the life experience of another group to absorb the traditions of that group. Twice I recorded tales in East Chicago from Puerto Ricans married to Negro women who had never heard, and expressed astonishment at, their husbands' narrations. Puerto Ricans and Mexicans share the same language and faith, but their folklore follows different channels. The Puerto Rican *botánica* or magic-herb store and the Mexican *curandera* or magic healer are separate and distinct. *Susto* has special connotations to Mexicans and Mexican-Americans, who believe that *susto* is induced by some supernatural or magical means; but the Puerto Rican lawyer representing the Latin American organization of Gary and East Chicago and who knew all about the *botánica,* drew a blank on any special significance of *susto,* and was astonished to learn that his Mexican secretary did react to the word.

Folk prejudices as well as cultural inertia contribute to ethnic separatism. In a conversation with Katie S. about the soul food prized by the colored people, I thought to ask her if she had ever tried Mexican dishes. Yes, she had tried *tacos* and rather liked them until she heard they were made from dead cats. Calling on a Slovak celebrating his fiftieth wedding anniversary, I elicited no folklore but did receive one double-barreled folk hatred: "I never see a picture like mine [of his golden wedding] for a Czech; they have twenty wives, like niggers."

9. THE URBAN SYNTHESIS. Yet if the migrant groups in Steel City never penetrate each other's folklore, or perhaps even each other's homes, they do share the environment, the living experience, and perforce the lore of their new abode. People are marked by living in Gary or East Chicago, for these are uncommon cities, just as the Upper Peninsula of Michigan is an uncommon region leaving its imprint on all its inhabitants. The pervasive themes of Gary-East Chicago binding its people into a new folk community are steel, crime, and the racial-ethnic mix.

Steel created Gary, and the great mills whose furnaces must burn twenty-four hours a day is the number one fact of life in Gary and its environs. Some day perhaps an urban folklorist will write a "Folklore of the Steel Industry" to match Mody Boatright's *Folklore of the Oil Industry*. Meanwhile anyone can hear little stories about steelworkers, for instance about problems in communication. A Romanian crane operator worked for thirty-nine years in Inland Steel without learning English. During my stay an injured worker brought to the infirmary at Inland could not make his ailment known, although a nurse present tried speaking to him in Polish. The staff had to send back to the patient's unit to learn he was a Serb. These incidents get talked about and lay the ground for a new body of anecdotes based on the age-old motif of language misunderstanding. The human side of steel inevitably involves ethnic and racial humor and *blason populaire*. Crime stories and fears are an outgrowth of the contemporary industrial city and the Negro ghetto. Everyone is apprehensive—whites and blacks—and talk swirls around hold-ups, beatings, and murders. One of my informants, Marty G., father of seven, was murdered with his wife not long after I recorded him: no clues, no motives. One evening when I was interviewing a group of East Chicago Serb adherents to the mother church, one man present, a policeman, interrupted the thread of our discussion to tell about several recent crime incidents. At the time I was impatient to get back to our main topic, but now I realize that he was dealing with a central theme of Gary-East Chicago lore. One incident dealt with the refusal of a storeowner and his wife, who had just been robbed, to identify their Negro assailant, found with their goods and the owner's wallet in his car. After the suspect's release, the police officer asked the couple why they had refused to make the identification. "Well, we have to live there after you leave. Let them have a few bundles of clothes. Better than to have his friends come back and burn the place down."

A brief summary of a long evening's conversation with three southern-born Negroes, all steelworkers, may further illustrate the newly evolving urban synthesis. They were my friend Harold M., an official in a labor union; Ben D., a former professional gospel singer now preacher at the Macedonian Baptist Church; and Ben T., his former manager and now his deacon. The first half of the conversation turned on life in the South, on methods of cotton-picking, frauds in the poultry business run by Italians in New Orleans, and managing spiritual singers. During these recollections I was able to record half a dozen familiar folktales, such as "Dividing Souls" and "Why the Fox Has a Short Tail." For the second part of the evening the talk shifted to northern life, the labor unions, the Syndicate, and the political machine. Ben T. made sweeping and authoritative pronouncements: eighty-five percent of the people in Gary were from the South; Gary, and the world at large, were run by syndicates. He and Harold fell to comparing personalities in the unions and swapped accounts of the attempt by Democratic party forces to bribe union officials to swing votes against Dick Hatcher. Union grievance committeemen had each been given $250; half of them simply pocketed the money without acting. Ben talked at length about "snitching." Down south the black snitcher ran to Uncle Charlie, who protected him from the law, but up north the whites were the worst snitchers. The snitchers often had done the job themselves. One who was caught begged not to be sent to the "Peniten" but to the State Prison, because he knew he would be killed by the people he had snitched on. Ben ended these remarks by saying that Gary is the city of steel and that life revolved around the pay check every two weeks. Harold, a good talker but no storyteller, did think of two steel mill stories, one about an eccentric worker called "Old Man Shouting Robertson" and another about a lazy dog named Superintendent.

The full measure of talk, grossly synopsized here, suggests the shift from southern memories to northern conditions in the minds of migrants from the South, and the dominant themes of the races—petty and major crime and work in the steel plants, generating factual and finally fictional anecdotes. In the course of my sojourn I heard two fantasies in what may be an evolving legend of Richard Hatcher, the first Negro mayor of Gary. The more naturalistic ascribed to him a romance with a Jewish woman in Glen Park, which had gained him the Jewish vote, ordinarily bitterly anti-Negro. The second, propounded by a visiting television personality calling himself Psychic, held that Hatcher was actually the reincarnation of a southern white slave owner. This I heard from Harold M. Separate and divided as are the ethnic-race groups of Gary, all share participation in and reaction to, the election of their Negro mayor. From this shared experience emerges the lore of the city.

These currents of city talk sometimes carry floating seeds of legend. On three occasions I heard the related legends of the Vanishing Hitchhiker and La Llorona, localized on Cline Avenue in East Chicago and the swampy Cudahy strip between East Chicago and Gary. A young Mexican-American, Tilly L., told me that her brother, a cab-driver, had been interviewed on television after picking up a woman often sighted and picked up on Cline Avenue by passing motorists, who found her gone from their vehicles when they arrived at the address she gave them as her destination. The newspapers had publicized the story. The related incident concerned a passionate murder of a woman in Cudahy whose wraith was frequently seen and identified by the Mexicans with La Llorona, the weeping lady-ghost mourning her lost children. An elderly but vigorous Mexican, Victor L., who narrated to me his life story for two hours without drawing breath, knew at firsthand the Cudahy murderer, a fellow-worker in the mill, and had seen his shooting of a husky man who tried to stop him the night he ran amok. Victor's son, born in East Chicago, explained that La Llorona was adapted to local events.

    10. EXCEPTIONS TO STEREOTYPES. A plurality of cultures exists in Steel

City, going their own ways and not simmering in a melting pot. But if it is a mistake to treat all these folk cultures as equal in their rate of acculturation, it is a comparable error to treat all the individuals in the same cultural group as interchangeable parts. In the American scene—with its high mobility and unexpected juxtapositions, accentuated in urban settings—endless surprises occur. The individual breaks out of his stereotype frequently enough so that deviation itself becomes an acceptable concept.

A number of examples came to my attention in the Gary-East Chicago field trip. The most dramatic involved the Polish precinct-worker of the Democratic party, Marion Tokarsky, who broke with her ethnic, political, and religious allegiances to make common cause with the ghetto Negroes and support the Negro mayorality candidate. Here was an unpredictable phenomenon, the Polish Catholic immigrant befriending her Negro enemies and explaining to them the supernatural-Catholic basis of her decision, to which they responded in the style and manner of the Baptist congregation. Other illustrations of deviancy can be given. The seventy-five-year old Mexican *curandera* in Indiana Harbor, Mrs. Tomasita G., who dictated formulaic cures for *susto* in Spanish into my tape-recorder, proved to be a Mormon. On Sundays she made two trips to Highland to attend services at the Mormon church there, although the old Catholic church was just around the corner, and her foster-son and his wife came across town out of loyalty to that church, when they could have gone to a nearer Catholic church in East Chicago. The president of the Northern Indiana Political Action Alliance that Marion Tokarsky addressed was not a southern or northern Negro but a native of British Guiana, who in his youth identified with the British ruling class and looked down upon the East Indian servants on his plantation. When Edward B. came to the United States, he was astonished to discover that Negroes were second-class citizens. He had married a Negro woman from Georgia.

In the *Indiana Alumni Magazine* I read about Fedor C., who had come to America as a refugee from the Nazis and Communists, knowing no English. He had worked in the steel mills, taken courses, and become chairman of the political science department at the Northwest Campus of Indiana University. In Gary I spent an evening with Fedor and his wife Astrid and discovered that, while no fact in the magazine account was untrue, the stereotype presented was completely false. The couple were gifted and attractive intellectuals, university-trained, cosmopolitan, and sophisticated. Their life stories, which they told readily into the tape recorder, are extraordinary human documents; but they have no relation to the conventional saga of the immigrant. Again, from Victor L., Jr., I heard contradictions of the Puerto Rican stereotype, for instance, that all Puerto Ricans had Negro blood and hence would move into and marry within the American Negro community. There were indeed Puerto Rican Negro couples whom I met in East Chicago. But Victor knew whereof he spoke, for he was an Indiana-born Mexican married to a red-haired, fairskinned Puerto Rican girl, whom he had to court in the face of protective Castilian-type chaperones.

The answer to the original query, "Is there a folk in the city?" must clearly be yes. Perhaps it is best to say that there are many folk groups, who in Gary and East Chicago are becoming a city folk. But city folk are different from the country folk of yesteryear, and the folklorist exploring their ways must drastically revise his own traditional concepts of the folk and their lore. Yet the city is indeed a proper field for him to cultivate. If in North Uist, with its population decimated and a century of intensive collecting already achieved, John MacInnes can still say that he will never plumb all the layers of tradition, imagine how many lifetimes would be needed to explore the multiple folk cultures of Gary and East Chicago.

APPENDIX

The tangible results of this field trip—on which this paper is based—are nine tapes of twelve hundred feet played at one and seven-eighths speed and one tape of choral singing played at seven and one-half; notes on some fifty-three interviews; a diary written each evening running to ninety typed pages; and a box of books, pamphlets, leaflets, typescripts, and even a Puerto Rican straw hat and record album, given me by my new acquaintances—often books cherished and dear to them—as evidences and documents of their traditions and assertions. The interviews are divided as follows: Negro 15, Serbian 8, Mexican 7, Puerto Rican 5, Croatian 5, Greek 3, other 10. "Other" includes a Romanian couple, three Poles, two Italians, two Slovaks, one "Mexican hillbilly," and a daughter of a Sioux Indian mother and an Italian father. "Interview" is a formal word covering all kinds of meetings, sometimes with one, sometimes with several persons present, sometimes a chance encounter, sometimes an arranged appointment. Besides personal talks of some intimacy, I should also include attendance at four Negro church services on successive Sunday mornings, at a Negro choral performance, and at a program on Negro history given in Negro churches on two Sunday afternoons; a tour through Inland Steel, a luncheon-seminar and convocation lecture for and by Mayor Hatcher, for which I flew from Gary to Bloomington and back one day on the Indiana University plane; a spirited local production of "The Roar of the Greasepaint, the Smell of the Crowd," which as a review pointed out, curiously fit into the Gary milieu; and a Serbian musical program at St. Sava Church.

Indiana University
Bloomington, Indiana

Prepared Comments by Linda Dégh

Dorson's field-fresh presentation of the new area of folklore study now under scrutiny is provocative enough to open up a new vista for the traditional folklorist. His field report is a powerful human document put together on the basis of impressions, observations, and tape-recorded disclosures of representatives of the multifaceted folk of the city. This account of a necessarily unorthodox fieldwork project reveals the deep concern and the sense of responsibility of the folklore scholar who for the first time finds himself facing the people of the poverty-ridden, crime-infested, ethnically and culturally mixed industrial city. It also reveals the search for understanding, the attempt to find the lore of urban life radiating through the dark shadows of urban tension, and to discern folk tradition in day-to-day practices, common conversations, gossip, religious belief, and the personal documents of life experience.

Dorson's use of the only feasible method of collecting in a complex industrial community, that of the casual participant-observer who makes a nonselective, around-the-clock record of even the trifles of daily life, was successful indeed. By virtue of his being an outsider to the Gary-East Chicago community and its ethnic and racial groups, while at the same time equipped with experiences in traditional communities elsewhere, Dorson was able to see what a native observer—or the folklorist concerned with one isolated aspect of the traditions of the area—could not have seen so clearly. The diagnosis of Gary and its people was the summation of three weeks of random observation. Yet the statements and the conclusions offered might well be used as a point of departure and a guideline for the future study of urban folklore.

I would like to discuss two main points: the problem of urban and modern industrial folk and their folklore, in general, and my own field research in the Gary-East Chicago area covered by the paper under discussion, the so-called Calumet region, in particular. The question "Is there a folk in the city, is there place for the folklorist in modern industrial society?" is a recurrent one as urbanization spreads and brings about tremendous changes even in the peripheries of Western civilization and within the most resistant core of traditional folk culture. This question, however, immediately raises two others: "What do we mean by 'folk'?" and "Just what do we want to study when we scrutinize the folk in our role as folklorists or regional ethnologists, folklife researchers or students of Volkskunde?"

"Folk," in the traditional sense, means the *vulgus in populo*,[1] the lowest layers of modern society as they developed in the immediate postfeudal period. It means rural people—agriculturists, merchants, craftsmen, small entrepreneurs, and have-nots—living in little communities in the countryside, the inhabitants of farmsteads, villages, townships, and small towns. Relatively isolated from the more progressive urban centers, the folk is old-fashioned, depending to a great extent on traditional economy, skills, ideas, and life style. It accepts outside impulses only to a limited extent, adjusting them to the traditional pattern. Ever since the late nineteenth century, the folklore scholar has been interested in the vanishing relics of the traditional and self-contained

---

[1] Eduard Hoffmann-Krayer, "Naturgesetz im Volksleben?" *Hessische Blätter für Volkskunde*, 2 (1903), 60.

ways of life preserved in various isolated enclaves within his own national culture. He has searched for what was old (and thus venerable) when collecting in the field and has tended to ignore anything new and modern. Thus, the picture drawn by the traditional folklorist is based on the notion of a selective and preconceived search for the idealized past, rather than on first-hand observation of the facts of folk life as they are. Accelerated industrialization gradually reduced the folklorist's hunting grounds and forced him to give up field collecting for historical sources, or for a reconsideration of the aims and scope of his discipline. It seemed hard to part with the old concept of folklore, and folklorists have insisted on pursuing the lore to where it had retreated and might for a time survive because of unusual circumstances. Tolling the bells for the "dying folk tradition" has alternated for a century with the triumphant discoveries of traditional folklore forms—ballads, songs, and *Märchen*—still remembered by city dwellers. The German colonies in eastern Europe and the different ethnic groups in the United States are among the best-researched relic areas. Both of these show similarities in the conservation of an earlier stage of the mother culture, while the mother culture itself has followed the natural course of further change and evolution.

In Europe serious research on urban folklore began during the late 1920s. In northern and western Europe, where the classical peasant culture began to wither away at a quite early date, we find numerous books on industrial workers' folklore, as well as monograph studies of city folklore.[2] These works, however, based on research in cities with several hundred years of historical continuity, are for the most part historical in orientation; so they do not bring us very far in the formulation of a new folklore theory to meet the needs of the modern folklorist. Almost simultaneously on both sides of the Atlantic, the sociocultural changes following World War II made folklorists realize the necessity for broadening their field of study. The modern, complex, pluralistic industrial society became the focus of attention. The increasing mobility of the population, the process of cultural hybridization and acculturation, and—more than anything else—a superior technological civilization forced the folklorist to face the facts of the present. The new trend, called *Gegenwartsvolkskunde* (contemporary folk culture) in the German-speaking countries, switched the emphasis from the past to the living folk traditions as reflections of modern society. These traditions were conceived of as the vehicles of expression for modern groups of people, instead of a moth-eaten hoard of defunct survivals.

Because of its unique features, the United States is the most appropriate testing ground for the elaboration of a new theory for our discipline. This country reached the highest levels of industrialization in a relatively short period of time. Within a period of less than eighty years, industrial cities mushroomed around factories, supplying them with manpower. This process is a continuous one, and it is still absorbing a wide variety of cultures before the very eyes of the observer. People of rural and immigrant background on all levels and degrees of acculturation settle down, form groups, split into subgroups, fuse with other groups, or dissolve and submerge, enriching the greater national culture with their most resistant folk traditions. Traditional as well as urban folklorists can find abundant material for case studies in this living laboratory.

What is "folk" for the contemporary folklorist? A group of people united perman-

[2] For relevant data see Linda Dégh, "Comments on Marcus S. Goldstein's 'Anthropological Research, Action, and Education in Modern Nations, with Special Reference to the U.S.A.,' " *Current Anthropology*, 9 (1968), 256–257.

ently or temporarily by shared common experiences, attitudes, interests, skills, ideas, knowledge, and aims. Those shared attributes are elaborated, sanctioned, and stabilized by the group over a period of time. Any such group or any communally shaped cultural trait might be the subject of folklore study. Not the *vulgus in populo*, but the cultural variables of a broader ethnic and national context is the focus of research. This type of study cannot be carried out, as formerly, by the solitary folklorist who could work conveniently in a small, isolated village. A whole team of specialists—native speakers of the immigrant languages and experts on the different regional groups—must join forces in a cooperative project. Intensive single studies of each group and its affiliations, incorporated into urban folklore monographs, might eventually allow us to grasp the entire life, function, and quality of the cultural conglomerate of the folk in the city.[3]

As to the question of the kind of folklore the complex industrial city has, I want to speak about my own findings among the Hungarians of the Calumet area.

As a native of Hungary with field experience in a great variety of Hungarian peasant and urban communities, my initial goal was to trace the acculturative process that transformed the Hungarian peasant into the Hungarian-American steelworker over a span of some forty to sixty years. What has happened to him? What has become of him? These questions were considered in terms of three factors and their consequences for change: (1) the environment (2) language and means of communication, and (3) social status. Being familiar with regional Hungarian folklore, I started with inquiries about traditional folklore genres as I knew them in their native villages. And I failed. The first two weeks of collecting were full of disappointment because the situation was totally different from anything I had ever encountered before. People's attitudes were different, and they were utterly uncooperative. They could not comprehend what purpose their information could possibly serve. They had learned from experience to be suspicious of talking to strangers. The principle, "Do not let anyone invade your privacy," encouraged them to hold back anything that might shed an unfavorable light on their lives. The hospitable country man can certainly not be compared with the hard-boiled city-dweller.

But even when people did occasionally open up, their information was anything but folklore. What I was doing was sociology, local history or the like but definitely not folklore. I began to feel somewhat guilty about wasting time by attending all kinds of gatherings from Sunday school to funerals, from bingo parties to social evenings in old folk's homes. I spent a good deal of time just hanging around, just being there, waiting patiently for something to happen. I was alert to gossip, followed up rumors, grabbed every opportunity to make people talk about themselves and about others. I have listened spellbound to the fascinating autobiographies that people so generously narrated. Life certainly can be more adventurous than a novel.

Once, however, I suddenly became aware that what I was doing was in fact, folkloristic research. One of the life stories I recorded turned out to be a popular performance, functioning and varying as a folktale would in any traditional community, with the participation of a suitable audience, and elaborated along the lines of tradition. I realized then that it is necessary to learn the cultural environment of the community before one can really find out what its folklore is. It would be a futile effort to learn anything

---

[3] This type of approach is discussed in Linda Dégh, "Approaches to Folklore Research among Immigrant Groups," JOURNAL OF AMERICAN FOLKLORE, 79 (1966), 551–556.

before understanding the basic attitudes, reactions, philosophy, education, home economy, and other small matters measured against the old country ways and the ways of the new environment. Accordingly, I worked out a detailed fieldwork guide for myself, which I have used consistently in the field.

There are no people without tradition. But tradition means conformity to a definite pattern developed over a long period of time by the participation of many generations. What happens to the body of tradition when its bearers leave their country, either as individuals or in small groups not powerful enough to continue on in the tradition? Uprooted Hungarian peasants were by no means homogeneous when they settled in the Calumet area. They came from different regional Hungarian cultures and had to conform to the ways of their fellow workers and neighbors; however, all Hungarian-Americans become culturally homogenized under a cultural umbrella called the Hungarian-American culture. This institution enforces its fabricated cultural features on immigrant life and thus lays the foundation for the folklore of Hungarian-Americans. By means of the ethnic churches, language courses, books, periodicals, the Hungarian Family Hour broadcast, and other mass media—as well as the organized ethnic rituals (vintage celebrations, Christmas carol singing, commemoration of national holidays) and benefit associations—this pattern became the most characteristic trait of the Calumet Hungarians, as indeed of all Hungarian-Americans. The establishment of a similar generalized pattern is probably typical of most other ethnic groups in the United States. This pattern represents an ideal rather than actual and valid Hungarian image, but because it overlaps with and, in fact, discredits the genuine folk tradition, it has acquired tremendous importance. No folklorist in Hungary would ever collect the syrupy middle-class pseudofolklore collected from immigrant groups in the United States—the pop-folksong records, Gypsy music, faked "Hungarian" national costume patterns, and patriotic literature of obscure local poets—because they do not affect peasant culture. I agree with Dorson that these as well as other objects and ideas brought back from visits to the native country reinforce national consciousness and are, therefore, essential to our considerations; however, they are not folk tradition. Nevertheless, linked with the cultural variables developed in the different local clusters and depending on the relationship with other immigrant and native groups, the attributes of this artificially constructed image might someday become a source of a new folk tradition.

As for the retention of the values of the parent cultures by continual reinforcement and for the maintenance of cultural pluralism in the Calumet region, this seems to be a fact valid mainly for the immigrant generation. As Moore has rightly pointed out, "The Calumet region became a mixing bowl, rather than a melting pot, of races and nationalities. Melting pot suggests a oneness of features and characteristics produced by a simultaneous amalgamation of different elements. This did not occur in the Calumet area. Instead, the movement of the population groups into the region during the first fifty years was such that each had the opportunity to make its presence felt."[4] It is true that the immigrant generation did not change its essentially peasant attitudes. The generally known facts of immigrant readjustment—language learning, adoption of different food and dress habits, and acquisition of new technical skills—remained imperfect even after fifty to sixty years. In the case of the Hungarian immigrants, we can speak only of attitudinal changes that affect mostly the material life of the immigrant generation. Approaching the problem of immigrant adjustment as a process of accul-turation, assimilation, and integration, we cannot speak of cultural pluralism without oversimplification. Assimilation generally occurs with the first American-born gene-ration, whereas integration becomes complete by the second.

If folklore is the product of the life of its bearers, it must reflect this life. Among the traditional forms of folklore I collected were a great number of anecdotes, belief legends, folk medicine, and folk religion items, many songs and a few ballads and ritual songs, along with a rich treasury of customs and attitudes. As far as specific Hungarian-Amer-ican genres are concerned, I had a rich harvest in dialect stories, jokes, and experience stories of all kinds, as well as customs and rituals borrowed from the multiethnic environ-ment. All of these are very much alive and have their communal use and value. I would hesitate to call any of the immigrant genres new, since they all had their traditional parallels in similar old country situations.

The existence of experience stories in folk culture has been recognized for a long time, although folklorists paid little attention to them as long as the *Märchen* was their main attraction. In recent years, however, the genre has been described and analyzed, and some collections have been published. The experience stories are by no means moribund, and their elasticity has allowed them to adjust better to modern develop-ments than most other folklore forms. They can be characterized largely by three main topics: (1) the tragic, thrilling or humorous narration of an extraordinary experience in everyday life; (2) narration of experiences during a temporary absence from the com-munity; (3) narration of life experiences in newly formed communities. The last topic is what we find in an agglomeration of people of diverse ethnic backgrounds. Each im-migrant or newcomer to the urban environment has his own story that can contain a single account of great importance to him or a series of episodes from his life. These, of course, become folklore only if they follow a certain pattern and become stabilized by frequent repetition as a result of public demand and communal approval.

My final comment concerns the social value of the kind of folklore that develops within the milieu of the industrial community. Undoubtedly, the social importance of urban folklore forms is not equivalent to that of the classical *Märchen* or heroic song in their heyday. The contemporary folklorist is not looking for creations that are estheti-cally perfect according to his judgment. In search for folk expressions in the bosom of urban life, he wants rather to find out what type of folk attitudes and ideologies are characteristic of his urban folk. The great industrial cities in the United States offer the modern folklorist two typical fields for research: the study of ethnic residues and interethnic acculturation reflected in folklore materials; and the study of the impact of urban life on folklore. The two are intimately related.

BIBLIOGRAPHY

Conrad M. Arensberg and Solon T. Kimball, "American Communities and their Variations," in *Culture and Community* (New York, 1965), 95–210.

Hermann Bausinger, *Formen der 'Volkspoesie,'* (Berlin, 1968), 212–223.

Leo A. Després, "Anthropological Theory, Cultural Pluralism, and the Study of Complex Societies," *Current Anthropology,* 9 (1968), 3–16.

Richard M. Dorson, "Immigrant Folklore," *American Folklore* (Chicago, 1959). See bibliog-raphy to chapter.

Joshua A. Fishman, *Hungarian Language Maintenance in the United States* (Bloomington, Ind., 1966).

E. C. Hughes and others, eds., *Race and Culture* (Glencoe, Ill. 1950).

Emil Lengyel, *Americans from Hungary* (New York, 1948).

Tamotsu Shibutani, *Improvised News: A Sociological Study of Rumor* (Indianapolis and New York, 1966).

Melford E. Spiro, "The Acculturation of American Ethnic Groups" *American Anthropologist,* 57 (1955), 1240–1252.

Ingeborg Weber-Kellermann, "Probleme interethnischer Forschungen in Südosteuropa," *Ethnologia Europaea,* 1 (1967), 218–231.

Emilio Willems, "On the Concept of Assimilation," *American Anthropologist,* 56 (1955), 225–226.

Indiana University
Bloomington, Indiana

Prepared Comments by Leonard W. Moss

My sociological colleagues assure me that when there is nothing else to attack in a paper, challenge the sampling procedure. Somehow, somewhere it has to be wrong. In anthropology we can always question the theoretical position taken by the speaker. Contemporary student activists would attack by dismissing the whole paper, the speaker, the meeting, and the world as irrelevant. I am truly uncertain what mode of critique I should adopt. Perhaps the safest ground is to challenge the speaker on what he did not say and what he did not intend to say. Here one can build the horsiest straw man and whip it dead into the ground. Mixed metaphor? No, true to the social sciences, a neologism!

One might assume that Professor Dorson's paper is based on an unsophisticated acceptance of the folk-urban concept as suggested by Redfield and many others in the social sciences. This would presume a pure folk at one end of the continuum and Volkswagens at the other end. I must then attack Professor Dorson's title as a phony. Is there a folk in the city? The answer is obvious, for folk is people and that is what the city is all about to everyone except bureaucrats and census takers. Professor Dorson and Doctor Dégh have tackled a terribly difficult problem. It is far easier to collect folklore and be objective about its contents in the Outer Hebrides than it is in Gary, Hamtramck, Oshkosh, or Belt Parkway. In treating with the verbal lore of a people, we are touching the very heart and guts of a culture. The attitudes, values, and beliefs transmitted at the knee of the mother constitute, for the most part, the nearest and dearest expressions of mankind. The ultimate common values of a people as a whole are embodied and emboweled in the oral tradition. This is equally true of people living in the shade of the Ituri Forest, on the edge of the Kalahari Desert, on the Abruzzi highlands, or in the smog-filled, peeling-paint households of Gary. We are dealing with the hopes, aspirations, norms, and day-to-day mishmash of people.

In the urban setting the collection of folklore becomes a terrifying problem. Imagine the "simplicity" of collecting oral tradition in a milieu dominated by media of mass communications. Professor Dorson has given us a good start in the attempt to sort through the welter of materials. It is most difficult to separate what is transmitted through kin lines from what is communicated by unrelated people living near one another.

How does one trace the combinations and permutations of the lore that is part of mass culture—in the broadest sense of both mass and culture? Couple this with the phenomena of ethnic hybridizing and lore that crosses class lines, and one begins to perceive the enormity of the problem.

Though Professor Dorson has noted the difference between working abroad and working at home, I must note that it is far more difficult to collect on the local scene. And the mere act of checking into a downtown hotel does not remove one from the home front. You have never really left the pad. There is, somehow, the lack of total immersion that takes place in a foreign environment. The folklorist or anthropologist living abroad has the opportunity to collect his wits on the rare occasion when he can sum up the present experience in comparison with the yesterday of his cultural past. Living in the morass of urban existence gives us pause, but not the pause that refreshes.

Professor Dorson places heavy reliance on the use of a tape recorder as a collecting instrument. This device is a useful and welcome adjunct to field research; yet, I shudder at the ultimate effects of wholesale notetaking. We are heading for an era when we shall have warehouses full of information on tape, punch cards, and all of the other glorious paraphernalia of "modern" research. Then some lunatic will turn loose a group of aspiring doctoral students on the ultimate "Great Project . . . in the sky, by and by." This will entail the correlation of everything with everything else, in hope that the great computer of the future will spew out something meaningful. One is reminded of the computermen's bit, "GIGO—*Garbage In, Garbage Out.*"

Many points of focus are possible in the study of urban folklore. Professor Dorson glosses over one sore point: crime in the streets. In the case of homicide, criminologists note that 60 to 75 percent of all murders take place within the family or circle of friends. I do not suggest that crime and violence are not problems in our society. I do suggest that it is important to sort fact from lore in these touchy areas.

One basic problem lingers in my simplistic mind. When will those of us engaged in folklore tackle the truly important problems? Some years ago anthropology came to grips with the problem of turning ethnography into ethnology. How long will it take folklorists to make the meaningful step toward that end? This is not meant as a criticism of Professor Dorson's fine paper. I choose, instead, to castigate him for what he has not done. He did not set for himself the task of comparative analysis and theory building. As a leading authority in the history of folklore and as a major folklorist, he owes us much more than proof that folklore exists in the city. He owes us more than a series of vignettes and anecdotes, no matter how interesting they may be. Professor Dorson has avoided facile generalizations and for good reason; yet, he has also avoided the creation of genuine hypotheses that could lead to exciting and fertile research beyond the point of collecting and categorizing. Without classification we wander in a morass of unordered data. If we stop at classification, we commit taxonomic suicide. If we are unprepared to venture forth with hypotheses that lead to theory building, then we are reduced to mere dilettantism.

Many important questions remain in the field of urban folklore. In a world dominated by rapid change, what is the mechanism of *retention*? For example, one might cite the Marrano converts of Spain, who cling to elements of Judaism after nearly five hundred years. We must learn more about the phenomenon of diffusion. We know next to nothing about ethnic hybridizing. We have not scratched the surface of the ways new lore is created.

Outside the world of academic folklore, there is a cruel world replete with problems. In our day we are beset by racism, economic deprivation, violence, prejudice and hate, overpopulation, and war. If words and music, blowing instruments and shouting in church, and having steel companies sponsor books on urban folklore would influence in any way the problems that beset our society, then I would urge we all shout, sing, speak, read, and so on. I think, however, in our culture other techniques far more productive than those presently used by folklorists must be applied. How is one to sway a culture loaded with urban problems, whose Congress lops untold billions off of a meager urban budget at the same time that it swells an already bloated military budget? In a culture that gives toy tanks, cannons, and guns as gifts to celebrate the birth of the Prince of Peace, people will pay scant attention to books on urban folklore.

Wayne State University
Detroit, Michigan

Reply to Prepared Comments by Richard Dorson

Moss's comments seem so unrelated to my paper that I can make little comment in rebuttal. He asks for "comparative analysis and theory building" and "the creation of genuine hypotheses." Since the Gary-East Chicago field trip was conceived to test several hypotheses, which Dr. Dégh and I have both set forth, and since it produced for me, after a twenty-three day field trip, a whole set of theoretical concepts, outlined in my summary ten points, which could consume several lifetimes of investigation, I must for once be reduced to shocked speechlessness.

One matter I would like to amplify, this suggestion of mine for a book of urban folk traditions as a means of developing an interethnic and interracial community of interest. The idea grows out of one field discovery, the cherished esteem of The Book as a cultural artifact representing the unique inheritance of the ethnic or racial group— a very special, little known, usually obscurely printed book. Why not a book representing each of the major folk groups of Gary-East Chicago, so that the pluralistic cultures will lavish their affection on a tome representing them all? With the steel companies as the logical publishers, since they created this divided community. The reference librarian at the *Gary Tribune* informed me that the series they had run on nationality groups in the city continued in greatest demand of any of their features. I make this suggestion half-seriously, recognizing that the practical and intellectual difficulties would be formidable, but responding to the impulse of our symposium for specific thoughts on reducing hostilities and building bridges in our cities.

Dégh's paper emphasizes a point of utmost consequence to which I completely subscribe: the necessity for an altered role and broadened vision of the folklorist as he addresses himself to the "cultural conglomerate" of city people. In the end we may find that we are not dealing with such different classes of material as we had encountered in the countryside: the immigrant experience-story replaces the *Märchen* of old. I am not so sure as she is that we can, or need to, separate a pure folk tradition of peasant culture from the pseudofolk products depicting and memorializing that culture. My own thinking now turns to the "unofficial culture" rather than remnants of peasant culture. How we distinguish the official from the unofficial culture is a theoretical problem of its own. The urban folklorist will not want for field data or intellectual challenges, so long as man lives in cities.

Discussion from the Floor

George McMahon:—When I first heard of folklore in the city, I thought of collecting what you or Dr. Dégh mentioned, vanishing relics and idealized past. But what I was hoping eventually that both of your presentations would do, and I don't think you did it for me anyway, was to show how you can begin collecting folklore of the culture that is developing in the city. I don't think either of you did that. How would you go about collecting oral traditions that are right now developing, you know, in Jeffries Project or on Third Avenue or on John R. Street?

Dégh:—This is exactly what we are doing; first we must collect ethnographic data. We can't find out what its folklore is before we know the field. This is a new field for us.

Aili Johnson:—I'd like to make a comment. I think that if we're going to study John R. we ought to study about Bloomfield Hills in exactly the same way, and Grosse Pointe, too. We should compare the folk of Bloomfield Hills and Grosse Pointe with the folk of any area in Detroit and see what the changes and differences are. One will find a good many ethnic groups, if you want those, but you also will find certain other patterns. Are they similar? In what way are they different? Why study one type of life in the urban community and not the other? Would that be useful in helping solve our urban problems: studying different groups, such as economic levels, not usually investigated by folklorists?

Moss:—I think in defense of Dick Dorson's paper, he makes it eminently clear that he does not limit himself to a single group within the community.

Stekert:—I think what Mrs. Johnson was saying was that we should study the folklore of what is sometimes referred to as the "dominant culture" of the society as well as the urban ethnic groups.

Dorson:—Yes, the executives as well as the employees.

Robert Tremain:—How much communication is there between these ethnic groups? Is it fear or is it total ignorance, or what is the situation?

Dorson.—That's a long story. There's violent hostility among certain groups; there are all these animosities. But, on the other hand, there are bridges that have been built. It seems to me that one has to be careful about generalizations.

Arnold Pilling:—I would like to comment on a recent Detroit phenomenon, which I think might have some utility as a source of folklore. There has been established in

Detroit a rumor control center. I understand that at the center a telephone operator is at the opposite end of the line to write down rumors, listing their time and date of hearing, where they were heard, and where the person telephoning lives. It seems to me that the availability of such precise material should not be overlooked. The rumor control center material may easily be useful in telling us something about the dynamics of folklore. I assume we all agree that rumors are in a folklore area. I think we know relatively little about the dynamics of folklore, how folktales spread, and how they modify in spreading.

It seems to me that we have here an easily available source on urban folklore. It would be tragic if these records were lost. If nothing more can be done at this time, we should urge that the records of this rumor control center be saved for later mining. Enough data are apparently preserved so that students might later isolate motifs and write of their changes as they move from one location and time to another. Some of these rumor control center data have been noted recently in local newspapers, but more analytical treatment is necessary. I think that we have very meaningful material here. It certainly should tell us something of today's urban folklore.

Unidentified black woman from Detroit:—I'd like to ask Dr. Dorson a question. I notice you talked about the Negro church and what you found there. What about the other segments of the Negro community. Did you get any experience there?

Dorson:—Well, I had some contacts. I don't know that there'd be enough to make any large generalization about it, but there seems to be a trend to imitating middle- or upper-class white culture. I think that's pretty noticeable. I went to a Trinity Baptist church, and I was informed about a book, again a reference to "the book," which was available in a certain drugstore (I never was able to get ahold of it) informing Negroes about certain cultural traits they should divest themselves of in order to become accepted into the white community. Most unfortunate kind of publication, it seems to me, but anyway there it was. It was certainly having an influence in the culture. Some of the traits mentioned were—I think—loud talking, loud laughter in public places, the whole series of these things, or the wearing of large hats with extravagant colors. That's one kind of possible trend I could mention. Of course that's a very large question.

Same black woman:—I just want to know what way these things are used in social relationships of the people that you're studying. It seems to me that cultural traits can be absorbed by other cultures, have different meaning assigned to them, that the same meaning can exist in two completely different cultural traits at different times in a people. It seems to me, then, that the kind of difference between what we call folk from what we call urban is the difference in the way we relate to each other as persons, the meaning of social relationships. And to study the folklore, or the tradition, or how certain cultural traits are maintained you must look at this deeply-rooted meaning of the relationships people have for each other. I think the difference between what we call the ghetto community or the urban community is more than just economic difference. It's a whole set of relationships that have a meaning—what the other person means to you, what social relations mean. I don't see how the kind of study you're doing is rooted in that kind of thing.

Dorson:—I'm not sure just what kind of personal-cultural relationships you're speaking of. Maybe I could give this example of Marion Tokarsky, the Polish woman, who made common cause with the Negro community in Gary and in East Chicago. She presented her story to the Northwest Political Alliance group which was composed almost entirely of Negroes, some Puerto Ricans. Now she presented it to this group really in the form of a church service, I would say. I don't know if I'm speaking on your point, but the relationship was effective within the terms of a traditional institution central in the Negro community. This was the way in which they would understand this message, and the way in which the bridge was built between this Polish Catholic woman and the Negro Baptists. Well, that would be one kind of relationship that certainly enters into our investigations.

Morton Leeds (Washington, D.C.):—There is one thing I'd like to say. Someone raised the issue of cross-culturation of groups. This is occurring at all points in the daytime at work, and it's the obvious thing we should always remember. Now the question we could ask ourselves in this kind of study is to what extent do we communicate across cultures in the daytime, to what extent do we not communicate. Because, if you remember, our personal choices at the lowest tension levels are for evening communications with people like ourselves. This is one of the great problems that we as a society face because we tend to drift back to our lairs and go back to the people we are most comfortable with. Now this becomes a social rather than a purely anthropological or folkloric problem, and it is also an economic problem. So you have the interpenetration of at least three different levels of the society.

Dorson:—How do ethnic groups get together, how do they communicate, what are their interpersonal relationships? I think that's what the question is. And it seems to me there is relatively little communication other than on the job. Then it's a retreat, if I can use that word, back into their familiar cultural traditions. For instance, I was told that there is very little joke-telling on the job in the steel mills because ethnic jokes are regarded as a divisive influence, so the management doesn't want this sort of thing. So they don't have this common community of storytelling. Some groups have a good deal more than others, like the Greeks, whereas the Croats will tend to mix. But again you can't generalize.

Second unidentified black woman from Detroit:—I have a question. Last week I worked with a preschool teacher who happens to be white, and we got into a discussion as to what was racism. And she said it was any relationship between any kinds of people, either good or bad. I sit here and listen, and presumably people are trying to solve social problems. I was wondering when is someone going to begin to look at what racism is, because obviously it is not a recent phenomenon, so it has its roots and genesis very long ago in America. And if we look at the institution of the black church and know that, again, its genesis is rooted in slavery—when are people going to deal with what is racism because here, too, there are many things in folklore I am sure that perpetuate racism. And I think that this certainly is a task for the folklorist as well as the anthropologist, and I wonder when this is going to happen.

Dorson:—That's exactly what we're doing. We're dealing with the materials that reflect racial and ethnic folk culture, divisiveness. I think perhaps racism is too strong a term. It's lost its charge, I think, by being used in too many contexts. We were talking here about ethnic or group folk cultural traditions and perhaps trying to look at them positively as well as negatively. It seems to me from what we found that one group knows little about the cultural traditions of another. And they don't understand or appreciate the best of what the other tradition has to offer. That might be our way out.

Moss:—It's obvious that Professor Dorson has been collecting some of the materials you allude to. I am reminded of one point where a Slovak, pointing with pride to a picture of his golden wedding anniversary, says that this could not have happened to a Czech since they have twenty wives just like the blacks. So he disposes of two peoples at one time, and within that expression it is obvious that he is establishing a nexus of social relationships within which he interacts. It is within this kind of guts of a folk culture that you find relationships established. When you hear a Sicilian say, *"Lite tra padre e figlio, non ci vol consiglio,"* you know damn well he means, "There's an argument between father and son. Outsiders keep out, this is family."

ROGER D. ABRAHAMS

The Negro Stereotype
*Negro Folklore and the Riots**

DISCUSSIONS OF THE RIOTS of the last few years almost always turn to some expression of what Negroes are doing to themselves. A recurring note is that the rioters are playing right into the hands of the bigots by conforming to the stereotype, by being irrational and destructive and falling into thievery. There can be little argument against this, because thievery and destruction do occur. The riots, however, simply announce to the white world that life in the ghettoes may seem to have changed because of recent legal decisions and governmental actions but that it hasn't. Ghetto Negroes are beset with the same economic, social, and psychological problems as before. The only changes that have occurred are in the extent of hope and the depth of resultant frustration.

The riots are not revolutionary; they put no program into effect, and they exhibit only a spasmodic plan of attack. They do publicly proclaim, however, that the American Dream is still being pursued—and still being frustrated. Stokely Carmichael says just this in his book *Black Power,* "In America we judge by American standards, and by this yardstick we find the black man lives in incredibly inadequate housing, . . . in segregated neighborhoods and with this comes *de facto* segregated schooling, which means poor education, which leads in turn to ill-paying jobs."[1] This is the essential "message" of the riots. Robert Fogelson, a historian of the riots, points out,

Far from rejecting the national ideology, the rioters demanded that all citizens fully honor it; they insisted on changes in practice, not principles. . . . The rioters made it clear to reporters during the riots and to interviewers afterwards that they expected the rioting to improve their position by arousing white concern. They could not know then—and indeed they may not know now—that, if anything the whites, though more concerned, are also more intransigent. Put bluntly, the Negroes delivered a protest, but the whites did not hear it.[2]

* Professor Abrahams' paper was first written in 1967; and, more than the others included here, it was geared to contemporaneous events. His later work, *Positively Black* (Englewood Cliffs, 1970), contains some of the texts presented here and many of the same ideas, but it is not focused solely on the riots of that time.

[1] Stokely Carmichael and Charles V. Hamilton, *Black Power* (New York, 1967), 155–156.

[2] Robert Fogelson, "Violence as Protest: An Interpretation of the 1960 Riots," unpublished manuscript (1967), 16.

The whites did not read the message clearly because in rioting the ghetto Negro acted in a manner that whites were able to categorize as typical. The whites viewed these acts of protest as further examples of the disorganized, dishonest, and immoral life-style of the blacks.

How did the rioters get caught in this misunderstanding of motive? The answer lies in the ambivalent image of themselves that Negroes have developed under the stern tutelage of whites. The slaves, once deculturated, were provided with a stereotype of themselves, which they learned to accept or "accommodate" to. At the same time, however, slaves developed a mechanism of fighting back. Though they accommodated to the stereotype image, they converted their supposed animality, supersexuality, and childishness—their thievery, laziness, and strong smell—from negative to positive attributes. Thus Negroes have been able to use the stereotype as an aggressive weapon against the very society that imposed it.

This operation is costly, however, for it still adds up to an acceptance of the white stereotype. There must be an ambivalence about conforming to the stereotype since both the white world and important segments of the Negro community continue to regard such traits as negative. Furthermore, the acceptance and conversion of the traits lead to activities and attitudes that are uncreative and unfulfilling, indeed, noticeably destructive and all too often suicidal. The destructive activities of the riots are similar to those portrayed as "heroic" in many Negro traditional narratives. In a very real sense these fictions are related to Negro actions, for they have been one of the primary devices by which the Negro self-image has been formulated, transmitted, and maintained.

I.

Many scholars have suggested that there is an intimate relationship between the problems faced in common by a group and the communicative interaction they develop. What interests folklorists most is the structure of the communications of culture as the communications become repeated—and therefore, by definition, traditional. Any group with a sense of community will announce this sense by borrowing or developing traditional communicative devices. The devices, in fact, define the group and become its folklore. We tend to look to peasant communties (or, more recently, to aboriginal groups) for folklore, because the members of these groups and their ancestors have existed for such a long time together under the same conditions that they have a great number of shared expressions and practices. But there are groups arising in heterogeneous city cultures ("special interest groups," "subcultures," or "part-time folk communities") that have their traditions as well—hippies, spelunkers, church, club, and lodge members, astronauts. A member of a heterogeneous society may belong to many different groups of this sort and share in all of their traditions. These groups have expressive traditions arising out of, and primarily concerned with, the common activities of the members. The amount of folklore and the degree of its persistence within a group is in direct proportion to the amount of time members spend together and the number of values and activities shared within the group.

A group's feeling of apartness or common purpose may arise simply because of the shared interests of the members (as opposed to the lack of interest of "the others") or it may occur because of the danger of a common activity. In certain cases, physical and geographical separation increases the sense of community; in other cases, a certain sense of community is created when cultural disparity is observed in a pluralistic situation and one of the groups is denigrated for these differences. This commonly brings about a defensive sense of group cohesiveness, a degree of homogeneity even in the midst of a culturally heterogeneous milieu. This cohesion becomes more profound whenever the existence of the group or its most deeply held values and practices are threatened. In the urban milieu, sense of community and of cultural homogeneity is felt more deeply in minority groups; this is, in part, a reaction against the anxieties arising from being a minority and the recurrent threat posed by the surrounding society to the existence of the group and its members. Where the group is threatened, traditional expressions are often the most salient means of proclaiming and reinforcing group identity.

Viewed in this way, the study of the expressive culture of minority groups can cast important light on community values and activities and point to those places where cultural disparity between the minority group and dominant society is most deeply felt. But such an enclave, given its minority status, is commonly subject to greater stresses from outside forces than is any other kind of subculture, and in many cases it reacts with traditional expression, more intensive in aggressions and defenses and more complex in functions than that found in any other type of subculture. The lore of a minority group must convey not only its esoteric conception of itself, proclaiming its ideals and taking care of its day-to-day interpersonal problems; it must also cope with the exoteric stereotype imposed upon it by the dominant culture.[3]

Expressive folklore confronts three kinds of problem situations: those arising from disruptive forces operating within the group, those stemming from the confrontation of man and nature, and those stimulated by a threat from outsiders. Expressive folklore is a composite term for the traditional activities that attempt to control the uncertainties arising from all these situations. The nature of the folklore of a specific group, therefore, will directly reflect the kinds of tensions and anxieties experienced in common by the members of the group.

The folklore of all communities will reflect problems of the social, natural, or external sort; but because of varying situations the range, intensity, and focus of these problems will differ from group to group. Most peasant groups, for instance, faced with the necessity of wresting a living from the soil will have a wealth of traditional expressions of knowledge devoted to the recurrent problems posed by the destructive aspects of nature (storms, droughts, sicknesses). At the same time interpersonal problems may be equally important to these groups and in such a case will result in the presence of numerous traditional mechanisms for the preservation of group harmony (proverbs, games, and so forth). But pressures from other groups outside the community will be nominal in such cases. On the other hand, for minority groups in the urban milieu the threat of nature is negligible while the problems of out-group exclusion are primary and pervasive. In one fashion or another, the lore of the minority group reacting adversely to social isolation must cope with imposed social distance or rejection, commonly maintained and rationalized through stereotyping by the majority group.

"A stereotype," as defined by Gordon W. Allport, "is an exaggerated belief associated with a category. Its function is to justify (rationalize) our conduct in

[3] William Hugh Jansen, "The Esoteric-Exoteric Factor in Folklore," *Fabula: Journal of Folktale Studies*, 2 (1959), 205–211.

relation to that category."[4] By centering on rationalization processes Allport points to the often unconscious nature of attitudes and consequent trait-assigning in stereotyping. Robin M. Williams, Jr., developing upon this, points to four ways, both conscious and unconscious, in which stereotype is enunciated in Negro-white communications.

Accidental-indirect—"Phrases . . . equating whiteness with purity or desirability and blackness with evil" or "whites telling Negroes jokes about Jews, Italians, or Catholics, or confidential statements such as 'You Negroes are all right with me, but it's those Jews I don't like.'"

Accidental-direct—Racial testimonials in which "whites seek to establish rapport by making favorable categorical statements of their preference for Negroes or by making assertions that Negroes are not inferior to whites"; and racial slips, "unintentional phrases in the speech of whites that carry epithets or other expressions that are disparaging."

Intentional-indirect—Stereotyped preconceptions, such as "white people who expect all Negroes to be able to dance and sing, . . . or who think that each Negro knows all other Negroes, or who believe that Negroes are lazy, ignorant, and happy-go-lucky . . ."; and caricatures of the Negro, "the way Negro life is parodied in the media of communication."

Intentional-direct—Jokes, songs, and stories disparaging Negroes; and the intentional use of racial epithets. [5]

Because their use is intentional and at times deliberately pointed, jokes and other traditional channels for verbal aggression often serve as the most direct and potent medium for disseminating stereotype notions. Though such slurs are "intentional," they nevertheless have an important unconscious dimension observable in the "Rastus and Mandy" cycle of jokes long used in the southern United States as a means of illustrating the Negro stereotype. In their great emphasis on the supposed sexual freedom of Negroes, these jokes betray the fear and fascination of sex, characteristic of the sexually protected and repressed.[6] Consequently, these jokes are a means by which sexual restrictions can be bypassed, at least vicariously, while at the same time the attribution of "deviant" sexual activities to Negroes can be used as a device for maintaining their subordination.

In fact, most of the traits of the Negro stereotype may reflect a similar mechanism for exercising antinormative motives for ambivalent purposes. Stereotypes held by the dominant group commonly reflect the most positive traits of a culture rendered negatively. "Negative stereotypes used by majority-group members . . . to stigmatize outgroups usually are the reversed images of dominant positive traits. The epithet of laziness reflects the value [and the burden] of industriousness. Ignorance contrasts with the virtues of competence, education, self-improvement. Dishonesty is the opposite of upright, moral, fair dealings."[7] The force of the negative stereotype rises from its ambivalence, that is, from its ability to promulgate high values through their negation, to use the improper actions in a cautionary fashion, to impute the rejected activities to a subordinate group, to maintain social distance and rationalize subservience, and all the while vicariously

[4] G. W. Allport, *The Nature of Prejudice* (Reading, Mass., 1954), 187.

[5] Robin M. Williams, Jr., and others, *Strangers Next Door: Ethnic Relations in American Communities* (Englewood Cliffs, N.J., 1964), 44–46.

[6] John Dollard, *Caste and Class in a Southern Town* (New York, 1937), 168–170; Robert Seidenberg, "The Sexual Basis of Social Prejudice," *Psychoanalytic Review*, 39 (1952), 90–95.

[7] Williams, 40.

enjoying the exercise of the otherwise forbidden motive. One may have cake and eat it, too.

II.

This study, however, is not so much concerned with the establishment, maintenance, and dissemination of the stereotype of the Negro as it is with the ways this combination of traits has been received and manipulated by Negroes. We are dwelling here in the realm of what John Dollard has called the "lore of accommodation."

Accommodation attitudes are those which enable the Negro to adjust and survive in the caste situation as it is presented to him. Originally the alternatives to accommodation were successful conflict with whites or extinction. There was little prospect of success in conflict . . . so the only possible alternative was adjustment to the situation. . . .

Accommodation involves the renunciation of protest or aggression against undesirable conditions of life and the organization of the character so that protest does not appear, but acceptance does. It may come to pass in the end that one identifies with it and takes it into the personality; it sometimes even happens that what is at first resented and feared is finally loved.[8]

The theory of accommodation is an extremely attractive one for an understanding of Negro-white relations, especially in regard to the amazing conformity of Negro personality types and certain of the stereotype traits. The theory is so attractive, in fact, that Stanley M. Elkins devoted a large section of his book *Slavery* to an exploration of the psychological dimension of the accommodation pattern. But Elkins' point of view is almost as ignorant as Dollard's in regard to the defensive-aggressive direction that apparent accommodation features may take. Only in a footnote does Elkins acknowledge that subservience may be used as an aggressive weapon, and he was driven to this through the suggestions of the psychoanalyst Bruno Bettelheim. Elkins notes, "This involves the principle of how the powerless can manipulate the powerful through aggressive stupidity, literalmindedness, servile fawning and irresponsibility."[9] He might have added to this repertory of aggressive-defensive traits most of the others in the Negro stereotype—thievery, sexual abandon, childishness, and so on.

The use of these traits for aggressive purposes has a certain irony to it, and does permit hostility to be directed toward the very source of the group's greatest frustrations. But the ego gains derived from such activities are small and short-lived because they do not generally register any reaction in the white world, except to confirm stereotyped notions. Even though the traits are converted, the argument is still being waged on white man's terms. The actors exhibiting such traits continue to function as miscreants, not only in the eyes of the white world but also to the preachers and matriarchs within the Negro community. Furthermore, the aggressions allow little of the long-term gains needed to build a stable and meaningful self-image. It is difficult to embody such an image in negations. The aggressions seem to be directed only at the white world; but given their continuing negative associations, even in the minds of the aggressors, they become in part self-castigating. Their rhetoric is a confused one, for they seem to say two contradic-

---

[8] Dollard, 250, 255.
[9] Stanley M. Elkins, *Slavery* (Universal Library edition, New York, 1963), 132–133.

tory things at the same time: "Look how big, brave, and dangerous I am" and "Look how degraded and worthless I am." No wonder their message calling for recognition and power, when expressed in terms of riots, is misunderstood.

III.

This self-defeating aggression pattern seems to have arisen early in the New World Negro experience. In the activities and fictions of the ante-bellum and Reconstruction periods, the traits of the stereotype converted were those that could be expressed most easily in a covert way: laziness, childishness, irrational beliefs, and "misuse" of language. In the 1940s and 1950s, more active though still covert activities developed, like "Pushin' Day." Negroes took off from work, going to the most crowded stores in town to do some "pushin'," which can be done without much fear of arousing attention or reprisal. More recently this type of aggressive activity has been more overt, in sit-ins, marches, and most recently in riots. This changing approach to the problem is strongly reflected in traditional narratives as well.

The two types of stories of greatest currency in Negro groups, urban and rural, have been trickster tales and jokes. These humorous story types are aggressive in their conception and allow the storyteller and his audience to channel frustrations with greatest economy. At one time tales of the trickster in the guise of Br'er Rabbit were quite common. In these Rabbit goes through a series of adventures in which he is able to dupe animals larger and more powerful than himself, sometimes Lion or Bear, sometimes the Farmer. To get away with his tricks, Rabbit must not only have audacity and drive but also the self-serving purpose and direct expression of hungers characteristic of the child. And it is in the guise of the childish creature who really cannot be held accountable for his actions that we commonly observe and judge Rabbit. This childish behavior and approach to life is, of course, one of the major characteristics imputed to the Negro.

This conversion technique is even clearer in the nonanimal trickster tales in currency since Emancipation. The most widely found trickster of this class is the slave John (or Tom or Efan) who crops up in many stories in direct confrontation with his "ole Marster." Though in some tales Marster outwits John, it is usually the other way around. In the most commonly found story in this cycle, "The Coon in the Box," John is forced into playing the role of a clairvoyant in a bet between Marster and another white planter. Marster says that John has supernatural power of vision, and the other man bets that John is a fraud. They get an object and put it into a box. John, through trickery, finds out what is in the box and names it at the appropriate time. This happens again. A third time, a raccoon is caught and put into the box, and the other white man takes precautions that John cannot cheat again. John, in desperation, when forced to admit that he does not know the contents of the box, says, "Well, you got this old coon at last." And so again he and his Marster win.[10]

This story emphasizes, through the punchline, that John is to be regarded as a representative Negro in conflict with the white world. And his activity is once again directly related to a facet of the Negro stereotype—in this case, the pro-

[10] Richard M. Dorson, *American Negro Folktales* (New York, 1967), 126.

pensity of the Negro toward childish belief in various kinds of occult powers. This ironic transformation of stereotype is true of virtually every trait of this sort. Laziness, stupidity, and thievery are all constant themes of the Marster-John cycle, used by John as a means of getting the better of Marster. Richard M. Dorson, for instance, prints a number of stories in which John becomes a thief and has to talk his way out of punishment when caught. John's trickery is usually expressed verbally.

John stole a pig from Old Marster. He was on his way home with him and his Old Marster seen him. After John got home he looked out and seen his Old Marster coming down to the house. So he put this pig in a cradle they used to rock the babies in in them days (some people called them cribs), and he covered him up. When his Old Marster come in John was sitting there rocking him.

Old Marster says, "What's the matter with the baby, John?" "The baby got the measles." "I want to see him." John said, "Well, you can't; the doctor said if you uncover him the measles will go back in on him and kill him." So his Old Marster said, "It doesn't matter; I want to see him, John." He reached down to uncover him.

John said, "If that baby is turned to a pig now, don't blame me."[11]

But the most aggressive type of Marster-John story is that in which John not only gets the better of Marster but in the process causes him to appear ridiculous. This type, still abundantly evident in Negro repertories, commonly turns on some kind of obscene reference in which Marster is not only made the fool but his masculinity is placed in question.

There once was a Negro slave named Tom who was so smart that his Master told everyone in town not to make any bets with him. It so happened that another white man in town wanted to buy Tom. So the original Master told him, "O.K., I'll let you buy Tom, but I must warn you never to make a bet with him." So the white man said, "Oh, I'm smarter than a nigger any day." He bought Tom and just as sure as life, Tom shortly thereafter propositioned the man. He said, "Master, I'll bet you anything that you're constipated." The white man said, "What? No, I'm not. I know I'm not constipated." Tom said, "Well if you're not constipated I'll bet you a thousand dollars that by twelve o'clock you will be." So his Master said, "All right, you've got a bet."

At twelve o'clock Tom came back. He told his Master that he had to test to see if he was constipated. The Master asked, "How do you do this?" Tom explained that he would have to pull down his pants and let him stick his finger up his ass. The Master agreed to this. Tom did it, and said, "Well, you're not constipated." Master said, "Well, I guess that means you owe me a thousand dollars." Tom said, "All right." The Master went off happy because he had won the bet and outsmarted Tom. He happened to be bragging to a friend about this and his friend said, "What? Man, Tom had bet me *two* thousand dollars that by twelve o'clock today he'd have his finger up your ass."[12]

Just this kind of aggression is directed against the white man in another widely found series of stories centering on "White Man, Nigger, and Jew" or in Texas, more commonly "White Man, Negro, Mexican." These are Negro versions of the international type of jest that plays off the cultural traits of three or four different ethnic groups or nationalities (like American, British, French) with the intent of illustrating the superiority of one's own group. The stories focus on stereotypic traits, and as in the other story types discussed they take some element of the Negro stereotype and make it into a power device showing the Negro to be su-

[11] Dorson, 137–138.
[12] Collected from Arlette Jones, Houston, Texas, December 1965.

perior. In the following example, the purported strong smell of the Negro is utilized to show the Negro's great masculine power.

Once upon a time there was a white man, a Mexican, and a Negro. They were in a contest to see who was the mustiest. So they tied a goat in the back of the house and said, "Now we'll see who is the mustiest." The white man went around the back of the house and the goat just sniffed a little. The Mexican went around the house and the goat sniffed a little more. The Negro went around the house and when he came back the goat was dead.[13]

The important term here is "musty"—used rather than "smell" or "odor"—for "musty" has strong sexual connotations, especially in a joke about goats. This joke is therefore something of a sexual boast. The Negro is, in a sense, beating the goat at his own game while putting the white man and the Mexican to shame.

Sexual superiority, the most common trait assumed by Negro men in these stories, is often found in combination with toughness and "style."[14] In these jokes, sexual superiority is used as an aggressive weapon; most of the jests involving three men turn on the sexual proficiency and superiority of the Negro male, illustrated either in the larger size of his genitalia or in his greater sexual capacity.

A man put up a sign outside his farm offering a reward of one-hundred dollars to anyone who could make his alligator reach a climax. Three men came to try. They were a white man, a Mexican, and a Negro. The white man went in and stayed for fifteen minutes. He came out all tired and ragged. The score sheet reported: "Man—one climax. Alligator—none." The Mexican went in. He stayed for an hour. He came out haggard and disheveled. The score sheet read: "Man—four climaxes. Alligator—none." The Negro went in. He stayed two hours, three hours, twelve hours, a day, a week, two weeks. He came out neat as a pin, cool, calm, and collected. The score sheet read: "Man—fifteen climaxes. Alligator—dead."[15]

Three men were sent to court: a white, a Negro, and a Mexican. They got to court and the judge said, "If you have fifteen inches of length between you, I'll let you go." The judge called for the bailiff to measure the penises. So he measured the Negro's and it was seven and one-half inches long. Then he measured the Mexican's and it was five and one-half inches long. Next he measured the white man's and it was two inches long. That was fifteen inches. Therefore they were set free. When they got outside the court, they all started laughing and bragging. The Negro said, "You'd better be glad mine was seven and a half inches." The Mexican said, "You'd better be glad mine was five and a half inches." The white man looked at them and said, "Both of you have better be glad that I was on hard."[16]

But this kind of aggressive statement of superiority in competition with whites is giving way to a further and even more overtly aggressive joke type. White man and Negro meet (usually a city Negro with great style and audacity); they have a fight when the Negro steps out of line, and the white man is warned against reprisal by some very tough action and statement on the part of the Negro. In a story recently found in both white and Negro repertories the southern white man shoots an apple while it is still in the air to show the out-of-line Negro what he can expect if he continues to act insolently. The Negro answers this by picking up the apple

[13] Collected from Ann Jennings, Dallas, Texas, January 1966. For another reporting, see Arthur J. Prange, Jr., and M. M. Vitols, "Jokes Among Southern Negroes: The Revelation of Conflict," *Journal of Nervous and Mental Disease*, 136 (1963), 162–167.

[14] Roger D. Abrahams, *Deep Down in the Jungle . . . Negro Narrative Folklore From the Streets of Philadelphia* (Hatboro, Pa., 1964), 65–88.

[15] Collected from Betty Wagner, Prairie View, Texas, December 1965.

[16] Collected from Ann Tate, Houston, Texas, December 1965.

and throwing it up in the air, taking out his knife, throwing it up too, and having the apple come down already peeled.[17] But this message is even more baldly stated in a tale recently collected in Texas.

One time there was a white man's rooster and a colored man's rooster. White man he went to the store and bought him a damn strong man's rooster. Colored man went to the store and bought him one of them poor-ass damned roosters. Damn white man's rooster wanted to get up on the fence every morning and wanted to fight. Get up on the fence and look at the little colored man's rooster and go, "Cock-a-doo. Who wanna fight?" The colored man's rooster, "I do" [spoken loudly and high]. The white man's rooster would then just beat the goddamned shit outa that son-a-bitch. He goddam hollered and cussed but never could do nothing with the white man's rooster. Now this went on for two days. Two days later he got tired of seeing that white man's rooster beat shit outa his, so he went down and got him something. He went down and got him some spurs—you know, like a fighting cock has—and put 'em on his little rooster. Well, that rooster jumped up on that fence and went, "Cock-a-doo. Who wanna fight?" "Urrumh," went the little colored man's rooster and just tore into him like a cat into a rat and just tore him to pieces. And that white man was afraid to buy another rooster.[18]

These stories illustrate the depth of the problem of Negro-white relations in the continuing situation in which whites seem to ask for acquiescence and subservience on the part of Negroes. The narratives show that the violent direction of recent Negro reaction to this situation, which refuses them a sense of cultural and individual self-respect, has been anticipated in their in-group humorous inventions. They directly portray Negro-white confrontations and show means by which Negroes feel they may gain the upperhand.

   IV.

   To see these stories only as a reaction to white subjugation would be a vast over-simplification. Lack of ego identification, especially with lower-class Negro men, arises from the combination of a lack of employment opportunities for the men and a matrifocal family system that encourages active distrust between the sexes.[19] This distrust, furthermore, prevails between age groups and between the religiously inclined and those who reject religion, with its focus on the preacher. Consequently, there is considerably less of the sense of group cohesion that one finds in other minority groups, and a real lack of leadership. Because the Negro has identified so strongly with the image imposed by the whites, his rejection and conversion of the stereotype can only be seen as a hesitant first step toward achieving a sense of personal and cultural identity.
   The present lack of group identity is seen fully in these stories. They are totally hostile in their tone. The image of Negroes portrayed in them, though presented in positive terms, is still basically the stereotype imposed by the whites. Lack of group identity is further observable in the almost complete absence of definition of the stereotypes of other peoples. Insofar as there is a stereotype of the Mexican, for instance, it is just that he is somewhere between the white man and the Negro in his capacities. And the white man is simply defined in terms of what he lacks and the Negro has.

---

[17] Abrahams, 226–227.
[18] Collected from Curtis Willis, from Florida but living in Austin, Texas, September 1967.
[19] Abrahams, 19–40.

This does not mean that Negroes do not think and express themselves in negative stereotypes of other peoples; rather, as a subordinated group their vocabulary of stereotyping traits is severely limited. As noted above, stereotypes when developed and utilized by superordinate groups reflect the values of the group expressed in negative terms. But when the negative traits of the stereotype become converted into positive characteristics, it is hardly possible to reverse the argument. Though smell may become a positive characteristic, the argument that cleanliness is a negative trait simply is not available to the Negro storyteller. He must fasten the trait of sexual ineffectiveness on the white man as a result of his not smelling "strong." In other words, he has no developed sense of values beyond what is provided for him—and negatively—by the white man. The majority group's stereotypes assign traits as if they were "qualities conceived as if somehow inherent in the objects."[20] Negroes, insofar as they stereotype at all, can only conceive of theirs in terms of traits that they—the Negroes—have and the other groups do not. This paucity of stereotyping vocabulary emerges clearly in Williams' book. He shows that the Negro has a stereotype of the white, but it is limited to statements like "white man hates me."[21] Burma seems to argue the opposite, that Negroes have as much stereotype humor as whites, but his examples focus on the absurdity of "Jim Crow" situations, that is, those places where white man shows his hatred.

A limited vocabulary of stereotype is not true of all New World Negro groups, not even those with similar histories. In the British West Indies, for instance, there is a large corpus of stories that not only articulate this same struggle of Negro and white but do so with a more clearly defined conventional characterization of the "Buckra Man" planter. Furthermore, in these islands one of the major forms of humor is the same kind of trio contest jokes, with the important difference that the three involved are men from different islands—for instance, the 'Badian (Barbadian), the Vincentian (from St. Vincent), and the Trinidadian. The differences are expressed in terms of dialect and of stereotype traits. The 'Badian is crafty and sharp, the St. Lucian is lazy and dumb, the Trinidadian a thief, and so on. One, therefore, cannot help relating these lacks in American Negro storytelling techniques to the void of group sense and the lack of depth of cultural identity felt by the community, as well as to the degree of rejection by whites, a rejection so stigmatizing and persistent that it has limited all recognition of other white traits.

This difference has been pointed out often, most recently by David Lowenthal in his discussion "Race and Color in the West Indies."

Perhaps the most significant difference [between West Indians and American Negroes] is what the names themselves imply. To most white Americans, a Negro is still a Negro first and a man afterwards; the West Indian is a man from the outset in the eyes of the community and, therefore, to himself. The word "Negro," explains a Guyanese poet, is "a label denoting a type of human being who was part of a black minority in a white majority." In America "Negro" means problem. It had no application to the people living in the Antilles, where they form a black majority. Within the West Indies most designations are geographical. A black or colored man from Jamaica or Martinique is simply a Jamaican or Martiniquian; it is the white man who must establish his special identity. In the United States the

[20] Williams, 40.
[21] Williams, 247.

opposite is the case. "Southerner" is invariably taken to mean "White Southerner"; the southern Negro is simply a Negro from the South.[22]

Lowenthal's point stresses an important feature of the American Negro's lack of identity, his sense of being without a place both geographical and social with which he may identify and be identified. Without this, he seems incapable of seeing himself in terms of a distinct minority or ethnic culture. Lacking this, he can't conceive of the distinctiveness of other groups as well; consequently, he uses a joke form that in most groups is an "ethnic joke" but which in his jests is shorn of any ethnic contrasts. The Negro jokes do play upon distinctions, but they are social rather than ethnic ones.[23] Given their restricted and subordinate state, Negroes have tended to see life in terms of social polarities: themselves as the excluded "have-nots" and the establishment whites as the "haves." Between the poles, as these jokes illustrate, the Negro has been aware of ambiguous groups, peoples not "white" but somewhat above Negroes in terms of social acceptance. In the big Eastern cities, these ambiguous groups are commonly Italians, Jews, or Chinese, while in the Southwest the intermediate people are Mexicans. But, as these jokes show, these other groups are ill-defined in regard to distinct cultural characteristics; they are only seen to be between the Negroes and whites, both in terms of social acceptability and in ability to perform certain acts of an ambivalent nature.

In this inability to distinguish groups in terms of linguistic or cultural disparity, Negroes are different from other so-called minority groups, like Jews and Mexicans. In Texas, the social and economic situation of the Mexican is not very different from that of the Negro. However, "the Mexican-American . . . is quite aware of ethnic stereotypes. In contrast to . . . the Negro use of stereotypes, the Mexican-American jokes involve clearly defined ethnic slurs: the Englishman is arrogant and overbearing, the American is a checkwriting millionaire who doesn't mind the cost, the Jew tries to push down the entry price into Heaven, while the Negro is the happy-go-lucky, crap-shooting comedian."[24]

The major difference between the situation of the Negroes and that of Mexican-Americans is that the latter have remained in an area they once dominated and with which they are still identified (and are able to identify themselves). Further, though they are relegated to persistent second-class social status throughout the Southwest, they see around them evidence of their own continuing cultural presence—such as in the use by Anglos of Mexican-style houses, furniture, and clothes and in the overwhelming regional popularity of Mexican cuisine.

That this continuing feeling of cultural identity is bound to a sense of place was dramatically illustrated in recent events in New Mexico. While Negroes were rioting to demonstrate the degradations of their mode of existence, destroying the very places—the ghetto—with which they are identified, Reies Tijerina was orga-

[22] David Lowenthal, "Race Relations in the British West Indies," *Daedalus* (Spring 1967), 609.

[23] I am deeply indebted in the following argument to Américo Paredes. We were both participants in the symposium, "Folklore and the Social Sciences," sponsored by the Social Science Research Council and the Wenner-Gren Foundation, at which I read a paper containing part of the present argument, and he served as a discussant. He has kindly permitted me to incorporate many of his suggestions in the revision.

[24] Américo Paredes, "Prepared Remarks on Abrahams' and Fogelson's Papers," unpublished manuscript (1967).

nizing a guerrilla band and "recapturing" Kit Carson National Forest from the
gringo Forest Rangers, proclaiming Mexican-American sovereignty over the
land under the provisions of the Treaty of Guadalupe-Hidalgo. This action arose
out of a sense of mission and was accompanied by the appropriate manifestoes of
purpose. In contrast to the protest-rioting of the Negroes, the Mexican-Americans
were actually in revolt. Both riots and revolutions are aggressive acts, directed at
"the enemy" whites, but one was an act in the spirit of rebuilding a world once
lost, and to do so with a plan in mind, while the other, reacting to restrictive po-
licing, struck out blindly, destroying and looting.[25]

This feeling of lack of place is not unnoticed by Negroes. In fact, it is a constant theme in the Black Nationalism and Black Power movements. It is also a
theme in some jokes of the type commented upon above, like the following:

There was a Mexican, Frenchman, Chinaman and Negro sitting under a shade tree shooting the bull one afternoon. So they got to boasting about their countries and the Mexican
said, "Hail to the green grass of Mexico that has never been surpassed by any country."
The Frenchman said, "Hail to the great flag of France that is a symbol of power." The
Chinaman said, "Hail to the Great Wall of China that has never been scaled."
Next it was the Negro's turn to boast but he hesitated because he couldn't think of any-
thing to boast about. So just about the time he was fixing to give up he saw a black bird
that was flying over at the time, so he said "Hail to the black bird who flew over the Great
Wall of China, shit on the green grass of Mexico and wiped his ass with the great flag of
France.[26]

V.

Negroes, like Mexican-Americans, have commonly been regarded as a minority
group, but the two exhibit such different relationships to the majority group and
its culture that the very definition of minorities is called into question. The element which ties together such diverse "minorities" as Jews, Italians, and Mexican-
Americans seems notably lacking among Negroes—that is, a sense of cultural
identity distinct from that of the dominant culture. These other groups, when
threatened by the culture of the majority, begin by clinging to characteristics that
emphasize their cultural distinctness. Further, they develop (or develop upon)
stereotypes of the individuals in the outside group, the very ones who are surrounding and besieging them. This is the primary attribute of the true minority
member: he sees himself besieged, hemmed in, his cultural existence imperiled.
He is on the inside, keeping the invaders and the despoilers out. But Negroes, in
accepting the white stereotype and the American dream, see themselves as outsiders waiting to get in.

This does not mean that there has been a total definition of self in terms of
white man's values and life style. It has become evident in recent sociological
surveys that the point made in the Negro-as-bird joke (that the Negroes have no
pride in their "place," no historical and cultural roots to rely upon, and little self-
confidence in their present life style) is bringing about a reaction in the man in the
street. This reaction calls not only for the defiant gesture but also for the fabrica-
tion of roots—by learning African history and Swahili, by adopting West African

[25] Charlotte Darrow and Paul Lowinger, "The Detroit Uprising: A Psychosocial Study," unpublished manuscript (1967).
[26] Collected from Wardell Jones, Los Angeles, 1959 (text contributed by Ed Cray).

modes of dress, and by forming a Black Nation here. Those who are working in the ghettos report that "9 out of every 10 youngsters in Harlem are now black nationalists" and further that "nationalism comes in a variety of brands, ranging from a positive identification with Afro-American history and culture, to the more racist varieties that call for separation."[27]

Such a position, while it emphasizes the major ways in which Negroes differ from most ethnic minorities, moves Negroes who feel this way into the position not of membership in an assimilable minority but rather into the position of deviants—those who are branded by majority culture as acting in an abnormal or antinormative fashion. Deviants, when they form communities, define themselves in terms of how they differ from mainstream culture, not in how different they are, as minorities do. In other words, deviant communities look on the culture of dominant society as wrong, and define themselves by trying to up-end the values and characteristic activities of the dominant group. Minorities, on the other hand, make no attempt to either bring about change or to argue against the culture surrounding them. They do not understand the others and thus fear them, defensively cohering in the face of the threat of a cultural dominance that in most cases will eliminate them anyhow, at least those minorities which are city enclaves. Both minorities and deviant groups are defined in terms of disparity from dominant culture, but deviants work offensively, challenging the presuppositions of the majority, while minorities seem to ask simply to be left alone.

VI.

The Negro jokes we have reviewed are examples of one of the ways in which Negro-white relations are handled through an aggressive and ironic approach to life. Jokes, by their very nature, deal in the stereotypes we commonly call by their more literary name, "conventional characters." A joke commonly turns on a witticism and is consequently focused on character interrelationships (without much depth of characterization, since the roles are representative, conventional). The jokes quoted above also show that these interrelationships often turn into confrontations, conflicts that are usually resolved by the witticism, which points to the triumph of the witty or the strong. But jokes are short, and therefore any illustrative actions are limited.

There is another group of traditional narratives that arise at the same joking occasions but which are long, describe a series of episodes, and focus on heroic actions rather than on exercises of wit. They present values in terms of actions more fully than the jokes. These recitations are called "toastës" or "toasts" by many of the raconteurs who perform them. They are performed in rhymed couplets, are commonly multiepisodic, and often chronicle the deeds of some "big man" as he expresses himself with "style." The toasts are widely found among American Negroes, especially in the cities and in prisons.[28] These poems reveal ghetto Negro values even more than the jokes. They are more aggressive

[27] Martin Duberman, "Baby, You Better Believe," *New York Times Book Review*, January 21, 1968, p. 8.

[28] I have described their presentation and their compositional elements, and printed a number of texts from South Philadelphia in my book *Deep Down in the Jungle*, 99–173. See also Bruce Jackson, "Circus and Street: Psychosocial Problems in Folk Narrative," unpublished manuscript (1967).

in tone and diction, though the hostility is not so clearly focused on the white world. In the toasts one can find the clearest exposition of the patterns of approved actions that have been pointed out as correlates of the riots.

Most of these epic poems glorify the man who is "tough," aggressive, masculine, powerful, easy to aggravate and quick to fight, criminal, and amoral. Any kind of restraint is a challenge to the hero. The most widely known of these individualists are "Stackolee" and "Shine," both of whom become involved in epic contests that allow them to exhibit their masculinity in a dramatic fashion. Stackolee, beside killing a number of people who offer him only the slightest insult, has a gun battle with "Bully Lion" in a bar called "The Bucket of Blood."[29] "Shine," the only one of the toast heroes who actively contends with whites, has a series of wild conflicts with the captain of the *Titanic,* his wife and daughter, and finally a shark. One of the lesser members of this pantheon is the outlaw "The Great MacDaddy," whose activities and attitudes are capsulated examples of the deeds of this bad-man type of hero.

> I was standing on the corner, wasn't even shooting crap,
> When a policeman came by, picked me up on a lame rap.
> He took me to the jailhouse 'bout quarter past eight,
> That morning 'bout ten past nine
> Turnkey came down the line.
> Later on, 'bout ten past ten
> I was facing the judge and twelve other men.
> He looked down on me, he said,
> "You're the last of the bad.
> Now Dillinger, Slick Willie Sutton, all them fellows is gone,
> Left you, the Great MacDaddy to carry on."
> He said, "Now we gonna send you up the way. Gonna send you up the river.
> Fifteen to thirty, that's your retire."
> I said, "Fifteen to thirty, that ain't no time.
> I got a brother in Sing Sing doing ninety-nine."
> Just then my sister-in-law jumped up, she started to cry.
> I throwed her a dirty old rag to wipe her eye.
> My mother-in-law jumped, she started to shout.
> "Sit down, bitch, you don't even know what the trial's about."
> 'Pon her arm she had my six-button benny.
> Said, "Here you are MacDaddy, here's your coat."
> I put my hand in my pocket and much to my surprise,
> I put my hand on two forty-fives.
> I throwed them on the judge and made my way to the door.
> As I was leaving, I tipped my hat to the pictures once more.
> Now outside the courtroom was Charcoal Brown.
> He was one of the baddest motherfuckers on this side of town.
> The juries left out, and the broads gave a scream,
> I was cooling 'bout hundred-fifteen miles an hour in my own limousine.
> Rode here, rode there, to a little town called Sin.
> That when the police moved in.
> He was fighting like hell till everything went black.
> One of those sneaky cops come up and shot me in the back.[30]

[29] Abrahams, 123–136.
[30] The antipolice motivation expressed here is also a common rationale for the riots. Both fictions and actions reflect a real antagonism, of course.

I've got a tombstone disposition, graveyard mind.
I know I'm a bad motherfucker, that's why I don't mind dying.[31]

It is this "tombstone disposition" that seems most characteristic of these bad-men, because it illustrates a willingness to place one's life on the line, perhaps to die if only the dying can be done in proper style. And "style' 'in this case means not only heroic masculinity but conspicuous consumption. Life is seen in com-modity terms, with about as much worth as the personal limousine or the beautiful "threads" (clothes) these heroes are often described as wearing. The outlaw heroes are regarded as heroic not just because they act aggressively in the face of authority but also because they announce that they are pursuers of the American Dream, with its visions of perpetual plenty available to those who are willing to do the pursuing. These are the Negro entrepreneurs, those who are going to grab the goods even when society at large seeks to keep the TV sets and the beautiful clothes behind the glass windows of the department stores.

VII.

Though the Negro still seeks the promise of the American Dream, the Eden he pursues is no garden paradise but a city of gold, and his values are those of urbanites—not of peasants or would-be country people—exhibiting all of the characteristics that used to be termed "dandy" with emphasis on beautiful clothes and stylized manners calculated to attract attention. The Protestant ethic offers very little attraction. There are no frontiers in the Negro's world view, no new worlds to create for himself; paradise already exists, but on the other side of the dividing line. In this stylish world a job is convenient to supply money, but it is not a matter of pride (especially since the jobs seldom are prestigious) nor does one talk about it very much.

This is occasionally misunderstood by investigating social scientists. For in-stance, Charlotte Darrow and Paul Lowinger recently presented a paper on the values of the rioters in Detroit and noted that "some young Negro males prefer to give the impression to their friends and peers that they are not working when in fact they are . . . He says: I don't have a job. I don't work at something that is degrading and humiliating. But still, I have good clothes and a good car." Dar-row and Lowinger account for this by noting that "*because* having a good job is so important that an opposite effect takes over and there is a bravado about not work-ing."[32] They assume that having a good job is important, when it is not the job but the appearance of living the affluent life that is often most important. Afflu-ence is that much more dramatic if it can be had without work, if it is taken (as with badmen) or if it is bestowed (and not in the way or the quantity provided by systems of relief). The prestigious way of having style is by being "kept," and this is true not only of women but also of men.

The badman has been described as providing a pattern of heroic action, but his bold tactics are in direct contrast in certain important ways to another Negro hero

---

[31] Abrahams, 162–163.
[32] Darrow and Lowinger, unpublished manuscript.

type, the "cat." Where the badman works through violence and directed impulse, the cat works through wits and indirection. The cat has been effectively described by Harold Firestone.

> He strictly eschewed the use of force and violence as a technique for achieving his ends or for settling of problematic situations. He achieved his goals by indirection, relying, rather, on persuasion and on a repertoire of manipulative techniques. . . .
>
> He used his wits and his conversational ability. To be able to confront such contingencies with adequacy and without resort to violence was to be "cool." His idea was to get what he wanted through persuasion and ingratiation; to use the other fellow by deliberately outwitting him. Indeed, he regarded himself as immeasurably superior to the "gorilla," a person who resorted to force. . . .
>
> The cat seeks through a harmonious combination of charm, ingratiating speech, dress, music, the proper dedication to his "kick," and unrestrained generosity to make his day-to-day life itself a gracious work of art.[33]

The "cool cat" figures in many of the stories in the Negro storyteller's repertory. One series of jokes, for instance, has a formulaic opening like, "There was this cat from up North visiting his people down south, driving down there in Alabama in his brand new Cadillac and wearing his mohair coat and shoes shined like a mirror. . . ." These stories commonly turn on some way in which the "slick" manages to trick the white storekeeper "Mr. Charlie" into giving him respect and service. Furthermore, the cat emerges in certain notable toasts. In the toasts, as in real life, the cat and "the gorilla" often find themselves in contest with each other to see who can carry off life in the better style. This conflict is fully presented in the most popular of all toasts, "The Signifying Monkey and the Lion." The monkey is a well-known cool cat who gains his ends through indirection. This is exactly what "signifying" means.

> It was deep down in the jungles where the big coconuts grow,
> There lived the most signified monkey the world ever know.
> There hadn't been anything in these jungles for quite a little bit,
> So this monkey thought he would start some shit.
> So he hollered out to the lion one bright sunny day,
> Say, "Mr. Lion, there is a big burly motherfucker right down the way."
> Say, "Now I know you and him will never make friends,
> Because everytime you meet him your knees will bend."
> Say, "He got your whole family in the dozens[34] and your sister on the shelf,
> And the way he talks about your mama I wouldn't do myself.
> And one thing he said about your mama I said I wasn't going to tell:
> He said your mama got a pussy deep as a well."
> This lion was a mad son-of-a-bitch;
> He jumped up and made a big roar.
> His tail was lashing like a forty-four.
> He left these jungles in a hell of a rage,
> Like a young cocksucker full of his gays.
> He left in a hell of a breeze;
> He was shaking coconuts from the trees.
> The small animals got scared and fell to their knees.
> He found the elephant asleep under a big oak tree,

---

[33] Harold Firestone, "Cats, Kicks and Color" in *The Other Side,* ed. Howard S. Becker (New York, 1964), 282, 285.

[34] An elaborate insult contest with derision directed at members of the family (usually, as here, at the mother) of another in the contest. See Abrahams, 49–59.

Say, "You're the motherfucker talking about me."
But the elephant looked at him out of the corner of his eyes,
Say, "Go on, motherfucker, and pick on somebody your own size."
The elephant said, "My mother is very low sick and my brother lost his life;
I got up this morning and found another motherfucker fucking my wife."
Say, "I'm telling you now in front of your face so you can see,
This is no time to be fucking with me."
But the lion got back and made a forward pass
But the elephant knocked him on his hairy ass.
But he got back again and made a pass and the elephant ducked
And from this time on the lion was fucked.
They fought all night long and all the next day,
And I still don't see how that damn lion got away,
Because he broke both of his jaws and fucked up his face;
The elephant gave a yank on his tail and snatched his asshole clean out of place.
Then back-tracked him through the woods more dead than alive.
That's when the little monkey came on with his signifying jive.
Said, "Ha ha, motherfucker, look like you caught plenty of hell.
The elephant whipped your ass to fare-thee-well."
Said, "You left these jungles all highly sprung,
Now here you come back damn near hung—
With your face all fucked up like a cat's ass when he got the seven-year itch,
And you say you're King of the Jungle, say now ain't you a bitch.
And every morning I try to fuck a wee bit,"
Say, "Here you come with that Lion-roaring shit.
Say, "Your always around here roaring you're the king,
And I don't believe you can whip a god damn thing.
So shut up, motherfucker, don't you dare roar
Or I'll swing from these limbs and kick your ass some more.
And hurry up and get out from under my tree
Before I take a notion to shit or pee."
Now the little monkey got frantic and started to clown
When both feet slipped and his black ass hit the ground.
Like a flash of lightning and a bolt of white heat
The lion was on him with all four feet.
Then the little monkey with tears in his eyes
Said, "Oh, Mr. Lion, I apologize."
The lion said "Shut up, motherfucker, no use of your crying
I'm going to cut out some of this signifying."
So the little monkey knew what was coming and he had to think fast
Before this lion tore a hole in his ass.
So he said, "Mr. Lion, if you let me off here like a good gentleman should,"
Say, "I'll whip your ass all over these woods."
So the lion jumped back and stepped back for the monkey to fight.
And about this time this little monkey jumped damn near out of sight.
Damn near the top of a long tall pine swing down on a limb
Where he knew the lion could not get him.
Again he came on with his bullshit and signifying.
Say, "Now you kiss my two black balls and my black behind."
Say, "Yes, your mama got a cock big as a whale is true.
And your sister got a big cock, too.
And I started to stick a dick in your wife and the big cock flew.
And that ain't all—if you don't get out from under my tree I'll swing from one of
    these limbs and stick a dick in you."
Last time I was in the jungle, I passed the long tall tree,
The monkey was still at the top as happy as he could be.

> But you can bet your life even from that day
> The lion still wonders how that jive mother got away.
> Now if anybody asked you who composed this toast,
> Just tell him bullshitting Bell from coast-to-coast.[35]

Here is a clear exposition of the different approaches of the cat and the gorilla in the characters of the monkey and the lion (with the narrator associating himself with the monkey by calling himself "bullshitting Bell").

The monkey is often called a "pimp-monkey," but in ghetto-Negro parlance this is not necessarily a derogatory term. The pimp is the very epitome of the cat because he not only is able to get clothes and money through using his wits but does so by exploiting women. But just as the badman faces a moral problem by the easy and unconsidered decision to take through strength and to use violence, so the cat must decide that his style is best served through clever docility and persuasiveness. Occasionally, as when the monkey pleads for his life, he must become submissive; but clearly this act of submission is admirable if it is followed by achievement or maintaining of status. There are a number of toasts that turn on a sexual challenge from a woman (that is, a potential put-down). When the hero is a cat, however, the conflict commonly ends with a submissive act that allows him to achieve the life-style to which he aspires.

> Now this was while walkin' down L.A. street,
> I was broke as hell but my clothes was neat.
> I was broke as hell but feeling fine,
> Just put the last I had on a fifth of wine.
> So while I was standin' on the corner of Eighth and Grind,
> Leaning 'gainst a lamppost and a three-pointed sign,
> Thinking how I could make me some money
> When a little fine voice says, "Hey, honey."
> And I look around where I could see
> And no bullshit this was a fine redhead looking at me.
> She say, "Hey little daddy, when'd you get back in town?"
> You know I was gonna act like I was in the know
> So I said, "Baby I just got back a few days ago."
> She said, "Well I thought you and me was gonna out havin' a good time,
> Painting the town red buying whiskey, gin and wine."
> I looked at her, I said, "Girl, that sound all right,
> But shit, I lost all my money on them dice last night."
> She said, "Well, since I invited you out on this little spree
> You just fuck the time. Leave the rest to me."
> So now we made a few joints and headed for Beverly Hills
> Where you can't smell nothing 'cept roses and daffodills.
> She drove up front of her pad, said, "Daddy this is home sweet home."
> Said, "This is the castle, but inside's the throne."
> And no bullshit she had one of them red high tight pads, really corny and groovy
> Just like one of them big-shot pads you see in the movies.
> She said, "Come on in Bitty and play your favorite song."
> Say, "Hell, I'm change clothes but it ain't gonna take long."
> And she come out in one them gowns all skin tight
> And I jumped square and done kissed her and asked her politely could I spend the
>   night.
> She said, "Hell you can spend the night and the rest of 'em too,
> That's providing if you know what to do."

[35] Collected from Jimmy Bell, Austin, Texas, October 1960.

I says, "Now you wait a minute, whore, I'm kinda green,
You break this shit down and let me know what you mean."
She said, "Ah hell, I can find a grinder any time, that can grind for a while
But now tonite I want my love done the Hollywood style."
Say, "You got to get down on that floor on both your knees,
Nibble at this pountang like a rat nibbling at cheese."
Said, "You got to keep on nibbling and don't you lighten up and now drop
Till I pull on both your ears and say 'Daddy, please stop.'"
And that made me so mad that I began to shout.
I say, "Whore, I don't know what the hell you're talking 'bout.
Now I like cheese but I ain't no damn rat.
I go for a little piece of cock but not like that."
Say, "You're sitting up there looking good in your silk and lace
But you'll never get to sit your big ass in my face."
She said, "Well Bitty, there ain't nothing else you can do.
If you ain't gonna eat any of this cock I guess we through."
So I got my hat and coat and started to go,
But do you know I didn't get any farther than that whore's front door.
She say, "Hey wait a minute, little daddy," Say, "Wait just a minute,
You might wanna eat some of this if you know what was in it.
Hell, there's breakfast in bed for you and a diamond ring,
Bank-roll in your pocket and everything."
I looked at her and said, "Girl, eatin a little cock all I gotta do,
Shit, I don't see no reason in the world I ain't gonna string along with you."
So with my head hung down in sorrow
I'll be a playboy today, a cocksucker tomorrow.[36]

In toasts such as this, as well as in the jokes of the Harlem slick coming South, the appurtenances of the playboy are believed to carry power and self-respect with them, enough to overcome the aversion to the act of cunnilingus.

The cat is clearly a descendant of tricksters like Br'er Rabbit and the Slave John, for he lives through his wits and operates aggressively through indirection. In his city guise he offers a pattern of aggression and a life-style that continues to be attractive to members of ghetto communities. But there is a felt opposition between those who would follow the cat's lead and those who subscribe to the ways of the badman. In my study of one group of men in Philadelphia, the values of the gorilla predominated. The "Rat and Cheese" toast, for instance, in a version collected in Philadelphia concluded with the rejection of the woman's offer, and the signifying monkey is killed and jailed in some of the toasts. Furthermore, in the one story about Br'er Rabbit collected there, the wily animal is converted to a tough man who violently breaks up a party he has not been invited to. Though "flash" was valued in this neighborhood, toughness was more important, perhaps because most of my informants were ex-gang members. On the other hand, Bruce Jackson has found that in the toasts he has collected among prison inmates, less than 5 percent of his texts are devoted to badmen and a very large percentage depict the doings of pimps and slicks.[37]

It is difficult to meaningfully interpret the disparity in these traditions, but it seems possible at least to say that the two patterns of style and action have served as alternatives to the man in the street seeking self-respect and a feeling that he is in control of his own life by acquiring symbols of power and position. But both

[36] Collected from Bitty Brown, Austin, Texas, October 1967, by Anthony Lange.
[37] Jackson, unpublished manuscript.

life patterns have heretofore been directed inward, bottled up in the Negro ghetto. Stackolee kills and rapes other Negroes and the signifying monkey directs his wiles against a bully member of his own "jungle" community.

Recently both life patterns have been directed at the outside world, and it is difficult to decide which has caused greater reaction in the white community. The cat in the person of a Cassius Clay or an Adam Clayton Powell has suddenly forced himself upon the notice of whites, and they have no cultural frame of reference to understand him. Both Powell and Clay have constantly pointed to this cultural disparity, but their insights fall on deaf ears. Consequently, Powell is placed into a cat's blissful isolation in the Bahamas, surrounded by the happenings of the good life, while Muhammed Ali has his "world" heavyweight title taken from him for his "insolence." Such aggressive roles are not available to most Negroes; however, it has suddenly become possible to put on the mask of the badman in the licentious atmosphere of the riots. In such a situation, accomodation is forgotten and so is indirect attack. The symbols of power and place in American society are there in the store windows and in the counters, and they are grabbed.

The Negro, then, has been given an opportunity for making a choice, and he has taken it. But his patterns of emulation are still determined in great part by his conversion of the white stereotype. Furthermore, his actions are still only arrived at through chance and made only in reaction to past indignities. Through all this there is a suicidal note in the activities of his heroes, just as there is an element of the self-destructive in the riots. The tone of MacDaddy saying, "I know I'm a bad motherfucker, that's why I don't mind dying" is a clear expression of the ambivalence inherent in the Negro's situation. He accepts the immoral traits of the stereotype, turning them into positive attributes. Even badness is glorified if it enables one to partake more fully of the popular vision of the American experience. Crime, it is recognized, must be answered with punishment, even death. But death is one answer to the unmanageable conflicts of ghetto life, so badness may solve many problems.

The correlations between the conduct of the riots and the pattern of heroic actions are too insistent to ignore. Both in jokes and in real life, Negroes act in an aggressive, chaotic manner that results in much violence and self-destruction, with a minimum of lasting rewards. The Negro has held his hostilities in readiness. He doesn't make programs for retaliation. He doesn't have a clear sense of what he is fighting for, as he has no sense of identity except as described in white man's terms. Though he may feel he is striking at the white world, he turns any possibility of retaliation into an orgy of semidirected destruction (just a great big "Nigger Saturday Night" as someone described it). He hopes the white world will look on these riots and see what will happen if things are directed away from the ghettos toward the great white suburban world. But the message of hope and potential violence is bound to be misread, since it conforms so completely to the conventional role-casting of Negroes as irrational, thieving creatures.

There is one indication that the situation may change. Certain Negro militants have seen the self-defeating nature of the pattern but have recognized that the riots are at least a display of power noticed by the white world. They are channeling the aggressions outward, at least verbally. And they borrow the explosive, ambivalent rhetoric of the badman in framing their assault. Here, for instance, is a statement by a young Negro folksinger and writer.

I don't sing much now, because nothing short of destroying this country will satisfy me. . . . I love so intensely the beauty of humanity that I hate everything that frustrates, stifles, and destroys that beauty, and I will kill to see that it comes into being. To kill is often an act of love. And I learned that from a beautiful, shy young girl who is a guerrilla in South Viet Nam. She's killed 25 G.I.'s and I knew she knew about a love that I haven't experienced yet, but I look forward to experiencing it. I look forward to the day when I will place a person in my rifle sight, squeeze the trigger, hear the explosion and watch that person fall.[38]

The focus here is a bit more explicit, the diction a little more extreme, but the tone and the "I don't mind dying" approach is the same as in the badman toasts and jokes. The question that remains is whether this is a verbal rationale for a deviant stance or whether it portends future Negro activities. We do know that among the young in the ghettos the idea of black nationalism is becoming increasingly attractive. And we also can be sure that given the chance, ghettoized Negroes are going to continue to take every opportunity that arises to act aggressively while seeking a sense of power, place, and self-determination.

University of Texas
Austin, Texas

[38] Julius Lester, "Letter of Resignation to Broadside Magazine," Reprinted in *Sing-Out! The Folk Song Magazine,* 17 (1967/1968), Number 6, p. 41.

Prepared Comments by the Reverend Hubert Locke

I'm sure most of you know, but for Dr. Abrahams' benefit and for those of you who don't, I think I ought to make clear that folklore is not my field of disciplinary study, and so my comments may or may not be appropriate to this paper; but I leave that for Dr. Abrahams' response and for your discussion. Let me first acknowledge a personal debt of appreciation to Dr. Abrahams, if I may be allowed an expression that will only have meaning for those of you who have been privileged to see the paper, for this "stimulating" essay. He has brought, I think, a very interesting thesis to bear upon a wide range of folklore data, with some rather fascinating results. Let me say that I share his feeling that the study of folklore can provide really invaluable insights into the life style of black ghetto communities. And I think Dr. Abrahams has made a major contribution toward that end by bringing together the data amassed in his paper. My point of dissent and departure, therefore, is not with the data or with the application of the discipline of folklore to this data, but rather with the interpretations that have been drawn.

I want to do this in two parts. First, I want to raise a few mechanical matters about the paper itself and then to raise several questions about the overall thesis. There is a corpus of stories, some of which Dr. Abrahams has summarized, that reflect the sexual motif in Negro folklore; and I would really ask rather than raise an objection, as to whether these stories in fact have their origin in Negro folklore or in white tradition. My general impression is that most stories told about Negro characters with a sexual motif originate in white culture. This of course raises the question whether such data really reveal Negro aggression towards whites or white anxiety towards sex. Also, I would be interested in evidence that would substantiate the existence of what Dr. Abrahams describes as "Pushin' Days."

Let me just read these few sentences briefly. "In the 1940s and 1950s, more active, though still covert activities, like 'Pushin' Days' developed. In this, Negroes took off from work, going to the most crowded stores in town and doing some 'pushin,' which can be done without much fear of arousing attention or reprisal. More recently this type of aggressive activity has been more overt, in sit-ins, marches, and most recently, in riots." If I understand Dr. Abrahams' remarks correctly at this point, the implication is that this phenomenon actually existed in the forties and fifties as a more active, though still covert, form of Negro aggression. To the best of my knowledge, this phenomenon, at least in the North, was a widely held myth by whites, but never in fact existed as any conscious effort on the part of the Negro community.

I'm not certain how to interpret this comment by Dr. Abrahams: "To see these stories only as a reaction to white subjugation would be a vast oversimplification. Lack of ego identification, especially with lower-class Negro men, arises from the combination of a lack of employment opportunities for the men and a matrifocal family system that encourages an active distrust between the sexes. This distrust, furthermore, prevails between age groups and between the religiously inclined and those who reject religion, with its focus on the preacher." Now this is going to sound like special pleading I know, but I am not certain really how to interpret this comment concerning "the distrust between the religiously inclined and those who reject religion, with its focus on the preacher." If the evidence for this is the massive corpus of stories with the Negro preacher as the main character, I would suggest that these stories circulate mainly among the religiously inclined. Also, the theme in those stories that appear to be of white origin revolves around preachers and sex, while those communicated between Negroes generally depict the Negro preacher as an object of ridicule. But again I point out that, at least from my rather unscientific sampling, I find these stories more often circulated in church suppers than in any other institution I know.

All of this is really not to the point of my primary dissent from Dr. Abrahams' thesis, and that dissent I would describe as follows: At the risk of oversimplification, what I hear Dr. Abrahams saying in his paper is that the riots finally brought to the surface in an active and destructive fashion the latent verbal aggression that has always resided in the black mind, of which the folklore in the Negro ghetto is evidence. Again, I want to note this as a very interesting thesis, but it suffers, it seems to me, by reading too much into the riots. I'm not sure how much it reads into folklore, but I'm quite convinced that it reads too much into the riots. It assumes a sort of conscious collective rationale for rioting that just isn't there. At least in the Detroit riots, with which I am intimately acquainted, the post-riot studies failed to show such conscious rationale at all. In fact, the closer in time the riot arrestees were interviewed to the riot period itself and their subsequent arrest, the less rationale they were able to give for their actions. What the evidence seems to show is that the longer rioters have to think about their participation, the greater the rationale they are able to build for it. Accordingly, and on the basis of the Detroit experience, I would reject out of hand those theories that presuppose a riot rationale. I just do not see any evidence for it.

Now let me make clear, just as a footnote to my own footnote, that I'm saying this within the context of a scholarly meeting and not a black power rally. If I were at the latter occasion, I think I could articulate, too, the post-riot rationale that has emerged for these behaviors and do it with a specific and I think a very valid purpose in mind. But in the context of this study, I do not see what I would call this kind of collective conscious rationale for rioting emerging out of the riot community itself.

What I would do with the data Dr. Abrahams has presented—if you will forgive this arrogance—is to work it from an entirely different perspective, one which time doesn't permit elaboration upon, but which I think presents at least an alternative interpretation to that purposed here, and that is to see the dominant motif in Negro folklore as the motif of tragedy and the rather persistent death symbol—what Dr. Abrahams calls the "tombstone disposition"—which he finds in variants of the "Rat and Cheese" cycle, the Stackolee stories, and the Signifying Monkey saga. Now, if we pursue this option, that is of seeing the dominant theme in Negro folklore as the theme of tragedy, if we pursue this option, ironically we end up at the same point with Dr. Abrahams, for I see this tragedy motif as the recurrent theme in the philosophy of black nationalism: that is, the preparation for defense of the ghetto, the anxiety over genocide, the "we will die fighting like men" stance. I prefer this latter option, of seeing the tragedy-death symbol motif as a more accurate analysis of the meaning of that corpus of ideas and attitudes transmitted and communicated among Negroes, and the impact of that corpus on the development of a philosophy of nihilism in today's black urban ghetto.

Wayne State University
Detroit, Michigan

Reply to Prepared Comments by Roger Abrahams

Let me work backward, taking first the last point and then working back to the first, because I think these are excellent comments and they really focus upon the very crux of the matter, especially the last one. You mentioned that the major theme of these stories is one of tragedy. Now my training is not as a folklorist, actually, but as a literary man, and tragedy means something very precise in literary study. It means really a representative death in the midst of decay, bringing about regeneration through the representative nature of that death. The very central focus of tragedy, I therefore feel, is absent from Negro folklore. What we have rather is a corpus of lore imbued with the stuff of tragedy, which is pathos, that is, the tone of tragedy is pathos, the downward movement, and that indeed we do have.

But there's a difference, it seems to me, between death in the face of danger—as an illustration of adventure or as a statement of manliness—and the tragic vision. What we have here is not the tragic but the heroic. We have in Negro folklore the articulation of an essentially heroic vision. The heroic vision asks for the individual to subjugate himself to the group, to fight to the point of death for the group, and through death or through the possibility of dying, to ennoble the group image. I think that this is exactly what we have in Negro folklore. A heroic atmosphere is being created when a Negro raconteur says, "I'm a mean motherfucker and I don't mind dying." This is what he is saying it seems to me. That he is willing to take on any comers in any way possible to prove that he himself and Negro men in general are heroic and will fight for themselves and, perhaps by extension, for the group.

When I said that I saw a relationship between this Negro folklore and the riots, and that the relationship could be seen in terms of patterns of activity, I did not intend to say by any means that this was the rationale of the riots. In fact, if I could express it in these terms I would say it is the "irrationale" of the riot. What we are involved with is patterns of performance that are internalized, that are unconscious, that have been developed and promulgated in this heroic literature for at least twenty-five, probably fifty, or indeed maybe one hundred years—heightened, to be sure, by the urban experience and by the fact that in the urban milieu you have an actual face-to-face encounter with whites, and it's a recurrent thing. I'm not saying that this is the rationale of the riot but simply that the patterns I've seen in the folklore are also observable in the riots; and, therefore, they may be an expression of something that is internalized.

As part of the argument of my paper I point out the difference in Texas between the Mexican-Americans and Negroes in regard to these internalized patterns of action and thought. Mexicans find themselves in essentially the same second-class status in the Southwest, and yet you do not hear of Mexican-American rioting. But you do hear of them, like Reies Tijerina last summer, trying to recapture their land. I think land has a lot to do with it. What you have is the promulgation of a series of credos of what the Mexican-Americans stand for and what they're going to fight for. You don't have that among Negroes. And they go out, therefore, and fight in accordance with these pre-published credos. There you have the beginning of a rationale for revolt; and, as I say, I think this stems from the fact that in the Southwest every place the Mexican looks he sees reminders of his cultural heritage. In fact, whitey has been bleeding him there, and telling the world that he's been bleeding him. He eats Mexican food, he lives in Mexican style houses, the most "in" names for new developments are things like Lago Vista—and things of this sort.

One further thing, when I talked about aggression, I wasn't just talking about verbal aggressions. In these narratives we have the portrayal of aggressions that go far beyond verbalisms. They portray actions, too, and the actions portrayed in the most ubiquitous of these narratives are the very actions—but on a larger group level—that one can observe in riot situations.

In regard to the preacher tale, I can only say that my data doesn't agree with yours. In the two years I lived in South Philadelphia, it was the most common kind of tale and it was always sexually oriented and it was told by the man on the street. There was constant bad-talking of the preacher by the man on the street, especially by the man of words, and such a talker made his image by pushing off against the preacher, by making fun of him. "Pushin' Day"—I can only testify for what Negro students of mine have said in Texas, that this happened in Dallas all the time. In the North it may simply have been part of white folklore. It's the sort of thing that whites are certainly capable of conceiving and talking about.

But most important from the point of view of public understanding of folkloristic methodology, you point out that most of these stories arise in white communities and are picked up by Negro communities. It doesn't matter where they arise. I will be the first to agree that there is a very deep-seated white anxiety about sex and about a lot of other things. The important thing is that these stories are in active tradition among blacks. Now, there must be some reason why they are. People do not learn stories haphazardly. There are a lot of white stories that blacks have never picked up, elephant jokes for one thing. I'm not saying they didn't pick up any of them, but the phenomena was primarily white and middle class. So the important thing about these stories is not where they came from—indeed most of those I quoted are international and used for different purposes by different groups. That's the great thing about folklore. Essentially folklore is neutral in terms of values, but it is susceptible to being fed cultural energy and being, therefore, susceptible to cultural interpretation, and that's what we have here. We've got a lot of white stories here, but nevertheless, the way they're rapped out here, they're not white, are they?

Discussion from the Floor

Arnold Pilling:—I have the suspicion—let me state it as a mere guess at this point—that not only the major speaker and the discussant but also almost everyone else who has spoken on Negro phenomena today have touched upon one characteristic that those of us who are not from the cultural background involved seem relatively unaware of. When I first began to conceptualize this characteristic some years ago, I termed it—probably incorrectly—"speaking in tongues," meaning that in some instances a person in the urban Negro scene has an ability to use a special vocabulary or way of phrasing himself that the average person cannot understand. This use of a special vocabulary bars the average person from knowing what is going on.

Abrahams:—The average whitey.

Pilling:—No! No! My guess is that even the average person *within* Negro society does not know what is going on. I think what has been said today suggests that my old observation of "speaking in tongues" led to a relatively low-level generalization: What we may be dealing with is a characteristic of urban Negro society that places great value and prestige on a person who has a highly individualistic personal style of behavior. We find one expression of this in the "man of words." I think now we could validly group both the street operator (this "man of words") and the minister. In both cases they are using what their audience would hear as a special individual ability to use certain types of words. We also see this in the performance, in the physical posturing of some males, who show their style in large part by nonverbal performance.

Are we not possibly dealing with the general phenomena of high prestige being placed on a highly individualistic style, though, of course, a style within an accepted range of individualism? Another way of phrasing this is to say the individual performer in this context is attempting to communicate not with the words in their usual meaning but by means of communicating an impression. This impression is intended to set the performer aside as a special and separate person. The impression suggests to the audience that the performer is especially able to deal with concepts, whether the performer in fact deals with concepts well or not. But it is essential that under most circumstances the performer communicate in such a way that his actual meaning—if he has any—will not be easily understood. The special vocabulary means that the performer indeed has a highly personal style.

The actual product of this personal style as it comes forth from the "man of words" on the street or the minister in his store-front or church is in a way analogous to what has been charged as being present in Shakespeare's dialogue. The lines communicate by using symbolism. We are like certain criticized Shakespearian analysts who have been charged with asserting symbolism where Shakespeare may not have been conscious of the "hidden meaning." All of us are outsiders to these highly individualistic performers and can only attempt to guess at the intended meaning.

But in the present context I suspect it is not the meaning that is important. It is the fact that the performer has created a seemingly unique personal style. Does not this formulation seem to agree with your observation?

Abrahams:—I couldn't agree with you more. I will be personal about it for the moment; what I am trying to do in looking at this material and other materials of blacks in the New World is to try and find out where the intensity of the creative experience comes from, which we do not understand but which exists there. Because it seems to me that the first thing we must do as whites is to understand the intense creativity and hetero-geneity of Negroes. This is our burden, it seems to me. When I make these statements, I'm not talking to blacks; I'm talking to whitey. Throughout the New World, I've found (it isn't something just in the United States) there is exactly this attitude toward words and toward performance in general. There is a discrepancy between the average man and the high artist, the man of words (or the man of action, if he's a dancer of any sort or a stick fighter or something of that sort). In the United States, in Negro parlance, the word for this kind of verbal play on its lowest level is "signifying." What the man of words does essentially is to bring signifying up to a very high art.

Signifying is something that the white world cannot understand and cannot accept, and this is the reason why Cassius Clay and all these beautiful people are put down, because essentially they have brought signifying to a very high art. They're dealing in this kind of extremely subtle and yet extremely aggressive language, and it comes out nothing but arrogance to the white audience. As a result it is missed once again; cultural disparity completely precludes the possibility of understanding the essential creativity of this kind of performer. This is what makes me weep whenever I hear one of my Texas neighbors say to me, "Oh, they're so musical; oh, they can all dance," and you know, that kind of thing, because they're not really looking at the essentials of the creative black experience. They're looking at the externals of it—the externals that, of course, in their minds are tied to the old concept of "the happy, childlike people."

Now this brings about a respect for language as spoken. This means a constant willingness to engage in word play. Karl Reisman of Brandeis University, working on Antigua, a small island in the British West Indies, found exactly the same kind of thing. In the Creole situation you have a reduction of vocabulary; the outcome of the reduction is that you have a growing ability to speak in double talk, a growing ability to use words that mean a number of things in the same context. I'll give you one example that comes from Nevis, where they described this whirlpool effect out in the ocean; it is called a solfergut. That can mean either "soul forgot," the place where souls go, or it can mean "sulphur ghaut"—"ghaut" being the word for "wash" or the place where the water runs off. So "solfergut" can mean either the place where souls are forgotten or sulphur ghaut, the entrance into hell; and everytime they say this they can mean both.

But this is the kind of word play that we don't have in English very much, unless we run into a man like James Joyce, you see, who was willing to fight with words like this. We're so cognitively oriented; we've got to make all these distinctions all the time. We forget about verbal creativity when we do that. Black speech (it's probably of African origin because it is found throughout the New World) is endowed with this kind of creative ambience.

Herbert Bracken (black graduate student, Wayne State University):—One thing I was somewhat confused by; you made the statement in regard to Mexican-Americans knowing which direction they're going and what they're after as opposed to black Americans not really knowing.

Abrahams:—When they're involved in revolts. Well, you look at the history of Mexican-Americans in Texas or in New Mexico, and you'll see that over and over again there have been revolts against the white world, but always these revolts are preceded by a manifesto—sometimes four, and five and six manifestoes—and then action. And always the same kind of action, that is, a guerrilla action, going out into the country seizing a crucial fortress of some sort or another. You know what they picked on last summer—Kit Carson National Forest. It was just the symbol of it. They kicked out the gringo forest rangers, you see.

Locke:—We may be facing just a time gap here. It seems to me this is precisely the same phenomenon that is now developing in the black community. What you're going to see within the next few years is exactly this kind of phenomenon, the clear articulation of goals followed by a very well planned, well strategized, logistically carried out revolution.

Abrahams:—Well, apropos of this I'd like to point something out. Yes, there is a program developing, and it's developing around the concept of soul. "Soul" is a very interesting term because it comes from esthetics, just as "beautiful" comes from esthetics. These are esthetic terms for the good, for the good in performance, but now they don't mean good in performance only, they mean good in life. They're ethical terms as well as esthetic terms, and the whole business of Negro nationalism, black nationalism, and black power developing around the whole concept of soul turns on esthetic terminology. Which simply underlines what I was saying before, that it is the performer who is regarded as the bringer of good and is the "discerner of good."

Black woman from Detroit (Miss Dubarry):—What I wanted to point out was that the same sort of thing that is beginning to develop among the Mexican-Americans is also happening to blacks. I guess I really wanted you and Mr. Locke both to speak about what you were thinking of as the rationale for the rebellions; for example, the whole question of the people in the southwest area of Texas taking over. It's happening to black people also. We see, for example, African garb being very popular this year, the whole question of soul food being taken over. We see, for example, expressions on television used for advertisements; they're a part of our folklore, part of our everyday speech. I think black people feel that what's happening here is also a rationale for rebellion. We see whites sitting around talking about and trying to understand our culture without consulting us. We see white people getting large grants for example, to study us [laughter].

Abrahams:—Let me answer that. I think you'll find that black culture is not alone in this. White culture, especially northern European, whenever it becomes urbanized becomes a cultural ink blotter, picking up cultural elements from all over the place and leaving them dry, really taking the essential energy out of them. With popular culture, especially American popular culture, you have the effect of a gargantuan maw. You can see in the last few years numerous kinds of Negro styles, such as the samba, calypso, blues, and jazz—all kinds of Negro expressions—being brought into white popular culture, used up, and thrown away.

Locke:—In response to Miss DuBarry's point, all I'm trying to say really is two things. First, I think we ought to recognize that both in the black and white communities today (in the black community for the sake of politics and in the white community for the sake of, as you quite aptly described it, research interests) the rationale for riots has been a post-riot phenomenon. What has happened is that urban upheavals have occurred for the past four years, but black leaders have begun to give these upheavals conscious, systematic crystallization of meaning, direction and scope only after the fact. Now, I'm not saying that's good or bad; I'm just saying that's the way it's been. And it seems to me the difficulty (and this was really the heart of my complaint with Dr. Abrahams' presentation) is that while we have to understand these phenomena, we have to be very careful in discussing and communicating about them that we don't distort them, and I think increasingly that's what is taking place in American society. All sorts of rubrics are being hung on the riot phenomenon which the riot phenomenon just doesn't bear up under.

It seems to me that what we have to do is first allow ourselves (and that is something we can only do in these kinds of situations, removed from the ebb and flow of where the action is) to recognize that the civil disorders that began in this country—or whatever we should call them, riots or rebellions—began in this country in 1964, and in a sense caught both the black and the white communities by surprise. And that blacks have now discovered something about these disorders, and that is that they scare hell— which is a good theological term—out of white people; and therefore they have begun to give them a rationale, an interpretation. I think that is just a very sophisticated kind of political ploy (or pragmatic, if you will) which is going to be increasingly made. On the other side of the fence, a lot of the pragmatic value of that process is going to get lost, if we try to hang the interpretation of this phenomenon on too many other pegs that I think just won't bear the weight.

Leslie Shepard:—I just want to throw one small point in, but I think it's a very important one. We've had some very valuable contributions; we've had our attention drawn to areas that need to be investigated. What is worrying me most is the speed with which we can begin as folklorists to form stereotypes ourselves. The most dangerous stereotype is that it's only necessary to examine black folklore and you will understand what setting the city on fire means. After all, it's only a performance. But I don't want to sit in a theater in which the performance consists of really burning the place down. One of the forms of stereotyping that does take place in precisely this: "It is only this," or "If we only do that." I believe we have to be alive to the danger of stereotyping as folklorists, who are in fact subject to folklore processes, particularly in an area like a riot city. If one is to do investigation of myths and expressive language and performance, one might, for example, start with the liberal reaction to the riots, in which people have said, "Oh, yes, the Kerner report has given us all the facts, so it is only a question of white man's injustice to the black man." It is only a question of there being poor people, and so on and so forth. I suggest with all humility that these are dangerous stereotypes, which we have to look very closely at.

Aili Johnson:—I'd like to ask Reverend Locke a question. What can we as folklorists do in a very practical way—what can we do, let's say, when we come across rumors? Can we correct rumors on both sides and publish them so that they are known as rumors, labeled as such? For example, the story about how the riots in Detroit were started by some kind of spy in a white Cadillac from New York, people riding through. Many people heard versions of the rumor; sometimes it was seven, even fourteen Cadillacs, always white Cadillacs.

Locke:—You understand of course I speak again outside my area, so these comments may or may not be appropriate. But it seems to me there are two things we're discovering about our various disciplinary interests. One is how little the insights of a single discipline really interpret the phenomenon that is American urban culture. I would hope, therefore, that there will be a great deal of interdisciplinary communication and sharing of data and perspectives. This kind of data, for example, could be worked over rather thoroughly by a team of sociologists and clinical psychiatrists, perhaps, and theologians; because, I if I may get a personal plug in here, I noted in your response, Dr.

Abrahams, that we worked from two totally different interpretations of the meaning of tragedy and pathos. And if I brought some theological definitions of those two terms to bear upon the matter, I would come up with totally different answers. But I think that between yours and mine we might get a third insight that might come closer to what's really involved here.

Also, I am struck over and over again by the romanticizing of the urban ghetto. This especially impresses me when I read the literature of the social sciences. As a black lad who grew up in the urban ghetto in this city, I find what I read to be remote from what I knew of ghetto life. And I would submit that one of the exciting things I think folk-lore can contribute to this problem is a very scientific, if you will, process of amassing data and discovering repeated patterns that will help other disciplines come up with some realistic insights about ghetto life. Again, I would want to be careful about the interpretations that are given the data. But I think that just having a corpus of stories and the like is extremely important, although I would pay very careful attention—more careful, I think, than Dr. Abrahams would—to what in theological circles we call the etiological background. I think it does matter whether these stories originated in the black community or in the white community. I think that's absolutely crucial to the interpretation that's given to them. But at least the amassing of the data itself would be exceedingly important for our understanding of this phenomenon.

Leonard Moss:—Part of the problem Mr. Locke alludes to is that the anthropologists have run out of happy primitives to study in the Pacific Islands, so we are looking for them in the ghettos.

White woman from Detroit (Mrs. Weymer):—I'd like to ask that lady a question. I didn't understand your point. You seem to say that white people have no right to adopt aspects of your culture. Did I miss that entirely?

Dubarry:—No, Dr. Abrahams was saying why he thought the Mexican-Americans were rebelling and had developed a rationale for their revolts. I'm saying that the same things are happening to black communities that happened to Mexican-Americans.

Weymer:—Because the white culture took over the Mexican-American culture?

Dubarry:—Okay. So they take it over, but they don't want to call it Mexican-American culture. They don't want to give the Mexican-Americans credit for having a culture, or the blacks credit for having a culture, but yet they take it over. For example, the Beatles, you know, take over the rock 'n roll thing and make a great deal more money on it than any black person ever did. You know this causes the whole land question. In the South, you know, black people had land taken from them, and they all know and understand that.

Locke:—What I hear Miss Dubarry saying is that Mexican-Americans have suffered the same experience that black Americans have suffered. To which I would simply add that the movement, the pattern of response of black Americans is going to be the very same, that is unless white America wakes up. It is going to follow the very same pattern that Mexican-Americans have employed. We will move from what Dr. Abrahams correctly called at one point a sort of irrationale, a sort of blind destruction, to a very conscious, preplanned, well-thought strategy of revolution. And I think the signs of that are already large in American society.

ELLEN J. STEKERT

Focus for Conflict

Southern Mountain Medical Beliefs in Detroit[1]

THE DIFFICULTIES ENCOUNTERED by a Southern Appalachian family recently arrived in a northern urban center are hardly new. In her novel *The Dollmaker*,[2] published in 1954, Harriette Arnow portrayed the agonies of such migrants to the city with accuracy and eloquence. Eight years later Rupert B. Vance suggested that the most promising solution to the social and economic plight of the Southern Appalachian region was to move the inhabitants to locations offering better economic opportunities. As he put it, "Since the mountains are not likely to be moved, we proceed on the assumption that men can be moved."[3] Since 1950 over two million persons have moved from the southern mountains to our northern industrial centers; however, as the old adage says, it may be easy to take the boy out of the mountains, but not the mountains out of the boy. While numerous studies have investigated the traumas suffered by immigrants moving to American cities from lands across the seas,[4] far less has been done to document the situation of the native migrant who is moving with increasing rapidity from our rural regions to our urban centers. His predicament is certainly as bad as that of the foreign immigrant of the late nineteenth and early twentieth centuries. One could say the native migrant's situation is worse; he is often thought of as "quaint" and "pure" while down on the farm or in the hills, but nothing more than a social problem in the cities. It is as though we feel he should not have to make an adjustment, for he is the embodiment of all the American values of the past that we hold dear. He should know better than to dwell in ghettos, have employment problems, and be ridden with illness.

The migrant from the southern mountains comes from a culture alien to that of our large urban centers. This has been pointed out many times in studies such as

[1] This study was made possible by a grant from the Wayne State University Alumni Association. For details as to methodology see the Appendix.

[2] Harriette Arnow, *The Dollmaker* (New York, 1954).

[3] Rupert B. Vance, "The Region: A New Survey," in *The Southern Appalachian Region: A Survey,* ed. Thomas R. Ford (Lexington, Ky., 1962), 8.

[4] See, for example, Paul J. Campisi, "Ethnic Family Patterns: The Italian Family in the United States," *American Journal of Sociology,* 53 (1947), 443–449.

Pearsall's *Little Smoky Ridge* and Matthews' *Neighbor and Kin*.[5] It is also true, however, that the beginnings of a transition within the southern mountain culture began over sixty years ago, when the introduction of lumbering and mining began to change the basic social structure. Consequently, the southern mountaineer has been raised to believe in and live by old southern mountain values, only to find the society around him becoming just as alien as the society in the cities.[6] Informants interviewed for this study often strongly expressed the feeling that there was nothing to go back to in the South; the North and the cities, they felt, were their only hope, although not without conflict. Like the foreign immigrant at the turn of the century, the southern mountain migrant has often chosen the conflict and hope of the city over the apparent certainty of failure back home.

The differences between old southern mountain values and new urban values are sharply presented by Matthews.[7] She shows that southern mountain society traditionally regards the "community level" as the ideal goal; one does not wish to be thought of as different or better than the rest of the community. Ideally one must be an integral part of the community and not compete with his neighbor for status. One's identity, and thereby one's value to the community, is determined by "ascriptive qualities" such as birth, sex, and age. Thus, when the southern mountain family is faced with new values on moving to a northern city such as Detroit, they are confronted with acute conflict. Urban society's concept of what constitutes a person's identity and value is quite different from what the southern mountaineer has been accustomed to. In the city one strives to be anything but "community level"; in the city one's goal must be to achieve, to be "better than the next guy." The southern mountaineer finds that his identity, as defined in the mountains, has little meaning in the city; who cares whose kin you are or if you are the oldest son? The southern mountaineer in the city finds that his identity now depends on behavior he has not been taught to value, and he often ceases to care. To those who may object to this view and point to the men in grey flannel suits and mass conformity in "other directed" urban America, I would suggest that the urban dweller's conformity is seldom thought of in such terms by the urban dweller himself. No matter how conformist he might be, he likes to view himself as different. Perhaps more important is the fact that one gains what is actually conformity in the urban center by achievement; one must keep up with the Joneses. In other words, conformity and ascriptive status are not necessarily the same thing.

The conflict of values frequently becomes insurmountable, as Matthews points out, for "the intrusion of So-So families into a Go-Go society does not cause violence: it only leads to an enlarging of the lower strata of the Go-Go society."[8] The women, who have been taught to wait and suffer what comes to them, often do so; and the men, robbed of their ascriptive patriarchal status, simply give up. It seems ironic that the southern mountain migrant should travel from a culture

[5] Marion Pearsall, *Little Smoky Ridge: The Natural History of a Southern Appalachian Neighborhood* (Birmingham, Ala., 1959); Elmora Messer Matthews, *Neighbor and Kin: Life in a Tennessee Ridge Community* (Nashville, Tenn., 1965).

[6] See Thomas R. Ford, "The Passing of Provincialism," in *The Southern Appalachian Region: A Survey*, 9–34; and Rupert B. Vance and Nicholas J. Demerath, eds., *The Urban South* (Chapel Hill, N.C., 1954).

[7] Matthews, 134.

[8] Ibid., 145.

placing a premium on the "average" to an urban culture that places him in anything but "average" urban status. The very ascriptive qualities that made him blend into his mountain society make him conspicuous at the bottom of the class structure in urban society. Yet, he feels he must blend, and in urban society to blend means to be middle class. Thus he must accept middle-class status as his new norm. He must use nontraditional means, that of "Go-Go" and "achievement," to attain an old and traditional value, the "community level," and he is caught in a tearing and often destructive conflict.

The southern mountain white, because of his tradition of seeking "average" status, generally finds himself confused and leaderless in the tremendously complex structure of public services he must use in order to survive. The organizations that show concern for his welfare are mainly church groups—ironically, church groups far removed from the fundamentalist religious persuasion in which he was raised. The Catholics, Lutherans, and Methodists for example, whose worship appears stiff and formal to the more evangelically oriented person from the Southern Appalachians, are among the churches in Detroit most intimately concerned with his well being. The interviews I did for this study revealed no respondent who regularly attended a church in Detroit. This corresponds with Griffin's finding in Cincinnati and with the general decline in church attendance in the mountains as well.[9] All respondents had belonged to some fundamentalist sect in the South, and although they did not participate formally in church services in Detroit all regarded themselves as religious. All of the informants considered faith the most important factor in curing disease, and over three-quarters of them retained a firm belief in faith healing. The persistence of past religious attitudes, even in the absence of present religious behavior, is characteristic of the general tendency of the southern mountain migrant to hold tenaciously to his beliefs even when circumstances favor a change in behavior.

Religious groups in Detroit usually succeed in attracting the Southern Appalachian person to their churches for social but not religious activities. The religious southern mountaineer believes in the church primarily as a place of worship; yet he rejects the type of worship he finds in the churches that work for his well-being in the ghetto. This conflict is actually verbalized by many of my informants; one respondent who often goes to a nearby church with her children for community functions remarked, "I don't see why they don't just open a social center."

These "alien" churches appear to be the only present rallying point and focus for leadership for the Southern Appalachian migrant in Detroit. The traditional social organization of the southern mountain does not stress community leadership. The Southern Appalachian people in the northern city, therefore, are not well organized and, consequently, often feel overlooked by legislators. One Detriot religious leader who has been involved in attempts to organize the voice of white poverty in the city bemoans the fact that the southern mountain white population is too "timid" to organize and obtain funds from government agencies. Because they lack strong leadership, he says, the ghetto Appalachian whites have

[9] Roscoe Griffin, "Appalachian Newcomers in Cincinnati," in *The Southern Appalachian Region: A Survey*, 83.

to "sit back and let that money go to the Negroes. . . . They're growing Negro leaders while the poor whites go down, down, down."[10]

But lack of leadership is not a new phenomenon for the traditionally individual-istic mountaineer. Matthews points out that "certainly the absence of recognized leadership is another important expression of the value the deme places on keep-ing status distinctions to a minimum."[11] The traditional value of nonachievement is a constant torment to the southern mountaineer in the city. Not having an orga-nized voice, he feels slighted and bitter about welfare and poverty programs. Among southern mountain people in Detroit one often hears the expression, "In this city poverty is black."

The black American is not alone in the impacted urban poverty areas of the United States. Often, as in Detroit, both Negro and white Americans live side by side in the ghettos. Why, then, does the medically indigent Negro American utilize public health facilities in Detroit proportionately more than his white neighbor in poverty? My study was undertaken to answer part of that question; it was conceived as a preliminary investigation of the Southern Appalachian migrant to Detroit. Because most Southern Appalachian migration to urban areas has been both poor and overwhelmingly white, it is with this group that the study is concerned. The term "medically indigent" is used in this study to denote per-sons who are unable to afford medical expenses without financial deprivation, re-sulting in an inability to pay for the basic resources needed for subsistence.

My investigation focuses on the fate of traditional medical attitudes and prac-tices brought to Detroit by the southern mountaineer. It seeks to determine whether traditional patterns and values have helped or hindered him in receiving adequate health care. In order to limit the study to a specific medical condition— one for which public services are available to the medically indigent in Detroit— the areas investigated were restricted to those concerning prenatal care, birth, and infant care. But no area of culture can be studied in and of itself; the behavior and attitudes of southern mountain women in the areas mentioned cannot be separated from the greater fabric of the southern mountain culture from which they came.

Toward the end of the first phase of my research, I was told by a pediatrician in one of the large Detroit hospitals that if she had her choice she would rather counsel a medically indigent Negro mother than a southern mountain one. She felt that Negro women listened more openly and seemed to benefit more fully from her advice. Sadly enough, my study supports a part of her observation; medically indigent southern mountain women in Detroit do not seem to seek or absorb medical counsel. Even when their articulated judgments change in the urban environment, their attitudes remain those of past tradition. The southern mountain mother rarely seems to internalize the advice offered her by the city physician.

It is true that segments of the urban Negro population retain some of their medical traditions, just as segments of the southern mountain population do. Many Negro women in Detroit, for example, treat umbilical hernia by taping a

[10] Monroe W. Karmin, "Model City Muddle," *Wall Street Journal,* February 20, 1968, p. 17.
[11] Matthews, 78.

silver coin to the navel.[12] But the important question is how long traditions anti-thetical to good health care are retained. My study was not intended as a com-parison of the health practices and attitudes of the medically indigent urban white and those of the underprivileged urban black. Once begun, however, it was hard to ignore the fact that every single health service contacted reported that the overwhelming majority of the people who used their facilities was black. Where was the black Detroiter's neighbor, the southern mountain white, when it came to utilizing medical aid from which he could clearly benefit? Educated esti-mates are that Detroit's southern mountain population is presently about thirty thousand and will be double that number in a few years,[13] though I would put it between fifty and sixty thousand at the present time. This does not include the large numbers of people from the Southern Appalachians who have entered a higher socioeconomic status and live outside the city limits in areas such as Hazel Park, Warren, Wixom, and "downriver" communities. Traditionally the southern mountaineer has placed a high premium on the welfare of his children; of all the areas of health care, he is most responsive to hospitalization for birth.[14] Why, then, do the women not appear more frequently at Detroit's prenatal and child care facilities? The answer lies to a great extent in traditional behavior patterns and attitudes.

The Problem

It has been recognized that poor health is intimately related to poverty, and that poor health in the prenatal period is often linked with a high rate of perinatal and infant mortality.[15] Given these facts, it is extremely important for an ex-pectant mother who is living in poverty, or near poverty, to seek and continue care throughout the entire maternity cycle. It is important both for her sake and for the sake of her child. Yet southern mountain women in Detroit are not receiving this care, and there is no reason to believe the situation is different in other north-ern urban centers. The medically indigent Southern Appalachian woman is among those high risk cases who most need the comprehensive services of medical as-sistance programs such as the Detroit Maternity and Infant Care Project. The DMICP, begun in 1964 with the intention of reaching women from low-income groups, offers comprehensive care for the entire maternity cycle. Hospital cost is determined by the financial situation of the mother. The project is part of a federal program providing similar services in other cities.

[12] Reported by a nurse from the Visiting Nurse Association in Detroit, February 1968.

[13] Martin Corcoran and others, "A Transcript of a Meeting Held at AYEP on August 10, 1967, between Dr. Martin Corcoran of the Appalachian Foundation and MCHRD Personnel," a mimeo-graphed document prepared by the Area Training and Technical Assistance Center (Detroit, 1967), 10, 19.

[14] C. Horace Hamilton, "Health and Health Services," in *The Southern Appalachian Region: A Survey*, 219–244.

[15] See, for example, Howard L. Bost, "A New Outlook upon the Problem of Poverty and Health in Eastern Kentucky," *American Journal of Public Health*, 56:4 (April 1966), 590; Steven Pol-gar, "Health and Human Behavior: Areas of Interest Common to the Social and Medical Sciences," *Current Anthropology*, 3:2 (April 1962), 163; and Helen C. Chase, "Perinatal and Infant Mor-tality in the United States and Six West European Countries," *American Journal of Public Health*, 57:10 (October 1967), 1743.

Although C. Horace Hamilton reports that the perinatal mortality rate in the entire Southern Appalachian region in 1954–1956 was only 1.3 deaths per 1,000 births higher than the national rate (35.4), the majority of counties with rates from 9.6 to 14.6 above the national norm of that time are within the geographic area from which the respondents for my study were drawn. (The women interviewed for my study were, therefore, originally from high risk areas in the South.) Dr. Hamilton is of the opinion that a medical "revolution" occurred in the Southern Appalachians from 1940 to 1955. Unfortunately, his strongest arguments supporting this contention are statistics that reflect behavior patterns rather than attitudes. The percentage of children born in hospitals in the Southern Appalachians rose from 17.9 percent in 1940 to 89.4 percent in 1955. The percentage of infants delivered by midwives decreased during that period from 14.3 to 3.2 percent.[16] These statistics, however, seem to indicate only a small victory, not a revolution. Both the contact and the depth interviews conducted during my study indicate that the women are quite willing to enter a hospital to give birth (in contrast to a determined abhorrence of hospitalization for anything not considered as "natural" as childbirth).[17] But they still were extremely negative about prenatal and postnatal care. Thus a mother of three, whose interviews revealed she had probably suffered from toxemia and other complications during her first two pregnancies, still had no prenatal care for her third child and was admitted as an emergency case with severe complications to one of Detroit's large hospitals several months before the birth of the child. Her interview suggests she might have suffered a third time from toxemia. During her confinements for birth this woman had been informed of the value of prenatal and postnatal care.

It does not follow, then, that southern mountain mothers and their children will be in good health simply because the children are born in hospitals. Note the high number of handicapped and dead children, as well as the number of complications during pregnancies, reported in the Appendix. The women interviewed often expressed a desire to have their children at home, and probably would have, had it not been for the fact that the doctors they contacted refused to make home calls and that without a doctor attending birth certificates become a legal problem. Most of the women's interviews indicate that the advice given by doctors while the woman was in the hospital was often misunderstood, merely tolerated, or completely ignored after the mother and child were released. Time and again it was apparent that hospital confinement for a birth did not significantly change the general medical behavior or attitudes of the women involved. Thus, among the southern mountain women in Detroit, it appears that behavioral change, in this case hospital confinement for birth, neither changes basic attitudes, nor leads to additional changes in medical behavior.

Infant mortality as an index of general health has long been of concern to this country. Since the President's State of the Union Message in January 1968, it has become fashionable to lament the fact that the United States has fallen behind

[16] Hamilton, 221–222.
[17] An attitude also reported in Marion Pearsall, "Some Behavioral Factors in the Control of Tuberculosis in a Rural County," *American Review of Respiratory Diseases*, 85:2 (February 1962), 205.

other "developed" countries to fifteenth place in this respect.[18] The United States ranks (in order) behind Sweden, Netherlands, Norway, Finland, Australia, Japan, Denmark, Switzerland, New Zealand, United Kingdom, France, Federal Republic of Germany, Belgium, East Germany, and ties with Canada for the honor of fifteenth position. Our standing reflects a national problem. Prior to 1950 the trend in our infant mortality rate pointed to a decline that would have produced a rate of 15 deaths per 1,000 births in 1964. After 1950, however, the decline leveled off, giving us an infant mortality rate of 24.8 in 1964—9.8 above the projections from the 1937–1950 trend.[19] The projected rate of 15 was hardly unreasonable since in 1964 both Sweden and the Netherlands bettered that figure.[20] In addition, the statistical differences showing fourteen countries as superior to the United States in the area of infant mortality cannot be accounted for on the basis of discrepancies in definitions or of the manner in which the statistics were gathered.[21]

One reason why it seems significant to look specifically at the southern mountain woman is that she is part of a population usually lumped into the general category of "white southerners." This is not only a quirk of statisticians. Killian indicates that the general urban community does this too. They tend to lump all southerners into one category and call them disparagingly "hillbillies."[22] The patterns and values of the person from the Southern Appalachians—even those affected by the mining and lumbering industries—are often different from the traditions of persons from southern urban centers or the nonmountain areas of the South such as the Tidewater or Bluegrass country.[23] The southern mountain woman, therefore, is a hidden statistic in the southern "white, nonwhite" category. We must delineate her distinctive traditional patterns of behavior and attitudes relating to prenatal care, hospital delivery, and postnatal care, for she is a member of an increasingly numerous high-risk group in the poverty areas of our urban centers. If we understand her traditions we can begin to reach her and provide care from which she can benefit greatly.

Census tract "A" in Detroit, for example, one of several areas in the city where southern mountain people have moved alongside of poor blacks and the area from which most of the informants for this study were drawn, shows an infant mortality rate of 36.8 per 1,000 live births in 1966, compared with an overall city average of approximately 28.1.[24] The woman from the Southern Appalachians in this census tract is certainly a high-risk maternity patient. Recent statistics point encouragingly to a drop in infant mortality in large American cities, but according to Dr. Arthur Lesser, Deputy Chief of the U.S. Children's Bureau, this drop is largely the result of medical welfare programs. If Detroit's clinic clientele is any

---

[18] Chase, 1737.

[19] Iwao M. Moriyama, "Present Status of Infant Mortality Problem in the United States," *American Journal of Public Health,* 56:4 (April 1966), 623.

[20] Chase, 1737.

[21] Moriyama, 624.

[22] Lewis N. Killian, "The Adjustment of Southern White Migrants to Northern Urban Norms," *Social Forces,* 32 (1953), 67.

[23] See Polgar, 168.

[24] Detroit Department of Health, "Vital Events Which Occurred to Detroit in 1966," (Map) *Annual Report,* section 1 (Detroit, 1967).

indicator, it seems unlikely that there were many white mothers among the 700,000 to 800,000 women of low-income families who were served by the maternity and infant care projects to which Dr. Lesser refers.[25]

It appears that one of the primary reasons why the southern mountaineer does not take advantage of urban health facilities is that there is a deafness based on cultural factors affecting both the person from the Southern Appalachians and urban health personnel. Neither really seems to hear what the other is trying to say; all interviews, both with contact people and with informants, indicate a communication problem. Much of the difficulty seems to lie in a basic conflict between the traditional values and practices of the "medically educated" urban professional and general public and those of the southern mountaineer. Clearly, what one does not understand one cannot hear. It is pertinent, therefore, to discuss some of the basic life patterns and values of the Southern Appalachian resident and to attempt to relate these attitudes and modes of action to the mountaineer's medical situation in the city.

Medical Behavior in the City and Prior Tradition

It appears that the general pattern of maternity behavior among first-generation southern mountain women in Detroit is to have little or no prenatal care, to be hospitalized for the birth, and to have little or no postnatal care. This also seems to be the current pattern in the South today. Most of the Southern Appalachian women interviewed for this study would rather have had their children in their homes. One woman even told of a couple who served the southern mountain population in Detroit by delivering children at home; the couple had no medical training, but their fee was cheaper than that of a private doctor. Most of the women interviewed preferred a private doctor to the series of doctors in a public clinic. Although they stressed their desire for personal attention, they also indicated that they switched doctors frequently. Most of them retained a basic distrust of physicians as well as a traditional modesty. Prenatal and postnatal examinations were regarded as humiliating.

These attitudes, and others, are part of the traditions the southern mountain migrant brings with her to the urban center. They are that area of Southern Appalachian folklore that falls under the category of beliefs or values, often manifesting itself in structured behavior such as that found in the practice of folk medicine. This study is concerned with both areas: that of traditional attitudes and values and that of folk or traditional practices (cures). The interviews in Detroit revealed both knowledge and application of a wealth of southern mountain folk remedies. It appears, understandably, that these are slowly beginning to blend with general urban folk medicine, which ranges from chicken soup to aspirin. But the retention of these southern mountain cures seems to be primarily a reflection of the persistence of basic traditional medical attitudes. A convenient metaphor would be to view the actual cures as entities embedded in a traditional body of belief to which they owe their existence. Without the attitudes the cures will not persist; consequently, while the actual practice of specific cures tends to change first (although

---

[25] Physicians International Press, "Cities Report Drop in Infant Mortality," *Ob-Gyn News* (March 13, 1968), 6.

southern mountain folk cures are by no means dead in Detroit), the traditional values regarding medical behavior resist change with a fantastic energy.

GLORIFICATION OF THE PAST. Most medically indigent Southern Appalachian people who have come to the large urban centers in the North have done so to escape an agonizing existence in the South. One informant succinctly stated why she had come to Detroit, "There was nothing down there, and I mean nothing!" The South, too, has been going through many changes, and often life is not as romantic in the hills as northerners might think. The northern city often presents a dream of better things for the southern mountaineer, who will be faced with a major adjustment no matter where he chooses to live.[26] In fact, the southern mountaineer most often has moved from a situation in which he was having to cope with the influences of urbanization anyway.

The imperative quality of the move to the northern city is coupled with a hope that often turns to bitterness in the reality of ghettos, which are hardly better than southern rural poverty. When the present offers excessive conflict, there is often an understandable retreat into old attitudes and traditional behavior. This is true of the southern mountaineer in the city ghetto. One of the outstanding themes in the interviews—an attitude encountered even with the most medically sophisticated respondents—was that the way things were done back home in the past was far superior to the present. I frequently got the impression from the southern mountain women with whom I spoke that if they had sought medical advice during their maternity cycle it was mainly because it "was the thing to do" rather than out of any conviction it would really help. Thus, the mountain woman clings to the past in two ways: first, she does not completely accept professional medical care, since her traditional attitude remains the same; and, second, she acts according to the dictates of her "So-So" culture by doing what is acceptable in her new urban, middle-class oriented environment.

The glorification of past medical practices showed up in several different ways. Often, after a large part of my questionnaire was covered and the interviews turned to the section dealing with common childhood ailments, respondents displayed an intense respect for the home cure and a disdain for anyone—especially city people—who "give in" and go to doctors. The general dislike, or at best indifference, toward the medical doctor and the common glorification of the skilled practitioner of home medicine in the South (usually an older woman) reflects this persistence of traditional attitudes. Often respondents spoke of the older woman who knew the folk cures as the embodiment of the perfect person, again a clear idolization of the past, "She was the greatest person in the world." Another evidence of the tenacity of the past is the tendency of most women to go back to the South for care when they are either severely ill or pregnant. It seems that, when the dream of the city dies in the reality of the present, the pain of yesterday fades away and the past is glorified.

An example of the persistence of past values can be seen in the case of D.G. She came to Detroit from Kentucky a few weeks before her first child was born because her mother was here. She had no prenatal care and delivered her child in a Detroit hospital. She lived in Kentucky during the entire second maternity cycle,

---

[26] See Vance and Demerath, *The Urban South*.

received no prenatal care, and had the child at home. Although the local doctor, whom the family had known for years, was attending at this second birth, D.G. suffered extensive injury to her reproductive organs. As she described it, "She [the baby] came right away. Of course as big as she was I didn't know then that everything tore out and the doctor didn't tell me or make any examination. He took the afterbirth and had C [husband] go bury it someplace . . . that dogs or nothing, you know, they couldn't dig it up" (Hand 59).[27] However, D.G. still feels that this second birth was her easiest, "I had a real easy time." She remembers it as her most ideal delivery, even though when she went for an examination in Detroit during her following (third) pregnancy, the doctor expressed concern about her ability to carry the child. D.G. eventually had to have an operation to repair the injuries resulting from the second birth.

For her third pregnancy D.G. had prenatal care and delivered in a hospital. A year later, she had her operation, "About a year afterwards I went in and they called it the suspension. They pulled everything up like it was supposed to be and put it back in place then stitched up down there where it was all ripped out and told me that I was just like a new woman." Several years following the operation she had her fourth child, had prenatal care, and delivered in a hospital.

The case of D.G. is interesting and typical. In the course of her four pregnancies she altered her pattern of behavior to comply with what medical authorities feel is correct procedure; however, her attitude has changed little. She still regards the second birth as the best, "natural," as she terms it, even though she is quite aware that she was harmed during delivery and almost lost her next child as a result of poor medical attention. ("Natural childbirth" to D.G. means that she had no medication; she was not referring to the voguish practice of "natural childbirth" followed by many urban women.) Though D.G. has altered her behavior pattern, she still clings to the old attitudes and values. Although she has spent most of her adult life in Detroit, D.G. like many others thinks of herself as in but not of the urban community. On the other hand, it appears that she idolizes the home community of the past, not the present; in Killian's words, "its norms [were] still praised as the best, even when they could not be followed."[28]

B.R. is another example of the tendency to hold to the past regardless of contradictory experience; she spent most of her interviews vociferously praising the positive value of doctors, but she often slipped into such statements as, "My mother didn't have all of this medication [and hospitalization] when I was born, so I don't think that I have to have it either." This is almost identical to Koos' New York State respondent who refused postnatal care in the name of tradition and mother by saying, "Nuts to him [the doctor], I said. I didn't see any reason to go—I felt fine, so I just didn't. I'm not going to do something like that when my mother didn't."[29] In the case of B.R., however, there is an additional factor that shows how she forgets important facts because of her need to glorify the past. B.R. implied that her mother had an easy time during her birth, but as the inter-

[27] This and subsequent numbers refer to the classification of folk beliefs in Wayland D. Hand, ed., *Popular Beliefs and Superstitions from North Carolina, The Frank C. Brown Collection of North Carolina Folklore*, vols. 6 and 7 (Durham, N. C., 1961 and 1964).

[28] Killian, 68.

[29] Earl Lomon Koos, *The Health of Regionville: What the People Thought and Did About It* (New York, 1964), 67.

view progressed it became clear this was not true. B.R. almost died at birth. It appears that she was born with an Rh factor complication, and would have died (as was the case with her two brothers) had she not been immediately rushed to a hospital for blood transfusions.

The persistence of traditions that sometimes, though not always, are at odds with rationality is a formidable factor. It appears that the more stress the individual confronts the more likely he is to fall back upon past patterns of behavior and past attitudes. In James Agee's *Death in the Family,* for example, the conflict between rural and urban southern mountaineers is a central theme. In this case the belief that the dead father returned to his home to say goodbye to his family is a very comforting idea and eases the grief of his kin. And birth, like death, is a time of adjustment and stress. It is easy to agree with Nancy Milio, who observes that "lower-class women are more likely to resort to their folklore for coping with crisis."[30] Living lives ridden with immediacies and emergencies in the ghetto, the southern mountaineers understandably rely on the patterns learned in the past. One does not have the time for the luxury of learning new attitudes.

PATTERNS OF MOVEMENT. In attempting to determine why southern mountain women do not use the facilities available to them in the metropolitan Detroit area, it is necessary to consider factors having to do with the city itself and relate them to the southern woman's traditional values and patterns. Although Detroit is an extension of their home communities, for many of these Southern Appalachian people the advantages of the city still are not at their disposal. The southern mountaineer is surrounded by invisible walls within which he moves. This is especially true of the mountain woman, who in this respect is not unlike most urbanites. She has, however, more limitations than most, for she is usually without transportation and money, and often has several small children to take with her wherever she goes. In addition, she is burdened with the traditional southern mountain assumption that she should stay home and not appear often in public. An extreme example of this was related by B.T., who told of a woman who was rendered entirely helpless when her husband died, for he had been the one who transacted all the business with the outside world, including grocery shopping.

In many ways, it is more difficult for a newcomer to find his way around Detroit than in other cities. This city's public transportation system is insufficient, costly, and difficult for the new arrival to master. The hospitals where a medically indigent woman can receive the best care are often located far away from her familiar neighborhood. Few women living in the area of the Riverside Church on the east side of Detroit, or south of Wayne State University in the central part of the city, can easily manage the six- or ten-mile trip to Mount Carmel Hospital in the city's northwest section, via a complex and often frustrating bus system. Few can manage even the shorter trips to Detroit Memorial or Hutzel Hospital in the center of the city. The southern mountain woman is often more familiar with the roads going back to the mountains than she is with the route to the hospital in Detroit. The difficulty is compounded by the fact that she probably does not even believe in visiting the hospital in the first place.

[30] Nancy R. Milio, "Structuring the Setting for Health Action," *American Journal of Public Health,* 57:11 (November 1967), 1986.

Some progress toward breaking down this territorial handicap has been made in Detroit. The Detroit Maternity and Infant Care Project (DMIC) has made it possible for half of the medically indigent mothers in the city to have all of their prenatal, delivery, and postnatal care in the same hospital. Before this project was established, a mother often had to go to three different health facilities and bear the difficulty of adjustment three times over. In addition to the DMIC, the ECHO project (Evidence for Community Health Organization) is trying to pinpoint the health problem areas of Detroit in hopes of placing health facilities in those areas, rather than attempting to move the population to the hospitals.

But even though one understands and copes with the problems of territorialism within the city, there is still the problem of traditional attitudes to be dealt with. Even the most "urbanized" informants—those utilizing health facilities most frequently and most effectively—showed a decided reluctance toward accepting them as proper. The informants often accepted the doctors' advice only when it suited them, and they tended to revere traditional medical practices.

THE ROLE OF WOMEN. In the Southern Appalachian region, the woman traditionally was and is the primary transmitter of medical lore.[31] All of the depth interviews revealed a past reliance on a mother or grandmother who "always knew" what to do for an ailment. It was also this woman's role to determine when to call the doctor. Such a determination was made usually only in the most pressing conditions, such as those under which Sue Annie counsels Gertie to get her child to a physician in *The Dollmaker*.[32] To the southern mountaineer, the point at which one calls a doctor is far beyond that when the urban, middle-class "native" seeks help. This is not to say that the acculturated urban mother does not do her own "doctoring" before, or instead of, calling a physician. She has a long list of home remedies; yet, she calls for medical advice far earlier than the newly arrived southern mountain mother.

The southern mountain woman in the city is placed in a difficult situation. She is hampered in fulfilling her traditional role as healer because she realizes that her home cures are considered "backward." Even if she wishes to use them, she finds that in the urban environment it is difficult to obtain the herbs and other ingredients for the traditional cures. One might think this would lead to the adoption of traditional urban cures, but it appeared in the interviews that obstacles to the use of old remedies lead first to experimentation—an attempt to find substitutes for the traditional ingredients used back home. Thus, L.H. used nail polish to heal a burn suffered by one of her children, and a number of mothers reported trying various commercial teas instead of the traditional catnip tea to make their babies "break out with the little red hives" (Hand 314).

The southern mountain woman in the city follows the traditional pattern in deciding when the doctor should be visited; she takes her child to the doctor, as one informant put it, "only when it is absolutely necessary." This condition of absolute necessity seems to hold true for her pregnancy as well, and it helps explain why so many southern mountain women do not have prenatal care and often appear as "walk in" patients at hospitals. "Walk in" maternity patients are those

---

[31] See, for example, Eugene J. Wilhelm, Jr., "Those Old Home Remedies," *Mountain Life and Work*, 44:2 (March 1968), 22.

[32] Arnow, 33.

women who arrive at the hospital when birth is imminent, often having made no prior plans with the institution for confinement. If the mountain woman waits until the last moment before she seeks medical aid for illness, it is not likely that she will look for help in regard to something as "natural" as childbirth until the last moment too.

Another adjustment the southern mountain woman must make when she moves to the city—especially if she is from a rural area—is to accept what might be called a different "cleanliness imperative." In the past, it has been her job to determine and maintain the cleanliness of her home and children. Urban Americans have a predilection for washing away their sins with an excess of soap and water; all good acculturated city folk know, according to the social gospel from the turn of the century, that cleanliness is next to godliness. The southern mountain mother, however, has come from a less compulsive tradition. But there is good reason for the Southern Appalachian migrant to be more careful about personal hygiene in the city than she was in the mountains. The dirt of the slum carries diseases of many people and is often more dangerous than the dirt of the rural environment. And although diseases spread in rural areas through such means as contaminated wells, one must admit that the necessities of personal cleanliness are even more important in the overcrowded ghetto. When a sink or toilet backs up regularly in an urban slum, it becomes imperative that a mother wash her hands before feeding her child. Thus the newly arrived mother must also adjust her role of housekeeper and change her traditional "cleanliness imperative" for a new one.

The southern mountain woman traditionally is the one who actively perpetuates the medical lore of her culture, but it is the man who is responsible for transportation.[33] In the mountains when the decision was made to finally consult a physician, the husband was generally responsible for getting the sick person to the doctor or bringing the doctor to the house. Women usually stayed at home and seldom traveled to unfamiliar places. In the city, with her husband out of calling distance, it is the woman who has to transport herself and her children to the doctor when she decides that professional attention is necessary. It is a great effort for her to thread her children through the red tape of public transportation and welfare procedures at urban health centers. Reluctant to seek treatment until symptoms reach emergency proportions and disliking anything that resembles "welfare" in the first place, she is further discouraged by transportation difficulties. It is understandable why many illnesses go untreated, and it is a wonder anyone is treated at all.

The traditional role of the woman in the southern mountains is obviously quite different from the role she is forced to assume in the city. Her function as healer is hampered until she learns to substitute new ingredients for unavailable ones in her cures. She must learn to use different patent medicines. Often these are introduced to her through mass media, and they are accepted in the absence of an older woman (the mother or grandmother) to advise her about home remedies. In medical matters the migrant mountain woman seems to be more influenced by her television set than by the abundant and inexpensive public health facilities

---

[33] See Pearsall, "Some Behavioral Factors," 203.

available to her. She is not used to the new responsibilities of the urban environment.

ATTITUDES TOWARD WELFARE. It would be an understatement to say that the southern mountaineer has not looked upon welfare programs with favor. This attitude is an important negative factor standing between the migrant mountain woman and proper maternity care. Although the resistance to public welfare programs in the South seems to have diminished,[34] there still appears to be a basic scorn of them among the Detroit migrants from the southern mountains. The women interviewed for this study cited pride as a primary reason for their absence from public health programs treating the maternity cycle. The following excerpt from an interview expresses in content and syntax the typical confusion and disgrace that is felt when seeking medical welfare assistance:

Well, down there you never take them to a doctor unless they are real sick, you know. . . . And I guess it would apply after you come here, too. And then a lot of them don't know what place maybe if they don't have no money and they would be in a city and everything strange and new to them, why they don't know that a there—ah, ah, not—nobody told them some of them that a you know there's ways of getting treated anyway whether you've got money or not. And a lot of southern people are, expecially the people from Kentucky, they have this pride—it may be a stupid pride in some ways, but they have this pride that they don't want to beg and they would maybe wait until the last minute you know, to take the child.

Such statements indicate that a combination of elements keeps the southern mountain woman from utilizing the services at her disposal. Among these factors, pride is quite important. Like most human beings, the southern mountaineer does not want to be regarded negatively; to him it is a reprehensible characteristic "to beg." He also feels it a negative characteristic to be thought ignorant and clumsy, to be viewed as a hillbilly. As one informant stated, "Most of the people [Southern Appalachian] are not as stupid as most city people think they are."

The humiliation of being treated with disdain because of what she feels is an unjust stereotype is probably another reason why the southern mountain woman refrains from using welfare. It does not matter whether or not the woman from the Southern Appalachians is in fact treated worse than anyone else; the southern mountaineer has been hypersensitive for years to the persistent stereotype of him as a hillbilly. This serves to alter his behavior patterns, if he feels threatened with possible insult each time he goes to a public health service, he will soon cease using such facilities. Watts points out the adverse effect of "time consuming travel and waiting for a cursory inspection or a single injection and a noncommunicative word or two from a physician,"[35] while Yerby acknowledges the reaction of the patient who is often treated as "an unfeeling lump of humanity [with] discourteousness or demeaning familiarity [by] the staff" of public health facilities.[36] The service provided for persons using the public health clinics is often far from ideal even for insensitive persons, but when people likely to overreact to impersonal treatment are involved, such service often discourages them from using the

[34] Ford, 13–14.

[35] Dorothy D. Watts, "Factors Related to the Acceptance of Modern Medicine," *American Journal of Public Health*, 56:8 (August 1966), 1212.

[36] Alonso S. Yerby, "The Problem of Medical Care for the Indigent Population," *American Journal of Public Health*, 55:8 (August 1965), 1215.

health facility. Clearly, the patient's self-image and fear of being stereotyped are extremely important in determining how he behaves.

Often in the interviews the bureaucracy of medical welfare facilities was mentioned as confusing and discouraging. What my informants considered red tape hardly helped motivate them to use the clinics for preventative checkups and often discouraged even emergency use. Nonmedical "doctors," often more accessible and friendly, were consulted by many informants in times of stress. Almost all respondents commented on the long hours of waiting, a complaint that has been reported in other studies.[37] One woman related that she had been made to wait, in Chicago, from eleven in the morning until midnight before she was given a bed in the hospital. She delivered her son half an hour after she was admitted.

The interviews indicated that these women felt they were being stereotyped and rejected. They often reported that the agencies and people they went to for help tried to "send me back home to have my baby" and acted as if the child were illegitimate. There are legal reasons for determining the residency and the status of a child, and often the medically indigent woman must be asked about such things; but legal necessities mean little to the mountaineer woman, and the impressions she receives are an important determinant of her future actions. When no explanation is given concerning why a question must be asked, and when the question is embarrassing in the first place, the result can be humiliating. The interviews indicate a severe gap in communication between the southern mountain woman and public health personnel, producing further embarrassment for the already self-conscious woman. Welfare is difficult enough for her to accept, but when it is accompanied by humiliation and lack of communication, acceptance becomes even more painful.

Perhaps part of the lack of communication stems from the fact that many clinic doctors are immigrants from other countries and that many native American doctors seem to have a distinct prejudice against "poor white trash." Often doctors and other public health personnel have little time and less inclination to explain what the treatment will entail in terms the southern mountain mother can understand. One informant reported her horror at receiving a spinal anesthetic for her delivery. Since no one had told her what the effects would be, she was terrified, certain that she had been paralyzed from the waist down.

It is not only the lack of communication, the waiting, and the impersonality of treatment that deters the southern mountain woman from using public health services. Sometimes it is the method of billing. During the weeks I was interviewing one informant, one of her children received a large gash on the back of his head. She took him to the emergency room of one of Detroit's major hospitals. He was released and asked to return after a week to have the stitches taken out. This woman, her four children, her husband, and occasionally her husband's brother and his wife live in a small three-room apartment. The family pays a hundred dollars a month for rent, and on good weeks—which are seldom—her husband brings home ninety-five dollars. One day when I returned to continue the interviews, I saw that the child had had the stitches removed, and I asked the woman how she had managed to get to the hospital. (I had volunteered to drive

[37] See, for example, Watts, 1212.

them when she expressed anxiety about not knowing how to get there by public transportation.) She did not answer at first, and only said that a few days before they had received a bill for twenty-two dollars from the hospital for the emergency treatment. Later she told me that her husband had removed the stitches himself. He had used the family nail clippers, kept on a dusty ledge over the door. There was another factor related to this home-doctoring: the hospital had instructed the parents to take the child to the division called "surgery" for removal of the stitches.

Two things helped deter the parents from taking the child to the hospital— and may have discouraged the family from ever using the hospital again. First, the billing procedure of the hospital dictates that bills be paid either by welfare agencies or by private individuals. There is no graduated scale for patients who are not totally covered by welfare or insurance. Perhaps 95 percent of that hospital's patients have their bills sent directly to a welfare agency. This informant and her husband were attempting to live without the help of welfare—although they had been forced to depend upon it in the past—and thus fell within that 5 percent of the hospital's patients who personally received bills for their treatment. The family's initial reaction to the bill was confusion and alarm. Twenty-two dollars is a significant amount to a family of six whose monthly income after rent is at best $280. They do not believe in owing money, but they could not understand why no adjustment was made for their financial condition. They had planned to pay the entire bill; however, one of the husband's coworkers told him that if he did not pay, the hospital would absorb the cost. To my knowledge the bill has not yet been paid. This family learned something about "appropriate" patterns of behavior in the city. What conclusions could they have reached except that one does not go to the hospital, that one should try to rely on welfare, and that one need not pay bills?

In addition, the fact that the child was asked to return to a section of the hospital called "surgery," was a horrifying prospect. Traditionally the person from the Southern Appalachians cites as one of his basic distrusts of doctors the idea that they will "cut on him" or perform surgery. Such statements recur with such consistency that they have taken on the status of proverbial expressions. While this dread was probably not the prime reason for the home operation with the nail clippers, it definitely was a contribution.

My interviews did not reveal the intense anti-Negro feeling reported by Killian among the general "southern white" population in Chicago.[38] Even after the riots of the preceding summer, it appears that the southern mountain migrant has less anti-Negro feeling than other segments of the southern population. The women interviewed, however, expressed some uneasiness about the fact that the majority of patients and professional personnel in the public health services were Negroes. This factor seems to have some deterring effect upon the southern mountain woman's use of the services, although other influences appear to be much more important.

More significant than the racial factor was the repeated expression of humiliation and confusion at having to face a new doctor on each visit to the clinic. The

[38] Killian, 68.

modesty of the southern mountain woman is intense. During my field trips to Kentucky in 1960 and 1961 I noticed that older women often changed clothes by simply putting on a dress over one already being worn. Also, I observed that it was unusual for persons to disrobe in front of others, even those of the same sex. The necessity of undressing is in itself painful, and it becomes even more so when one has to appear in such condition before a stranger—and a different one each visit. Most of the women expressed acute embarrassment about the pelvic examination. Several felt they had been physically hurt by it, and one woman commented that it "somehow wasn't right," having a strange man "handle" and "see" her just as if he were her husband. The most humiliating aspect of these examinations was the fact that the strangers were usually men. The southern mountain woman is not especially predisposed toward doctors in the first place, but she is even less enthusiastic about having to submit to what she considers a highly personal examination by a man. In her tradition prenatal counsel is given by a woman. Thus, the clinic situation intensifies the discomfort of accepting what is viewed as "welfare," and a visit is hardly an attractive prospect for an expectant Southern Appalachian mother.

It appears that no matter how good the public health facilities are they will do little good for the southern mountaineer unless some action is taken to provide solutions for the way in which transportation to the facilities can be obtained, change the manner in which patients are billed, shorten the time one is forced to wait for treatment, alter the impersonal way the doctor's treatment is regarded, and alleviate the embarrassment suffered from being examined by a new and usually male doctor each visit. All these problems reinforce the southern mountain migrant's feeling that "to beg"— to accept public health care—is degrading. That belief will not die until the behavior the southern mountain person views as "begging" is given some dignity.

ATTITUDES TOWARD DOCTORS. One of my informants explained that in the old days many people had already raised their families before they even saw a doctor. In fact, she said, "They didn't even know doctors was like normal people." The idea that physicians are not quite like everyone else still lingers in the mind of the southern mountain migrant in Detroit. Unlike many segments of the urban population, the southern mountaineer does not regard the physician as sacrosanct. Rather, the doctor is viewed in terms of the community values and is judged by his ascriptive rather than his achieved status. The fact that a physician has successfully passed examinations and mastered his profession means less to the person from the southern mountains than whose son the doctor might be and how he relates to others as a person. It appears that a general suspicion of doctors exists among those mountain people most removed from urban influences,[39] while a highly limited acceptance exists among transition groups affected by urbanization, such as the mining communities.

The characteristics for which a doctor may be valued and accepted by the southern mountain patient seem to have little to do with medical competence. The patient must be familiar with the physician and view him as a neighbor and member of the community. The doctor must take time to listen and talk with his

[39] Edward Suchman, "Social Factors in Medical Deprivation," *American Journal of Public Health*, 55:11 (November 1965), 1726.

patient and must explain things to him clearly. Matthews reports similar attitudes in the Tennessee community she studied.

> Ridge residents have a strong feeling against outside professional help. They prefer to use home veterinarians, home doctors, home preachers, and home undertakers . . . Most residents are horrified by the idea of being taken to hospitals, many of them exacting promises from kin that they will be allowed to die at home. They want "Doc ___" to treat them at home or in his county-seat office because they have "plowed many a day with him barefoot."[40]

One of the women interviewed in this study put it this way, "If they [southern mountain women] been to a doctor at all, they had a little coal-camp doctor; somebody they'd known all their life."

The fact that the southern mountain woman prefers a doctor she has known for a long time might account in part for her persistent search for private physicians rather than public clinic services in Detroit. In her quest she often goes from one doctor to another. Notice the use of the plural in the following quotation from a Detroit respondent, "Some [doctors] is good and some's bad but naturally the ones I would pick for myself would be the doctors that knowed me all my life." The search for a private doctor is partly the search for private attention. It is also partly an attempt to act like the "average," middle-class urban person. The attempt often fails because the doctor is not able to give the kind of personal attention the southern mountaineer wishes, and the fees, usually aimed at a middle-class income, are beyond his reach. All the women interviewed in Detroit had "shopped around" for a regular private doctor; yet, at the time of the interview only two had found doctors with whom they were presently satisfied.

The southern mountain women interviewed for my study pursued their search for a private physician with an almost frantic dedication. One woman had "gone through" more than five different private doctors in the course of a single pregnancy and finally had given up and returned to her home in Kentucky to have her child in a private clinic, attended by a doctor with whom she had gone to high school. This preference among some lower socioeconomic groups for treatment by private physicians rather than medical welfare clinics has been reported by Gallagher for the Midwest.[41]

In going the rounds of different private medical doctors, the southern mountain woman often finds her way into the offices of nonmedical "doctors," many of whom are outright quacks. (I use this term to refer to individuals professing medical skills and knowledge they do not have.) Because she does not like welfare medical care, and because she chooses a doctor for reasons that have little to do with his scientific competence, the southern mountain woman is likely to consult such "doctors." To her, they appear to give her the attention a medical doctor has failed to offer. The interviews showed that the respondents were unfamiliar with the qualification of medical doctors and did not feel their training was significantly different from that of osteopaths and chiropractors. Almost all of the respondents believed that the three were similarly trained, but that the medical

[40] Matthews, 111–112.
[41] Eugene B. Gallagher, "Prenatal and Infant Health Care in a Medium-Sized Community," *American Journal of Public Health*, 57:12 (December 1967), 2134.

doctor performed "surgery" and the osteopath was either a bone or foot doctor, while the chiropractor was a back specialist.

Marion Pearsall has described medical care in the mountains with particular reference to the maternity cycle: "[It is] still almost entirely part of the family system. . . . This is especially apparent in the area of maternal health and the rearing of children. Childbearing, for example, is believed to be such a natural function that it is not generally thought of as a matter for medical attention."[42] The southern mountain woman today brings to the city an indifference, if not disdain, toward doctors and a feeling that since maternity is a natural condition, rather than an illness, there is little reason to consult a physician about it. Since the one type of doctor she might have consulted is unavailable in the city—that doctor with whom her husband might have plowed—she often goes without medical care. The only chink in the wall of this nonmedical approach to maternity is the fact that most of the southern mountain women today are having their children in hospitals. It does not appear, however, that the basic medical attitudes have also altered. Most of the women interviewed would have preferred having their children at home, and they usually ignored advice given them during their hospital confinement. Often they returned to their homes in the South as the time for delivery approached, so they could be with the doctors they had known for years and with their mothers or other older women advisers.

Each woman interviewed had one or more stories to illustrate her feeling that she was treated badly by doctors. In one way or another, the doctors she visited did not meet her expectations of what a doctor should do for his patient. First, most of the doctors she visited treated her as though she were on "an assembly line." The feeling generally expressed was, "He made me feel as if he was trying to rush me out in order to get another one in." The best that could be said for one of the doctors was, "He was brief, to the point, and professional—which is about all you can expect from a doctor." Such statements clearly show the disappointment experienced by the informants. Somehow they had expected, but had not been allowed, to communicate with the doctor.

Although others have pointed it out,[43] it cannot be stressed too often that many of these women have much more to complain about than the actual physical problems for which they visit the physician, and that these other problems are part of what they feel the doctor is not allowing them to communicate. By not acting the expected role of "friend," the urban doctor often loses his southern mountain patient. If the urban physician does not want these patients to leave him, he must somehow find a way to fulfill their need for personal, meaningful communication. They have come from a tradition in which a mother, a friendly family doctor, or a faith healer has treated their illnesses in situations that involve intense and reinforcing personal relationships between healer and patient. The stresses of acculturation in the city intensify the need to seek aid; yet it is a sad irony that the sources of physical and psychic counsel usually have been left back in the southern mountains. As Koos states, certainly some of these problems are "unavoidable. It

[42] Pearsall, *Little Smoky Ridge,* 160.

[43] Milio, 1986; and James A. Kent and C. Harvey Smith, "Involving the Urban Poor in Health Services through Accommodation: The Employment of Neighborhood Representatives," *American Journal of Public Health,* 57:6 (June 1967), 997.

appear[s], however, that some of the 'scientific distance' between patient and physician was artificial, and could be reduced."[44]

What should the medical doctor's role be in treating those aspects of the patient's condition caused by the life situation and resulting in mental rather than physical anguish? If a physician does not satisfy her traditional expectations and help relieve her of emotional as well as physical stress, the southern mountain woman will continue to perceive his treatment as less than satisfactory. She will continue to shop around for new doctors in the city, return to her home in the southern mountains for treatment of severe symptoms, or retreat into the old attitude that doctors are not much help. If she chooses the latter two patterns, as in Detroit, she will only ask for medical care at the last minute, and then with reluctance.

Whereas the early doctors in the South went into the mountains and learned the traditional patterns there, today it is the southern mountain woman who must cross over into a new culture to find medical help. There were difficulties for the early doctors going into the mountains, and there are now difficulties for the mountain woman coming from her culture of southern mountain poverty into the urban doctor's office. The situation is reversed, but once more there are misunderstandings and differing expectations. It is paradoxical that most of the women interviewed showed some desire to learn accepted city ways, yet they were thwarted in many of their attempts. One middle-class urban value is the belief in physicians, but as an uninformed person the southern mountain woman cannot make the distinctions between different types of "doctors." Thus, she easily finds herself in the hands of charlatans who listen to her and talk with her in terms she can understand.

Another urban value the southern mountain woman quickly learns about is the respect for and the power of money. She soon discovers that money bought more in the South, even though there was less of it than in the northern city. One of her major complaints about doctors is that their fees are too high; yet she will often spend an exorbitant sum on a chiropractor and not regret one penny of it. The chiropractor has usually spent time with her; consequently, she feels satisfied with his care. But when a medical doctor charges what the mountain woman considers a large sum of money for care that does not include the needed (and expected) personal attention, a complaint understandably follows. After all, in a culture that considers money important, you expect it to buy what you deem valuable. None of the women interviewed recognized that their complaints were the result of their accepting the urban culture's value of money while retaining the value of personal medical attention from the southern culture. Such recognition, however, would hardly have eased their distress.

The charge against city doctors most frequently made by the women interviewed was that doctors were interested in money, not people or their health. As one informant bitterly put it, "Doctors are pretty much the same everywhere; they [only] want to be paid." Significantly, many of the women interviewed expressed the belief that people in higher economic brackets were better treated by doctors than they were. The idea that physicians are primarily interested in money has become a firm part of the southern mountain woman's belief. It was mani-

[44] Koos, 77.

fested in a number of different ways during the interviewing. One common feeling was based on the fact that doctors did not personally give them medicine but rather gave them a prescription to be filled at a drug store. As Koos puts it, "The idea of the family doctor as one who practices medicine in the home and is a walking drugstore has had to be revised sharply in recent years."[45] To the southern mountain woman under urban financial stress a prescription means more than just going to the drug store; it means lack of personal attention as well as a trip through confusing traffic, usually with several unattended small children at home (or dragging behind her), in order to spend additional money in an often overpriced local drug store. The anger at incurring this extra trouble and expense is expressed in the belief of one respondent that city doctors get "a fifty cent kickback" on each prescription, while in Kentucky, she said, the doctor will usually "give you his own medicine from his own supply instead of sending you for a prescription."

Another commonly held belief used to document doctors' greed for money is that a physician will usually make you come back, visit after visit, in order to earn more from your illness. The value of repeated visits is difficult for the Southern Appalachian person to accept.[46] Likewise, it is difficult for the southern mountaineer—who traditionally treats the symptom only when it is impossible to ignore—to comprehend the value of preventative checkups. He seems to perceive his physical well-being much in the same terms as his spiritual state, not realizing that if one "backslides" in matters of medical attention one cannot always be "saved." But the follow-up or preventative visit to the mountaineer is regarded primarily as another way for the doctor to make additional money. The belief that the doctor wishes his client to make a return visit in order to make money is reflected in some of the ideas the informants held regarding vaccination. They showed a feeling that vaccinations were given to make a person ill so he would need to see a doctor. The reason one got ill from vaccinations was that the doctors put "germs" in them or made them from snake venom, mold, or extract from the bones of dead horses. On the other hand, some informants indicated that doctors often gave injections that were "just water" so they could make an additional charge. Clearly, none of these ideas reflect the type of trust the physician hopes to elicit from his patients.

Among the mountain migrants, the intricate belief network supporting the basic feeling of distrust in the physician seems endless. Another common idea held by the respondents was that doctors, in addition to wanting higher fees, have some sort of sinister desire to "cut on you." This fear of surgery is compounded by the fact that it is usually performed in a hospital, and hospital stays (other than for birth) are dreaded almost as much as the surgery itself. One informant told proudly how her father-in-law left the hospital after refusing surgery, saying that he would rather "die at home," and did. It is no wonder that southern mountain women dislike having episiotomies, an incision of the perineum made during the second stage of labor in order to prevent laceration or tearing, such as D.G. experienced.

Several of the women interviewed complained that doctors required payment

[45] Koos, 62.
[46] See Yerby, 1215.

in advance for maternity care. Most of them resented being asked to pay for services before they were performed and expressed the feeling that if the doctor cannot produce the desired effect he should not be paid. One woman remarked, "Why should I go pay him in advance when I don't know what shape the baby would be in?" To these informants advance payment seemed to reflect distrust and suggested they were irresponsible "hillbillies." One woman indignantly said, "I trust him with my good health and he should trust me to pay my bill."

The medically indigent southern mountain family, like many families in the low socioeconomic group, has a set of priorities that places medical care well below the necessities of life. In order to encourage the rearrangement of priorities in the lives of the migrant southern mountain family—giving medical care the high rank it requires—the urban physician must offer something the mountaineer needs and wants. The physician who deals with southern mountain women in the city will have to be aware of the fact that he is assuming a role traditionally performed by an older woman in the family and that this role demands a personal commitment between patient and healer antithetical to the "detached" stance of the scientist. It would be good for the doctor to recognize the traditional modesty of the woman from the mountains and remember that in matters of maternity an older woman was usually the adviser and at delivery it was usually a woman who handled the proceedings. If he understands the patterns of behavior and attitudes of his patients, it will be much easier for him to reach them. He will be able to use folk cures that are not harmful, such as placing a knife under the mattress to ease labor (see Hand 48), to gain his patient's confidence, and consequently find it easier to replace harmful traditions with constructive practices. It would be best if he remembers that traditional behavior and attitudes fill important needs or they would not have persisted, and when attempting to alter them he must do so with practices and ideas that serve the same needs.

Koos points out that the physician is often more highly trained in the science of his profession than in the humanistic responsibilities of it.[47] It is true that the doctor often comes from a group that values success, and he finds it difficult if not impossible to communicate with the poor white. He may find it helpful to examine his assumptions about the southern mountain migrant for traces of stereotyping. For if the cycle of distrust is to be broken, the doctor will probably have to make the first move. It will be difficult, but important, for him to prepare himself personally as well as he is prepared professionally to treat whatever group needs his service. Part of this personal preparation is the objective study of the traditional beliefs and attitudes held by his patients. The doctor must also learn to speak their language so they can understand him—even if he has to talk about "opening the lungs" or "keeping the fever out of the brain." Once he learns the basic attitudes of his patients, it might occur to him, for example, that when a southern mountain woman submits to a pelvic examination it is often humiliating to her, as well as a sign of intimacy that may lead her to expect more understanding and personal attention from the physician than is actually received. Learning people's traditions is time consuming, but it would seem a necessity if the physician is to take the first step in breaking the patterns of medical behavior among groups such as the southern mountaineer. If the doctor learns how to communicate

[47] Koos, 146.

with and understand his patient, he will be better equipped to help ease the mental and physical anguish of the people who need his skills and time but cannot pay for them. If he can succeed in doing this, he will look more "like normal people" to those who regard him negatively.

SELF-DIAGNOSIS AND THE PERSISTENCE OF FOLK MEDICINE. The southern mountain woman appears to retain most of her traditional role as diagnostician in the urban environment. By the time she has decided upon a visit to a physician, she has usually diagnosed her own or her child's case and has often also determined what is necessary for a cure. One informant reported that she ceased going to one doctor because she felt he had failed to prescribe the "right" medicine for her. The description of complaints which the mountain mother gives the doctor is often difficult for the urban physician to comprehend, for she will often use expressions based on traditional attitudes toward disease. Any difficulty with breathing may be described as "smothering"; rashes must always be "brought out"; all manner of respiratory ailments may be called "pneumonia"; and "hives" can be "bold" hives, "little red" hives, or "stretch" hives. In order to understand the past medical history as well as the present complaint of a southern mountain migrant, the doctor must take time to understand both the terms used and the patient's feelings about the particular illness. One informant in Detroit reported that what she called "quick TB" was the most dreaded disease in her family. It was caused, she said, when a menstruating woman took a shower or was caught in a rainstorm. The blood flow would stop and "back up," resulting in sudden hemorrhaging from the lungs and death. Several women in her family had died from it. Fear of such medically undefined diseases is real and intense, as is the belief that one can correctly make the diagnosis.

The tradition of self-diagnosis is yet another factor discouraging the southern mountaineer's use of city physicians. It also appears to be a contributing factor in the patient's frequent switching from one private doctor to another. If the doctor cannot understand the patient's complaint and diagnosis, and if the patient cannot understand the doctor, it is unlikely that the two will have a satisfactory relationship. In addition, the tradition of not seeing the physician until the last minute makes the patient even less receptive to medical terminology and logic, especially if it contradicts the patient's own diagnosis and expectations for treatment. How can a southern mountain mother listen objectively to her doctor when she makes the visit, as one respondent described, under the following conditions: "Because when they [her children] are sick and need medical attention they need it at that moment, not a day or two days later."[48] The doctor is the last resort, rarely the first. One only visits him when there is something wrong.

These attitudes are often coupled with a fatalistic approach to life and death. Peters reports that no matter how satisfying the experience was with a physician, patients often would not return for treatment because they felt "fate" determined the outcome of the illness.[49] Fatalism is more pronounced among the older people from the southern mountains, but it still was detected among the young mothers in my study. The differing degrees of fatalism between the generations is well

[48] See also Gallagher, 2134.
[49] Ann DeHuff Peters, "Patterns of Health Care in Infancy in a Rural Southern County," *American Journal of Public Health,* 57:3 (March 1967), 421.

described by the following account telling when and why an informant finally took her son to the doctor:

A.   In the winter time pneumonia is very common.
Q.   What did they do for that?
A.   Well if it gets bad enough you go to the doctor.
Q.   When is bad enough?
A.   Well when a child is laying there tossing and turning and can hardly breathe and you get scared or [it] turns purple and starts strangling or something serious . . . Joe, he's laying in the bed and he's turning purple you know, and, ah, my mother-in-law runs in [and] instead of saying "you'd better take him to the doctor," she says "that's a dead baby, [name of informant], mark my words," and I grabbed Joe . . . and I ran, or partly ran, all the way to Doc [name] . . . I just thought to get him out of there, you know, I think I said "No, he's not dead yet," [and] off I went like a big bird.

The mother-in-law in this case represents the older tradition of completely discounting the effect of the physician in the face of what appears to be fated. The mother of the child remains fatalistic by not taking her baby to the doctor until the last minute, yet she is not ready to predict death in the name of fate until she uses the doctor as a last resort. This "last resort" pattern can be seen as an improvement, although not an ideal behavior pattern. It is related to and resembles the pattern of the southern mountain mother going to the hospital for birth but not for prenatal or postnatal care.

Self-diagnosis is often accompanied by self-medication, and it is therefore not surprising to find that all of the southern mountain women interviewed for this study had an extensive knowledge of folk medicine. Many of them openly acknowledged that they used the cures in the city, although they recognized the stigma attached to such actions. Generally, the effects of urbanization have begun to influence the folk medical practices and beliefs retained by these women, and it is probable that many of the changes had already begun before the move to the North. The number of cures, however, and the incidence of their use as noted in this study, indicate a significant retention of tradition among the southern mountain women. Some beliefs and practices were only vaguely remembered, while many were remembered and altered and others remained intact and were practiced in the city. Given the persistence of traditional attitudes and the other obstacles in the way of obtaining medical care reported in the earlier sections of this paper, it is not surprising that the cures have remained embedded in the body of beliefs surrounding doctoring and health.

Some cures show the effects of urbanization more than others. For example, the use of nonprescription medication appeared frequently in many of the cures reported by the women interviewed. The ubiquitous "baby aspirin" seems to have replaced such unavailable items as asafetida and turpentine. Castor oil and paregoric, although apparently not popular ingredients in cures in the old southern mountains, were frequently cited for various maladies. Drinking a few ounces of castor oil was recommended to induce labor, and rubbing paregoric on a baby's gums was said to be good for teething. With increasing urbanization in the South and the growing number of commercial outlets available, such patent medicines probably began entering the realm of southern mountain folk medicine long before the mountaineers began moving to the cities. But, since the

urban environment makes it easier to find such items, while also making it impossible to locate other cure ingredients, the use of patent medicines is further
encouraged. In the "old days," informants reported, a woman would drink herb
teas to induce labor (Hand 38–42), while a teething child might have its gums
rubbed with the brains of a rabbit (Hand 365).

Hand cites castor oil five times and does not list paregoric at all. The cure of
rabbit brains was not reported by any informant in this study, although a number
of teething cures unlisted in Hand were given, such as rubbing catnip tea on
the child's gums. Thus, the tendency to replace older ingredients with patent
medicines is exaggerated in the urban environment.

Another traditional medical practice altered by urbanization is the manner
in which a woman is supposed to be able to induce an abortion. The idea of abortion itself seems to have been encouraged by urbanization. Most of the informants
considered a large family in the city a burden and a sign of poverty. Most expressed the traditional belief that women should have many children, but they
also revealed their present conflict by saying they wished they had fewer, or that
they did not want more. When describing a family who had "made it" out of
poverty, one informant repeatedly noted that the family had only two children.
Abortion (as well as birth control) has become more acceptable to the younger,
urbanized generation of southern mountaineers. My informants generally believed that turpentine and quinine would induce abortion (Hand 22 and 23).
Since quinine was more readily available in the city, it was reported as being used
more often. The ways of inducing abortion by mechanical means seem to have
been altered slightly in the city, too. An older informant indicated that women
in the mountains would attempt to abort by breaking the "bag" surrounding the
unborn child with a splinter from an elm tree. Most of the women indicated that
they had heard of the same practice of breaking the bag but had been told that
a pencil should be used to do it.

Some women appear to have completely abandoned some cures because the ingredients are too difficult to find in the city, while traditional urban replacements
are more accessible. One woman, when asked what she would use if her child
had a cold, answered at once, "Baby aspirin and cough medicine." But when
asked what she had used down in the South she replied "Coal oil and turpentine
rubbed on the chest" (Hand 1130). Many herbs that were the basic ingredients
in teas and poultices used in the mountains are unavailable in the city. Occasionally
informants reported that they were able to buy such items as catnip tea in the
drug store; but generally these traditional herbs are difficult to come by, and the
cures for which they are used tend to die out. Informants reported, for example,
that it was generally believed in the southern mountains that all infants should
be made to break out in "little red" hives. If the infant did not break out with
these hives, the disease would "go in" and turn into the dreaded and fatal, "bold"
or "stretch" hives. In order to make the child break out, catnip tea was usually
administered (Hand 312). The informants believe that all rashes should be
encouraged, and that the more the rash is "brought out" (Hand 1803) the better
the chances for the patient's health. Nonetheless, most of the women were aware
that the children they had raised in the city without the benefits of catnip tea
never had the "little red" or any other hives and seemed none the worse for it.

Actually, it appears that catnip tea causes the "little red" hives. This particular preventative measure probably prevented the fatal types of hives just as much as it kept the houses safe from tigers. The cure seems to be dying in the city, not because of logic but because of the absence of catnip tea.

When ingredients are unavailable in the city, the cure will disappear, substitute another ingredient, or be replaced by another traditional cure not discouraged by the urban environment. The herbs for poultices, used for "risings" (pimples) by one informant when she lived in the mountains, were not available in the city. Thus, to bring the blemish "to a head," she substituted another traditional cure for which ingredients were available in the city. She spread the skin from the inside of an eggshell over it (Hand 1931). Almost all diseases have such multiple cures. Some of them involve a person with particular healing powers, who acts in a ritualized manner. In the city the absence of the herb called yellow root, used to make tea for "thrash" (Hand 399), did not bother the southern mountain mother who reported it as a cure. This fungus irritation, called "thrush" by doctors, has many cures in the mountains. One cited by informants involves a "thrash doctor," often a person who has never seen his father or who is a seventh son (Hand 221–224). These people with special powers are said to be able to cure an afflicted child by blowing into its mouth (Hand 413–419). One mother, however, perhaps because she knew few people in the city and could not find a "thrash doctor," used another traditional cure: washing out the child's mouth with urine (Hand 394). Similarly, if one cannot find a person with the power to stop blood (Hand 879–883), one can always treat the wound with cobwebs (Hand 861) or scrapings from a woolen blanket.

Changes reflecting the general influence of urbanization are common in the folk cures. At times the change is more subtle than the outright search for different ingredients or other cures. One respondent reported that pregnant women should not have permanents since the curl would not "take." This is perhaps a modernization of the older belief that pregnant women should not comb their hair ten days before delivery or it will either fall out or turn grey (Hand 15). Urbanization definitely has had a repressive effect on some beliefs associated with childbirth and child rearing. All of the informants indicated that they felt breast feeding was best for a child; that was the traditional way of feeding a child in the South. Few of them had breast fed their children in the city, although they expressed regret about not having done it. The major reason given for not breast feeding in the city was that it "was not done." Whereas the traditionally modest southern mountain woman did not hesitate to breast feed her child in public in the mountains, she found it an embarrassing thing to do in the city.

Hospital delivery of children has made continuation of many traditional beliefs and practices impossible. Practices such as burying the afterbirth (Hand 59) and putting fat meat down the newborn child's throat to clear out the phlegm (Hand 271), the belief that the first born child will be lucky if born in the father's lap (Hand 33), and numerous beliefs regarding the special powers of the child born with a "veil" (Hand 244 and 245),[50] all of which were reported by my informants, can hardly survive when births take place in the hospital. The tension

---

[50] See also Thomas R. Forbes, *The Midwife and the Witch* (New Haven, Conn., 1966), 94–111.

that results from thwarting these traditions in the hospital may well contribute to the informants' general preference for having their children at home.

Some traditional cures and patterns of action are not hampered by the urban environment and therefore will probably continue much as they were brought to the city unless the basic attitudes of the migrants change. One informant said the best cure for a child who has colic or who is "liver bound" is to hold the child upside down by the feet (Hand 287 and 319). A cure still used for nosebleed is to put a scissors down the back of the patient's neck (Hand 1893). Most of the women interviewed said it was extremely dangerous for a pregnant woman to reach high above her head, for such action would cause the cord to wrap about the unborn child's neck and strangle it (Hand 34). A dietary restriction reported by many of the women interviewed prohibited eating of fresh fruit or vegetables when pregnant. This does little for the vitamin intake of an undernourished woman, and an awareness of this practice would certainly be of help to the public health nutritionist. These are examples of medical beliefs not significantly affected by the urban situation and therefore persisting in the city much as they did in the mountains.

Some traditional beliefs survive in the city because they have been rationalized into forms acceptable to the urban dweller. One woman, for example, reported the old belief that it is bad to have teeth extracted during pregnancy (Hand 14). She claimed that her dentist told her not to have extraction done during menses because she would lose too much blood, and she therefore concluded that for similar reasons a pregnant woman should not have teeth removed before the birth of her child. Another woman explained that one should not cut an infant's fingernails (Hand 233 and 252–254). "You bit the baby's fingernails off because you could cut his fingers, you know, they were real tender and delicate." In urban society this explanation is much more acceptable than the belief that if a child's fingernails are cut with a scissors before he is one year of age he will grow up to be a thief (Hand 233).

Beliefs relating to the maternity cycle have persisted vigorously among the southern mountain women interviewed. Often—as was the case with the informant who cited her dentist as the authority for not having her teeth pulled— women claimed professional opinion as their authority for certain traditional ideas they still held. This might reflect a general uneasiness about the ideas or the inevitable tension of the interview situation. Almost all informants reported, for example, the belief that the sex of the child can be predicted by the manner in which the child is carried by the woman before birth, "high" or "low" (Hand 147). One woman, however, made it a point to explain that the nurses in the hospital where she delivered agreed that she would have a boy since she was carrying the child "low and broad."

The belief that a child can be "marked" by what the mother does or sees during the prenatal period (Hand 83–120)[51] was reported with rich elaborations by virtually every informant. This belief, more than any other investigated in this study, was expressed most often in the form of short tales or memorates. The stories told how the mothers' behavior during the prenatal period resulted in

[51] See also Charles H. Murphy, "A Collection of Birth Marking Beliefs from Eastern Kentucky," *Kentucky Folklore Record*, 10:2 (April–June 1964), 36–38.

"marking," ranging from innocuous birthmarks (Hand 85–113) to specific personality traits (Hand 83 and 84), to actual deformities (Hand 114–120). According to the informants, the child was often marked by the mother's cravings
during pregnancy. Thus, the mother's behavior during the prenatal period is traditionally considered important by the Southern Appalachian migrant.

The stories of "markings" were numerous. One woman told of a younger
brother who, "well, he just wasn't right" when born and died shortly after birth.
She blamed the deformity and his death on the fact that while her mother was
carrying the child she had seen youngsters killing bullfrogs. "You know how their
stomach looks," she said, and explained that her mother had vomited at the sight
of the dead frogs. The result, according to the informant, was that "this baby's
stomach wasn't even in the right place and his arms hung different." Another
respondent told how, when she was pregnant, she had seen a friend of hers lose a
leg while trying to "hop a train." When she rushed to help him he said, "Lord
have mercy, [name of informant], you['ll] ruin your baby!"

The belief in preventative medicine apparent in the use of catnip tea to prevent "bold" hives has not been translated into the use of medical services such as
vaccination for preventative means, nor has the concern for the child's welfare
reflected in the extensive body of lore about "markings" been converted into prenatal care for the mother and child. Stories about prenatal influences ease the
guilt felt at the birth of a deformed or dead child, but the vast number of beliefs
in the area of "marking" show more than an attempt to accommodate guilt. They
show a genuine concern of the mother for the welfare of her child. This concern
could be of help to public health personnel concerned with prenatal care.

There are numerous folk cures from the southern mountains that are not harmful in and of themselves. The practice of measuring an asthmatic child against a
stick—in the belief that when he grows past that mark his asthma will be cured
(Hand 829)—does not harm the child as much as not taking him to a physician
for treatment. Putting a red thread about a child's neck to prevent the mumps
from "falling" (Hand 1832) is not inherently dangerous, and neither is the
juice of a baked onion, recommended for pneumonia (Hand 1936). Informants
in this study reported all of these remedies. Beliefs not inherently harmful can
often be used by the physician to help introduce an unfamiliar medical practice to
the southern mountain patient. Similarly, the use of folk medical terms along
with urban terminology can be useful to the physician who is attempting to establish rapport. It would not hurt the urban physician to utilize knowledge of such
traditions in his attempt to treat his patients.

There are practices in the folk medicine of the southern mountain migrant
that are harmful. Giving a child turpentine for a cold (Hand 2204 and 1456), as
recommended by several respondents, can produce chemical pneumonia if it is
rejected by the stomach. The abortion practices described are hardly healthful and
can lead to serious infection and the death of both mother and child. The use of
baking soda to treat the inevitable heartburn of pregnancy (Hand 1614) is extremely dangerous in a high-risk population where toxemia is a constant threat.
The sodium intake involved in this cure causes the body to retain water, and
water retention is one of the major problems in toxemia.

A complex assortment of attitudes and traditional patterns of behavior keep the southern mountain woman from the physician in the city; consequently, self-diagnosis and self-medication continue. The folk cures of the southern mountains show some changes in the urban environment, but the conditions under which they are applied have not changed. There is still a basic resistance to physicians, only complicated but certainly not caused by the use of traditional medical practices. The continuation of self-diagnosis and self-medication is not surprising given the obstacles in the way of the mountain woman's obtaining medical care, and her glorification of past values and behavior. As long as the traditional attitudes remain, as long as there is little communication between medical professionals and the southern mountain migrant in the city, the folk cures will travel along with the traditional values, secure from the effects of modern medical knowledge.

Conclusions and Suggestions

How much of the behavior of the recently arrived migrant from the Southern Appalachians can be accounted for by the fact that he almost automatically becomes a member of what we politely call a "culture of poverty"? Certainly a good deal of his behavior is similar to that of other groups, such as Koos' lowest socio-economic group in Regionville, upstate New York. But we cannot explain away behavior simply by classifying it. The reasons for patterns of action come from beliefs rather than statistics, and in the case of the southern mountain migrant in Detroit the traditional attitudes and beliefs he brings with him to the city are a major part of the reasons for his actions. His problems cannot be fully understood simply by analyzing convenient statistical totals such as fetal deaths and neonatal deaths. Similar patterns of action and attitudes can be caused by dissimilar beliefs. The fatalistic world view of the southern mountaineer and of the Hindu might cause similar behavior; yet, they stem from sets of beliefs philosophically far distant. In order to understand behavior we must understand what is behind it, and to do this it is necessary to investigate traditional assumptions. Assumptions may control actions, and until the assumptions change the actions will alter only slightly. Thus, both helpful and harmful folk-medicine behavior will continue in the city as long as the traditional southern mountain attitudes toward health and healing remain.

The southern mountain migrant does not feel that he is a part of the city; he more often regards himself as a temporary urban resident and basically identifies with his region in the Southern Appalachians. It is natural that the feeling of not belonging in a new place will result in a continuation of past practices and attitudes. The necessary consequence of this situation is conflict. It is not surprising that the building in which hepatitis broke out in Detroit in 1967, causing a public outcry, was an overcrowded ghetto dwelling for southern mountain migrants. Southern mountain medical traditions and patterns of action in modern ghettos can only lead to sickness and misery. With the southern mountain population increasing in Detroit, the situation is not promising.

The general picture resulting from my investigation shows a persistence of tradition among the southern mountain women in Detroit and a use of old patterns of behavior and attitudes to cope with problems presented by the new urban environment. My study revealed a decided tendency to glorify the past, an acute difficulty in dealing with the urban environment even in basic areas such as transportation, a conflict in the demands of changing role requirements, an avoidance of medical "welfare" services, and an indifference or distinct dislike of doctors coupled with a strong preference for self-diagnosis and self-medication. In addition, there is some indication that in the northern city there is a tendency for the southern mountain woman to revert to medical attitudes and patterns of her parents' generation. This seems to be partly the result of a gap in communication between doctors and patients.

The tenacity of tradition is found in many areas of the southern mountain immigrant's life, but certainly no aspect is more significant than that of maternal and infant health in a population so prone to disease. The conspicuous absence from the public health facilities of the medically indigent southern mountain woman in Detroit can only be regarded as a social problem. As the southern mountain population in the city grows, so will the problem. The southern mountain woman's traditional values and patterns of behavior seem to prevent constructive contact with physicians during the prenatal and postnatal periods. During her pregnancy she most often seeks the advice of an older woman or a nonmedical "doctor." Frequently she will return to the Southern Appalachians shortly before giving birth.

It is possible to make some tentative suggestions about how to help the southern mountain woman alter her traditional patterns in the city. One of the best ways of reaching a group is by involving its members in what is to be done. Nancy Milio has succeeded in doing this with medically indigent Negro women in her Moms-and-Tots program in Detroit.[52] Given the reluctance of southern mountain women to travel outside their neighborhoods in the city and not to be seen in public when pregnant, it seems that a local center—partially staffed by southern women working with professional medical personnel—would be a logical solution to the problem of prenatal and postnatal care. Such a center could also run its own transportation system both to and from the hospital it would be associated with. In addition, ancillary facilities could be attached to this service, such as a day nursery to care for the children of mothers who are having checkups, a food and clothing distribution center, and a recreation facility. It would also be helpful to have a city information center and general personal counseling services within the center.

The southern mountain migrant is more responsive to verbal communication than to print. This is one reason why the personal interaction with the physician is so important to him. Doctors who treat this segment of the population should make an attempt to learn and to understand the traditional medical terminology and concepts of their southern mountain patients, as well as the tensions affecting them in the city. Fliers, posters, and billboards will have little effect in communicating to the pregnant mountain woman what public health services are available for her. It would be better to use the omnipresent television and radio as vehicles for transmitting information about maternity and infant care projects. After all, the Southern Appalachian region has had a long and distinguished history of oral tradition, and it would do no harm to capitalize on the receptive-

[52] Milio, 1985.

ness of the southern mountain immigrant to verbal communication. The use of public television and radio might also help those fortunate enough to belong to a higher socioeconomic level realize that there are others who live lives of continual and not so quiet desperation.

The most constructive innovation that can be made to improve the health of both mothers and infants in the southern mountain migrant group would be the establishment of a nurse-midwife program in Detroit. Not only would this permit the desired home visit and home delivery, it would also be in keeping with the tradition of counsel and attendance by a woman during pregnancy. The idea is not farfetched. Such a program has been successfully implemented in Leslie county, Kentucky by the Frontier Nursing Association,[53] and at Kings County Hospital in Brooklyn, New York.[54] It is a well-known fact that in west European countries a great deal of prenatal care is supervised by nurse-midwives, and sizable proportions of births are delivered by them. England, Wales, Denmark, and the Netherlands have flourishing nurse-midwife programs; all complications are referred to physicians, and a great number of the infants are born at home. All these countries have lower infant mortality rates than the United States, although we have 95 percent of our children born in hospitals.[55] The nurse-midwife program seems to be the ideal way of coping with the traditional attitudes that prevent the southern mountain woman from obtaining needed care during the maternity cycle, and it certainly would not jeopardize the health of either mother or child. Eventually it might even ease the "crisis in maternity care"[56] in this country and lower our infant mortality rate.

Some people are pessimistic about the future of health practices in the Southern Appalachians. Marion Pearsall has succinctly indicated the obstacles.

A history of difficult and limited access to good health services, hence a tradition of doing without; failure to identify certain abnormal states as true illness; willingness to accept and endure numerous symptoms fatalistically; heavy reliance on prayer and home remedies; lack of any real understanding or faith in modern medicine or its practitioners; and a general tendency to live from day to day, putting off decisions requiring purposive action.[57]

All of these obstacles do exist; however, some authorities have claimed significant results in changing medical and health patterns of the mountain people.[58] Nancy Milio's experience in Detroit and the findings of persons who have worked in the mountains indicate that it is possible for the southern mountain immigrant to alter his general attitudes and patterns of medical behavior in the city.

In the extensive public health literature concerned with the medically indigent, there has been a repeated call for "communication."[59] Although it is clearly a

---

[53] This program is outlined in *Today, Yesterday, and Tomorrow* (Wendover, Kentucky, 1963).

[54] Richard R. Leger, "Modern-Day Midwives in Demand at Hospitals That Are Short of MDs: Mothers-to-Be Prefer the Specially Trained Nurses," *Wall Street Journal*, April 19, 1968, p. 1.

[55] Chase, 1745.

[56] Leger, 1.

[57] Pearsall, "Some Behavioral Factors," 205.

[58] See *Today, Yesterday and Tomorrow* and Marilyn A. Jarvis, Mary Pullen and Jane Downin, "Health Larnin' in Appalachia," *American Journal of Nursing*, 67:11 (November 1967), 2345–2347.

[59] See, for example, "Report of the Program Area Committee on Child Health, APHA, 'Requirements for Data on Infant and Perinatal Mortality,'" *American Journal of Public Health*, 57:10

Good Thing to say "communicate," few depth studies have shown how to accomplish this goal with specific groups. The "culture of poverty" is not one but many, and similar behavior can easily be caused by totally different factors. Unless one goes beyond an outline of the symptoms and attempts to understand the causes of behavior patterns within the different cultures of poverty, "communication" will be all but impossible. The employment problems of the southern mountain male in the ghettos look much like the problems of the urban Negro, but closer investigation of the traditional attitudes behind these two similar behavior patterns might well dictate totally different methods for solving the problems of the two groups.

It is pertinent to indicate the special problems involved in "communication" with the southern mountain migrant. As with most groups, one must learn not only how to speak their language but when not to speak. Communicating with the southern mountaineer is a special problem, for we tend to think we should have no difficulty with him. He is deceptively the basic American, the relished Anglo stock, but his values and folklore are antithetical to the tradition of achievement and Go-Go in our urban centers. In the cities we have tended to overlook him because his skin color allows him to blend before he speaks. But when he talks and acts, he is as far from the American dream as is the black American. He is the hillbilly, the poor white trash who has somehow betrayed us all by not being the superfrontiersman. Our cities no longer want the frontier or its values, but the southern mountaineer wants the city. He needs the city. The frontier has passed, even in the South. The city must learn to speak and respect the language of the southern mountaineer in order to help him adjust to a new way of life. The city must learn to speak with the Southern Appalachian migrant without thinking of him—or making him think of himself—as having betrayed his "pure stock" by being lazy and stupid. He has much that he can give urban America, and we should not be impatient with him by underestimating the pain of his adjustment. And, just as with the black American, if we fail to learn the language of the southern mountain migrant, we will reap a bitter harvest from our isolated certainties.

APPENDIX

The purpose of this study was to report preliminary findings arrived at through analysis of data from the following sources: depth interviews of southern mountain women in Detroit; field work done in 1960 and 1961 by myself in Clay and Harlan Counties, Kentucky; published materials; and interviews in Detroit with persons having professional and nonprofessional contacts with the southern mountain population in the city. With only a three-month period to contact informants and conduct interviews of a highly personal nature, the number of depth interviews presented here is understandably limited, and the study does not attempt statistical analysis. In the future, with a larger number of interviews, data may be submitted for such analysis.

The interviews were based on a detailed questionnaire, but the questionnaire was not used as a rigid structure for the interview. Rather, it was conceived as a guide for material to be covered and was intended to be applied with compassionate human flexibility.

Approximately forty hours of depth interviews were recorded on tapes deposited in the Wayne State University Folklore Archive. They may be consulted for verification of the findings presented here. I might add that only responses given by more than two-thirds of the women interviewed are used in this report. Background data and identifying initials for these informants are given below.

(October 1967), 1848–1861; Yerby, 1215; Suchman, 1732; Watts, 1212; and Kent and Smith, 997.

Data on Informants Contributing Depth Interviews

Name	Age in 1968	Place of Origin	No. of Children	Children born in South	Children born in North	Regular Prenatal Care	Complications during Pregnancy
B.R.	31h	Pike County, Ky.	3 (1 hc)	2	1	1	yes
B.T.	33	Knox County, Tenn.	5 (1 hc)	2	3	..	?
D.G.	36h	Harlan County, Ky.	4 (1 d)	1 h	3	2	yes
J.B.	27h	Mingo County, W. Va.	2 (1 hc)	1	1	..	yes
L.H.	30h	Claiborne County, Tenn.	4	1	3	1 (husb. in Army)	yes
L.H.	25h	Henry County, Tenn. (Bluegrass area)	3 (1 hc)	2	1	..	yes
R.L.	55h	Carter County, Tenn.	1	1	..	1	?
S.G.	58h	Bell County, Ky.	4 (2 d)	4 h	..	..	yes

NOTE: h = born at home
           d = dead
          hc = handicapped

Medical consultation was obtained from doctors of medicine and public health nurses actively involved in public welfare medical services in Detroit. Most of these consultants were participants in projects involving maternity and infant care for the medically indigent.

Throughout this paper the terms "southern mountain," and "mountain," or "mountaineer," are used when referring to migrants from the Southern Appalachian region who are in low socioeconomic brackets. No attempt is made here to speak for the more fortunate who escaped ghetto life. Also, it is recognized that many of the patterns of behavior described in this paper apply to other socioeconomic groups as well. The attempt to relate these patterns to the past traditions of the Southern Appalachian region is in no way meant either to claim them solely for the mountain migrant or to stereotype him.

Wayne State University
Detroit, Michigan

Prepared Comments by Marion Pearsall

I hasten to acknowledge the general excellence of Dr. Stekert's study "Southern Mountain Medical Beliefs in Detroit." This is not the time to quibble about such things as the size and representativeness of her sample. The facts are there, in depth, and they are obviously real; however, it is the assigned role of a discussant to be petty, picayune, and peevish—which I shall proceed to be.

First, I would suggest that changes within the southern mountains began considerably more than sixty years ago. The Civil War (or what one of my favorite informants refers to as "the war between the Democrats and Republicans") had a devastating effect on even the remotest neighborhoods in the region. It, like other external forces that followed, hastened a process already begun internally, namely, the eroding of the subsistence base through subdivision and mismanagement of resources when there were no longer fertile new lands to take up. Both lumbering and mining reached the area within two to three decades after the war. In fact, lumbering reached its peak in 1909, almost sixty years ago; and coal (the principal mine product) was at its boomiest around 1920. Certainly, some kind of regular cash income plus everything that implies for participation in at least the lower fringes of modern American life has been essential to most Southern Appalachian families for about a century. So Dr. Stekert's "over sixty years ago" should read "well over sixty years ago." But I thoroughly agree that persons brought up to believe in and live by the old values (and many are so brought up) find life difficult today, whether they stay in the mountains or migrate to northern cities.

I come now to a point that keeps bothering me, though the problem may be more semantic than empirical. I seriously doubt that the community level is the average mountain family's goal, since in a very real sense there is no such thing as a "sense of community" in the smaller Appalachian towns and cities, let alone in the rural neighborhoods. True, there is a certain amount of pressure not to "get above one's raising," but the real unit for social control is the extended family, not the community as a whole. Some families obviously are achievement-oriented while others are not, though what constitutes achievement may be defined somewhat differently here than in other parts of the country.

The basic impression one gets is that of an emphasis on individuality, and what Dr. Stekert says in arguing that the conformity of "other-directed" urban Americans is more apparent than real is every bit as true in the mountains. One may say of the rural mountain man, too, that "no matter how conformist he may be, he likes to view himself as different." The conflict he faces on moving to the city is not that of a born and bred conformist who now must choose which of two opposing sets of values to conform to. It is more that of a born and bred nonconformist who finds that the beliefs and practices that have previously made him feel like a special and real person now get him into all kinds of frustrating and ultimately humiliating situations. There is no premium on being "average" in the rural South; quite the opposite. That many residents of the Southern Appalachians are average in a statistical sense is a very different matter. They may also invoke community norms at times as a sanction and justification for their own behavior, but this should not be equated with a positive desire to be "average" in their own or any other culture.

Overemphasis of this dubious notion of a desire to be average deflects attention from the truly important ideas introduced in the first few pages. The contrast between a society based on ascribed status and one based on achieved status is fundamental, although the actual situation is fraught with subtle complexities. Being a man, for example, is an important ascribed status in Southern Appalachian culture sufficing in and of itself to place a person in a superior position relative to all but a few (invariably older) women. But not all males are really men, since this is also an achieved status dependent upon certain skills (usually those associated with dangerous and physically demanding outdoor activities) and attitudinal practices (standing up for one's rights, telling off the boss, defending family honor, and the like). In fact, achieving status as a man is more important than achieving status through occupational and economic success; and, especially in urban settings, the two goals may be incompatible.

It is also important to note that social class distinctions are well established and recognized in even the most isolated sections of the Southern Appalachians. The migrant from this region does not necessarily "feel that he must blend, and in urban society to blend means to be middle class." But he does almost certainly know what class his family belongs to back home, and he knows that in the city he is treated like dirt at the very bottom of the social class structure. There is another factor here too; whatever his family's reputation back home, its members are at least known as individuals on a person-to-person rather than role-to-role or roleless cipher basis. Still, the basic problem seems to be that the skills and character traits that assured him status before do not ensure a comparable status in the city. He may or may not actively want to acquire the necessary new skills, but I am not sure this can readily be equated with any vaguely defined achievement or nonachievement value.

I am tempted to offer some of my own research data at this point in support of the observation that there is a basic communication problem whenever urban, upper-middle-class, scientifically trained health personnel meet persons from rural Southern Appalachia, but space does not permit. Instead, I will go on nit-picking with reference to the section on "Glorification of the Past." There is little, if any, glorifying of the past by real natives of the southern mountains; and the informant quoted to the effect that "there was nothing down there, and I mean nothing" is reflecting a general and quite realistic view. This statement (especially if it was echoed by others, as I suspect it was) should have made the author more cautious about labeling the observed behavior a glorification of the past, or a retention of old attitudes and values. It looks more like a plain case of homesickness and accompanying nostalgia.

I may be quibbling, but what is retained is probably not so much a set of medical attitudes and practices as an orientation toward home and family. Certainly those who remain in the mountains, although they still practice many traditional customs, do not particularly revere them. The culture is far more present-oriented than it is either past- or future-oriented. People live from day to day as best they can, not because they want to emulate the ways of their ancestors or, conversely, hope to achieve more prestige in the future but because they would like to go on staying alive. They do, however, have very strong family and locality ties—a fact that is dramatically demonstrated every weekend by heavy streams of traffic carrying migrants "home" to the mountains for brief, and sometimes fairly extended, visits. It is therefore not surprising that women in Detroit go back to Kentucky to have their babies even when they may be fully aware of the fact that they could get better medical attention in Detroit. It may well also be true that migrants living in ghettos actually do retain more of the traditional beliefs than their counterparts in the mountains for reasons of homesickness and as a defense against the frustrations of city life.

I would also quarrel with other statements, not so much because they are wrong as because they seem to attribute a unique kind of irrationality to people from the southern mountains. In the first place, as many studies of health behavior show, crisis behavior does not follow a simple regression pattern. Depending on the nature of the symptoms, almost anyone from almost any cultural background will use whatever modern medical facilities are available in the face of acute, life-threatening symptoms such as massive hemorrhage or extreme difficulty in breathing. For minor, chronic, and less obviously debilitating symptoms, traditional and less expensive measures are apt to be used. What the traditional measures are depend on the basic premises of the particular culture. That urban middle-class Americans turn to some kind of scientific or pseudoscientific source of help while persons from another culture turn to faith healers or herbalists may tell us something about these cultures. It does not tell us anything about the intelligence or rationality of individuals. Also, there is a fair amount of evidence that in time of crisis people use all sources indiscriminately. They go to a medical doctor, they pray, they buy something at the drugstore, and they whip up a home concoction that Aunt Julia would have sworn by except that she was opposed to swearing. I think the key here is found in the statement that "one does not have the time for the luxury of learning new attitudes." But I contend that if "the informants often accepted the doctor's advice only when it suited them," they were merely behaving like almost everybody else. Many studies document the obstinacy of lower class and peasant peoples in following medical advice. If we ever get up the nerve to conduct comparable studies of upper middle- and upper-class patients, I am sure we will discover that they, too, are apt to decide for themselves whether to obey the doctor's orders or not. Their alternatives may be different, but the underlying attitude is probably the same. Finally, we should not forget that today's "scientific" medicine will be tomorrow's "folklore" since science, too, is subject to fashions and fads; and a great deal in modern medical practice depends as much on cultural norms as on pure rationality.

I have reservations again with regard to the section on "The Role of Women." Since this is a study of maternal and early infant care, it is natural enough that mothers, grandmothers, and other women stand out as medical specialists. In fact, I wonder why nothing is said of the "granny" midwife. But the paper leaves an erroneous impression of the total medical system. It is acknowledged that men control transportation and therefore can exercise some authority in making decisions about where and when to seek outside help in time of illness, but the male role actually is considerably more active than the text indicates. With very few exceptions, midwives were and are women. Other than that, the field is wide open. Virtually all of the preachers noted for their healing powers are men, and most "thrush" doctors are men since being a "seventh son of a seventh son" is one of the leading criteria for this position. When it comes to "herb doctors," there were probably at least as many men as women.

Apart from the bias introduced by the focus on maternal and child health, the most easily transported health practices are also those associated with the family rather than with the various folk medical specialists. These *are* likely to be used mainly by women. But I am inclined to doubt that these women have any great trouble in finding what they want in the urban setting, since very few of them use herbs any more or know much about them. What they want and cannot get may be some of the older patent medicines of the Lydia Pinkham and Dr. Thatcher type, still available in a few country stores. For the most part, however, they are entirely at home with vitamins, Geritol, remedies for "tired blood," and the "mild diuretic to the kidneys," which are widely advertised on radio and television and are available in city as well as country drugstores. The only thing I wonder a bit about here is the lack of any reference to faith healing, though of course this would take the discussion away from the role of women. But many of the itinerant healers now operating in the Southern Appalachians have also practiced in the northern Midwest, where presumably they mingle with mountain migrants.

I take further exception to some of the interpretations in the section on "Attitudes Toward Welfare." I have a notion that it is the attitude rather than the object that bothers the migrants. For a good two or more generations, many people in the Southern Appalachians from the county judge to the most apathetic unemployed coal miner have felt strongly that the government should do something for poor people. It is being treated as an "ignorant and clumsy hillbilly" when all one wants is one's "rights" that raises Southern Appalachian hackles. Given the pride, sensitivity, and shyness of the migrant in an alien world that not only speaks a different language but insists on writing (rather than speaking) most instructions, the mountaineer quite naturally avoids officialdom.

The communication problem is very evident again here. The informants are probably reporting quite accurately when they say they were given no explanations—legal, medical, or otherwise—at the agencies where they applied for help. Professionals do stereotype and reject clients who are "stupid and ignorant." Which leads me to another point; namely, we need to study and perhaps try to change agency culture in the same detailed and dispassionate way we have been studying and advocating changes in lower-class cultures.

The statements about Southern Appalachian distrust of doctors and fear of surgery are certainly true. I would like to emphasize, however, that they are true because they are, or were, realistic. We have so far been talking about people from the Southern Appalachians as if they came from a different culture. To some extent they do, but the culture is a familiar one; it is American. The difference is that some of its beliefs and values hark back to the turn of the century. In those days and even more recently, many of the physicians in rural counties were poorly qualified to practice good or safe medicine. Even minor surgery was truly life-threatening, and hospitals were indeed only for the dying. The retention of such beliefs by mountain people is an example of cultural lag rather than cultural difference. There is no reason to doubt that, once they share a knowledge of good modern medical science with other Americans, they will make similar use of the system. The use may not be exactly what the medical profession considers ideal, but it will be in line with the practices of other increasingly demanding and increasingly skeptical consumers of health services.

The same is true with respect to the statements about modesty. Of course mountain women (and even more so their husbands) do not approve of the nudity and intimate physical contact required for a thorough medical examination. This is something physicians should be aware of and be taught to handle as tactfully as possible, but I doubt that it is any more a basic barrier to the use of health services for these women than it was for upper- and middle-class women twenty to thirty years ago.

The same notion of lag rather than fundamental difference is applicable to other parts of Dr. Stekert's study. A fair number of physicians in southern mountain counties still dispense drugs, but most do not. So present and future migrants probably will not expect this service, although they may continue to say they want it. Similarly, the idea of prevention of disease—or the taking of positive measures to maintain health—is very new in the region. It happens also to be relatively new within medicine itself, and Departments of Preventive Medicine and Schools of Public Health are still far from prestigeful within the medical profession. Why, then, do we expect semiliterate migrants from the southern countryside to embrace such programs enthusiastically? For them, getting a living is the basic concern. Next come the pleasures of life. Sickness is something that intrudes and must be taken care of when it interferes with other activities. Medicine is essential when necessary, but study after study in developing countries and here in the United States shows that (aside from true emergencies) other problems and other uses for one's money are more pressing.

Finally, let me react to the recommendations for changing the behavior of the physicians and others who work with southern migrants. I am not at all sure that if the doctor "understands the traditional patterns of behavior and traditional attitudes of his patients it will be much easier for him to reach them." I am certainly not opposed to teaching doctors some of the rudiments of folk medicine. I merely consider it more important to teach them first the concepts of culture and social organization, including the fact that they themselves are as culture- and system-bound as their patients. Then, to the extent that the doctor has a Southern Appalachian clientele, he can begin to pick up specifics about their behavior. But I believe that his personal behavior will continue to be more important as far as the patient is concerned than his knowledge of folk practices. Catering to antimedical beliefs is not the answer. From a medical point of view, the doctor is more likely to accomplish his curative ends by talking names and places and occupations with his patients as a means of establishing rapport than by engaging them in a conversation about folk cures. Even more will probably be accomplished once we make it economically, technologically, and socially easier for potential users to get to the appropriate health services than to use less effective sources of help.

University of Kentucky
  Medical Center
Lexington, Kentucky

Reply to Prepared Comments by Ellen J. Stekert

It is with the utmost respect that I reply to Dr. Pearsall's comments. I find little to disagree with, but much to clarify regarding my jagged prose. Dr. Pearsall and I are in basic accord on most of the issues raised in my paper; I believe that in most cases our minor differences are the result of misunderstandings rather than opposing points of view. She is correct in emphasizing that change began in the southern mountains more than sixty years ago. Today, life for many mountain people consists of coping with intolerable conditions that are actually the cumulative result of changes dating well before the Civil War.

Dr. Pearsall has clarified my hazy discussion of the important concept of community level. I was remiss in failing to modify some hasty oversimplifications. It seems to me that folklorists are surprisingly apt to practice some of the phenomena they study—in this case the process of stereotyping. I admit to traces of this academic culture lag. Certainly I am aware that distinctions exist within southern mountain culture and that such concepts as "average" and "achievement" can be thrown about all too blithely.

I believe Dr. Pearsall and I agree about what happens to the southern mountaineer once he reaches the city. He finds himself in an alien environment, one that imposes upon him values of little importance to him or his ancestors before the move to an urban center. The criteria by which he judged and esteemed himself in the mountains are quite different from those used to evaluate him by the "acculturated" urbanite. As Dr. Pearsall points out elsewhere in her discussion, it is important that we recognize two separate variables throughout such a study as this: that of time (what the values were in the past) and that of space (what the values were back home as opposed to here). In the worst cases, these variables affect the southern mountain migrant. He therefore faces conflict upon reaching the city, for he no longer is valued in his new community for the same things he was valued in the old one.

Both Dr. Pearsall and I failed to comment on the different patterns of adjustment between southern mountain men and women in urban surroundings. The women, it appears, attempt to adhere to their mountain role for a longer period of time than the men. The men, who act more independently, show signs of disorientation sooner than the women. High desertion rates leave many mountain women with burdens that intensify the conflict of traditions.

If I may be allowed to nit-pick back at Dr. Pearsall, let me refer to what I feel is her misunderstanding of my section "Glorification of the Past." Her comments are correct as far as they go, but it appears to me that she fails to recognize the subtle psychological state of mind I was referring to: a sort of fantasizing, rather than the holding of opinions one might act upon in the present. I clearly did not mean that any of the women I spoke to actually felt like returning permanently to the South; they came to the city because there *was* nothing better. But the necessity to think of something in a vague way as having been better, the need to remember the good without the pain, is often what leads to a retention of tradition. It is in this sense, that of wishing and therefore remembering the past as good, that I refer to "glorification" of the past. I do not use the term to reflect a firm attitude to be acted on in the present, leading back to the misery of the southern mountains. It is precisely—as Dr. Pearsall points out—because the southern mountaineer is firmly oriented to the present that he is able to see the past as good. Homesickness and ties to the South show that the southern mountaineer still looks to his past for relief from the pain of the present. Spatially he can occasionally return to family and familiar surroundings, while mentally (temporally) he can return to the wishful dreams of what might have been, or perhaps was.

As for attributing "a unique kind of irrationality to people from the southern mountains," that is certainly the last thing I wished to do. Rather, the point I wanted to emphasize was that tradition is always unusually strong among persons in crises. At such times human rational powers are of little help. It seems to me that this concept should not be underrated by folklorists. I might also point out that at the very beginning of my paper I tried to make it clear that the traits described as belonging to this small group of people were not peculiar to them alone.

Yes, as Dr. Pearsall observes, southern mountain people do behave remarkably like human beings, especially in crisis. But what is important to folklorists studying people in groups is the discovery of how individuals translate their human reactions into actions. One of the most important ways people do this is by use of their particular traditions. Each group has its own traditions, so that when a common human reaction takes place within two different groups, group members tend to react in ways partly determined by their culture and partly determined by their own psychological makeup. Under stress, individuals rely heavily upon tradition: if one feels ill in one culture, one might pray harder; in another, one might drink turpentine and sugar; in another, one might seek out a doctor; in some cultures, one might do all three.

Dr. Pearsall is quite correct in pointing out the important role of men in the general scheme of medical care in the southern mountains. Since my paper deals primarily with prenatal care and birth, however, it is understandable that women are emphasized, since in these areas the southern mountain woman is clearly oriented to a woman's medical counsel. Indeed, as I mentioned, the preference is so decided in these medical situations, that it appears women doctors would be the most effective in handling southern mountain women during the prenatal and delivery periods. The lack of reference to faith healing in the paper had little to do with the fact that such a discussion would have distracted from the consideration of the role of women. Little was found that related prenatal care and childbirth to this area of folk medicine—even though most of the women believed strongly in healing of this sort. Thus, the omission was due to the fact that faith healing seems to play little part in the area of medical behavior studied, although it still is important to the respondents in other areas of health belief.

Dr. Pearsall's point regarding culture lag rather than culture difference is extremely well taken. What today is modern, tomorrow may be considered "lag." It is important, however, to remember that much of what the southern mountaineer knows and experiences medically is the result of what might be considered "out of date" information. Such information, be it true or not, modern and voguish or not, still qualifies as folklore if it is learned traditionally; and it is with the dictates of tradition that the folklorist is concerned.

I agree with Dr. Pearsall's concluding statement that the personal behavior of the doctor is more important to the patient than the doctor's knowledge of folk belief; however, it does not hurt the doctor if he knows what to expect from his particular patient, especially in cases where he may not be able to obtain culturally embarrassing information from that patient or when he (even though an M.D.) might hold stereotyped ideas about his client's cultural background. Ironically, accurate understanding of the traditions of another culture often allows a person to deal with a member of that culture less in terms of stereotype and more in terms of individual qualities. I am certainly not advocating that medical doctors cater to "antimedical" beliefs. I simply wish to emphasize that not all traditional medical practices are harmful and that it is not necessary to "correct" all traditional beliefs. By showing some respect for tradition, the doctor can teach his patient more than by assuming he is treating a lout whose every tradition bespeaks ignorance.

Dr. Pearsall's sound and articulate comments are a rich source of ideas for future work. Hopefully the medical profession will take some heed, and in the future the health professional will be trained not only in the current technical medical information but in the basic concepts of cultural phenomena as well.

Discussion from the Floor

Leonard W. Moss (Wayne State University) :—On the point made by Miss Pearsall, it is not at all unusual to find a greater degree of retention among the old whites in the urban ghetto where the migrant brought with him the traditions that existed thirty, forty, or fifty years ago; while the village itself is undergoing dramatic change the villager who has moved to the city remains in a virtual state of arrest. Also, I'm not so sure I agree with that word "nostalgia," having interviewed an Italian cement worker just the other day, who spat on the ground as he cried out, "*Ammazza' Colombo*," a curse on Columbus. It was his desire to get back to the homeland.

Roger D. Abrahams (University of Texas) :—In regard to whether there is a focus upon being average or being a part of the norms of the community, or whether one emphasizes individuality. I feel that whether you are a member of the group, an average member, or an individual is determined by the specific situation the speaker finds himself in at that specific point. I believe that within every group, at least every group that I've worked with, especially in the West Indies, no matter how tradition-oriented a group is, you'll always find people who insist on the fact that they are individuals. There's one group in Tobago that I worked with, for example, who insisted upon certain kinds of group norms that emphasized the cohesion of the group in the face of outside pressures. This is the kind of group cohesion that tends to be defensively normative in certain very important regards, especially when facing members of the outside world—in this case, the collector. Yet, when I would work with one informant for any amount of time, after performing in public for some time he'd pull me off to the side and say, "Well, you know, Mr. Rogers, I'm a funny kind of guy. I don't exactly fit into this kind of community." The same thing happened over and over again. This was an attempt, even in this very cohesive community, to insist upon individuality under certain circumstances. We haven't really studied the circumstances under which a member of a group wants to appear to be conforming to the norms of the group or when he wants to appear to be an individual. But they're really two different roles, two different masks, which are being worn; and I think these are constants throughout all cultures.

Melvin M. Firestone (Wayne State University) :—I think there's too much of a tendency to view folk medical beliefs as basically nonrational in contrast to the rational western technical system, whereas indeed a lot of western medical beliefs are really folk beliefs and a lot of the ideas that you mentioned as being held in the Southern Appalachians are quite cogent. For instance, the idea of unnecessary cutting has been found to be quite true by certain sociologists who have been studying hospitals in the United States. There is a lot of unnecessary cutting. This is objectively true. Also, the idea of impersonality of the physician is something that is quite true and something that is receiving more attention and should receive even more, because as physicians get more and more specialized there is a tendency for them to become somewhat technical and the average patient feels he is an object, so this is true.

There was a film shown at the University of Washington in an applied anthropology course, called *Day Break at Udi*. It was supposed to be a classic in applied anthropology; it showed how these natives in Nigeria had their traditions changed to accept a prebirth clinic, a clinic where the women went for prenatal care and also had their children. The witch doctors were against this, and they were trying to frighten the women, but western technology and rationality triumphed. Finally the women did come in and have their children there. Well this was very fine and good, but a student who was a midwife and also a trained nurse said that there is a tendency, when you bring women together to have their births in the same place, for a good deal more infection to spread, infection that is chronic in such a situation because you bring all the infections into one place. Medical thought has it that persons in such a situation should be kept in separate houses. What you're doing here is establishing a practice for the convenience of the physician. So, you see, I feel to a great extent these local beliefs are much more rational, and one shouldn't implicitly make compartmentalizations.

Joani Blank (Public Health Educator, City of Detroit):—Since I am identified as coming from the public health establishment, I would like to say I agree with all the comments that have been made about doctors. Nurses, especially midwives, have one advantage; they are usually women. That was mentioned by Dr. Stekert in her paper, and I think that's something we can take a hint from in the public health establishment, the value of the woman as a professional to do certain kinds of tasks in relation to patients, just by the fact that she is a woman.

Stekert:—I also think it should be added that nurses are usually not regarded (nor do they on some levels regard themselves) as being from the middle class, or the "establishment." Very often nurses are from the very socioeconomic classes we regard as medically indigent. Consequently, the nurse can often act as a bridge between the doctor and his medically indigent patient.

D. K. WILGUS

Country-Western Music and the Urban Hillbilly[1]

COUNTRY-WESTERN MUSIC is currently one of the most important facets of the entertainment industry. It owes its status and respect largely to financial success, like most of the popular arts of America. Indeed, to call country-western music simply one form of American popular music is to make but one of the myriad and apparently contradictory statements that have been made about its origins, development, function, and significance. The history of this music and our attitudes toward it reflect the contradictions in the American character; that is, in the character of the country-western audience, the urban hillbilly.

The dichotomy in the term "urban hillbilly" expresses both the polarization of city and country and the accommodation of values represented in the hybridization of country-western music. I use the word "hillbilly" in all of its connotations—including Appalachian, southern, and backwoods or country—for they represent but degrees of the same concept and culture, and the different shades of meaning account for much that seems contradictory about the music and its history. Thus my topic cannot be narrowly concerned with migrants from the southern mountains to the northern metropolis; and, while it deals largely with the industrialization and urbanization of the southern regions, it is concerned ultimately with the urbanization of the United States. The South in general and the Appalachians and Ozarks in particular entered the game late, after their frontier folkways had developed and solidified for a longer period than elsewhere in the country. The shock of urbanization, therefore, was greater and the reaction more extreme.

The music growing out of the urbanization of the South was based on a number of traditions, many of them folk and regional, which were able to interact under a minimum of the standardizing influences exerted by the commercial music business. Yet for more than three decades country-western music has been intimately connected with the media of commercial entertainment. For these reasons it is, indeed, a laboratory for the study of some aspects of the American

---

[1] This paper was accompanied by the playing of a sound tape containing musical illustrations. The opening "theme" was "Detroit City," Bobby Bare, RCA Victor 8183 (1957). Subsequent footnotes will cite recordings, portions of which were played to illustrate points made in the paper.

character, particularly those related to the urbanization of the rural folkways. Because of the late collection and study of American folklore and because of limitations in scholarly outlook, conclusions concerning the early history and development of folk music in the United States are in many respects conjectural. Too often we must reconstruct the development by analysis of the very materials we need to understand in order to explain the development. We may conclude, however, that the early migration of British folk music to the United States was relatively uniform, but that by the end of the eighteenth century the North was receiving newer material and newer styles than the South and was under pressure to conform to emerging urban "popular" styles and to accept the products of the growing urban commercial entertainment industry. The South, on the other hand, tended to preserve and develop the older styles and to create its own materials because of its isolation from urban music. Consequently northern folk music eroded away; either it was lost completely, or it remained in vertical, family traditions, while performance styles more and more approximated urban norms—with the exception of certain pockets of geographical or occupational isolation.

In spite of oversimplification, this summary is broadly accurate. But oversimplification in this case can lead to misunderstanding. It neglects almost totally the interrelation of folk and popular music in the North, a development generally neglected in American folk and cultural studies. More important, it misrepresents the kind of isolation that operated in the South and the Southern Appalachians. To use the Appalachians as the extreme example, our summary perpetuates the notion that settlers flocked into the valleys and coves and then got stuck there. It would be more accurate to note that the settlers not only went where they did because they wanted to go but stayed there because they wanted to stay. They could have left. Many of them did, and many of them returned. By and large, the inhabitants of Appalachia were subjected neither to total geographical isolation nor to totally involuntary cultural isolation. That is to say, their geographical and industrial position permitted them to develop a degree of cultural isolation but did not prevent contact with elements of the dominant and developing American culture; their position made it possible for them to accept, reject, or modify many of its elements.

Thus, by the middle of the nineteenth century the South—approximately the area below Route 40—had preserved and developed a frontier agrarian culture. This culture was not uniform in all regions, no more than it was uniform within any smaller area or community. The regional differences in the culture are related to various musical styles and materials in early hillbilly music. But there was a uniformity in culture that was in turn reflected in music of the folk. The culture valued independence, self-sufficiency, honor, and loyalty (particularly to kin). The family was the economic and social unit, and children were economically profitable. The economy depended primarily on subsistence agriculture. Though the culture was work-oriented, life was attuned to natural rhythms, and leisure existed for traditional noneconomic pursuits. The frontier penchant for drink, violence, and rebellion was complemented by an evangelical religion dominated by the Old Testament. A rigid, patriarchal morality was accompanied by a deep drive for individualistic expression. Indeed, the society was one of extremes: sobriety and drunkenness, piety and hellraising, daily stoicism and orgiastic religious revivals.

One makes statements about the folk music of this culture with extreme caution. The secular musical tradition was almost completely domestic, performed by nonprofessionals. The repertory included both Old World and native American materials, though it is not possible to demonstrate when some of the latter entered the tradition. Few old ballads native to the area have survived. Performance, excepting shaped-note singing, was monophonic; melodies were largely modal, sung with considerable ornamentation and rhythmic freedom. The only instrument in wide use was the fiddle, and probably only for frolic music. The attitude toward secular music in general and the fiddle in particular varied from complete toleration to total rejection on religious grounds. But there was a strong, conservative tradition with ancient roots.[2]

A series of cultural shocks and alterations began with the Civil War. Of course the music and the cultural tradition of which it was a part had not been completely static, even in deepest back country, but change now became increasingly rapid. We can date economic changes, we can date song texts, but we cannot date changes in musical styles or even the introduction of musical instruments during this time. For example, the banjo and the Ethiopian minstrel songs were a staple of the urban tradition by 1850; yet we do not know when the southern white folk musician adopted them. What we do know is that by the end of the century they had become a vital part of the tradition. What we can do is recognize influences that were gradual, and influences that were resisted. We can summarize them as urbanization.

The war, as was the case with other American wars to follow, brought rural men into urban environments and men of different cultural regions into contact. After the war a pattern of immigration and emigration began. Northern entrepreneurs and technicians entered to exploit the South. Southern youths were leaving the area—largely for the West—but they were returning as well. Railroads furthered communication; in their very construction they introduced new cultural (including musical) influences. Logging, mining, and manufacturing plants were developed, altering the economy and the face of the South, without fundamentally changing the value system of its folk. It is in this atmosphere that hillbilly music developed and has continued to develop.

Listen to Bradley Kincaid, speaking as a successful professional performer in 1930 of "mountain songs" on radio and phonograph recordings.

There is a practice among recording companies, and those who are inclined to speak slightingly of the mountain songs, to call them Hilly Billy songs. When they say Hilly Billy songs they generally mean bum songs and jail songs such as are often sung in lumber camps and among railroad gangs. Such songs are not characteristic of mountain songs, and I hope with this brief explanation you will come to distinguish between these fine old folk songs of the mountains and the so-called Hilly Billy songs.[3]

Bradley Kincaid was a product of the settlement-school tradition, which was seek-

[2] "Johnny and Willie" (Child 49), Jim Bowles, Rock Bridge, Kentucky, recorded 29 August 1959 by D. K. Wilgus and Lynwood Montell; Western Kentucky Folklore Archive, UCLA.

[3] *Favorite Mountain Ballads and Old-Time Songs*, Book 3 (Chicago, 1930), 6.

ing to combat many of the effects of industrialization and is somewhat to blame for the paucity of information concerning various forms of music in the mountains in the early part of the twentieth century. But "mountain songs versus Hilly Billy songs" expresses the polarity between "mountain white" (the staunch Anglo-Saxon conservator of our ancestral rural values) and "hillbilly" (the crude carrier of filthy backwoods customs). "Mountain song" was of course but one of the terms (others were "Old Time," "Southern," "Dixie") used by recording companies in the 1920s to characterize their materials aimed at the white country audience. Archie Green has traced the term "hillbilly music" to an almost chance remark made at a 1925 recording session.[4] But the name certainly caught on because of its pejorative nature, and it is now rejected by the music industry for the same reason.

At any rate Kincaid was partially correct in assessing the sources of development of the newer musical tradition. Railroad camps in particular were important in the contact of the older white folk tradition with Negro work and social songs, as well as with all sorts of material carried by migrant workers. There were countless other influences and points of contact. Loggers brought in music; young natives rafted logs to cities and brought back music. The developing Negro tradition was available at many points—the rivers, the fields, the "Black Bottoms" of southern cities. We must not fail to note the influence of instrumentally dominated gospel song, which eroded much of the style of earlier religious music and tremendously influenced secular song. Urban popular song could be heard not only on visits to the city and through casual contact but from circuses and traveling troupes of entertainers. By approximately the end of the century, folk performers themselves were a part of the itinerant show business.

The tradition of wandering minstrel and ballad hawker is an old one, and the peddler of broadside ballads still operated in northern cities in the 1880s. The extent to which the wandering ballad singer of the South is a part of a continuing tradition is difficult to determine. We have nineteenth-century southern broadsides and songsters but precious little evidence of itinerant performers. When we do hear of the professional ballad singer, he is almost invariably included among the halt and the blind, to whom such an occupation was an economic necessity, a fact illustrating the frontier attitude toward musical entertainment. A number of early hillbilly performers belong in this category: Ernest Thompson, Blind Alfred Reed, Lester McFarland and Robert A. Gardner ("Mac and Bob"), and "Peg" Moreland. By 1909 Blind Dick Burnett of Monticello, Kentucky, was touring the South from Florida to Ohio, entertaining at fairs and school houses, selling his broadsides and songbooks, and staging fiddle contests. The fiddle convention or contest was not his invention, however, nor were all the "banjo minstrels" blind. The traveling medicine shows began to employ folk performers as part of their entertainment, and this encouraged youths to emulate them. Doctor Howard Hopkins—later a hillbilly performer in Chicago and elsewhere—recalls being entranced as a boy in Harlan County, Kentucky, with the performances of Dakota Jack's Medicine Show, which he joined later.

Thus there was a tradition of hillbilly musicians—professional performers of

[4] "Hillbilly Music, Source and Symbol," JOURNAL OF AMERICAN FOLKLORE 78 (1965), 204 ff.

material directed to a white folk audience—prior to World War I, the next shock and crisis of culture contact. For we must recognize that many of the early musicians in the commercialized tradition had not spent all their lives in isolated cabins so far back in the hills it took ten cents to send them a postcard. They had worked on the railroads; they had worked in the mills of the South, the oil fields of the West, the industries of the North; they had served in the Spanish-American War and in World War I. They were musicians looking for audiences, paying audiences, an important point in the process of urbanization. The acceptance of music as a career for a healthy adult—a violation of folk taboo—is but one of the tensions of the urban hillbilly.

Phonograph records and radio did not invent hillbilly music, but without them the tradition might have withered. The wedding was inevitable. We tend to emphasize phonograph recordings, mainly because they are surviving artifacts by which we can assess musical developments. But we have to recognize that, despite their importance in the spread and development of hillbilly music, phonograph recordings rank third chronologically among the media bearing the tradition and that their permanence causes us to underrate the other media. Professional country musicians performed first of all before live audiences. Even before the advent of radio some had moved beyond the medicine show, the school house, and the county fair to the vaudeville circuit—notably Uncle Dave Macon and the Weaver Brothers and Elviry. Except for a few early recordings of no historical significance in the development of the tradition, radio was an exploitative device before the commercial recording industry became a medium for the distribution of country performances. The tie-in of radio, phonograph, and personal appearances simply grew—as much through the efforts of the musicians as through the machinations of the media executives. Not that the musicians were not in many cases "used" by the executives. Unsophisticated performers realized pittances for properties of great value (for example, Andrew Jenkins), while others (for example, Jimmie Rodgers) became wealthy in a brief period. The point, however, is that the musicians were in many cases seeking exposure in the commercial media, particularly as an adjunct to personal-appearance fees.

It was no accident that the recordings of Eck Robertson and Henry Whitter in 1922–1923 were at the insistence of the artists, nor was it any accident that they were not exploited immediately by the Victor and Okeh companies.[5] It was no accident that Whitter came from a southern mill area and that a southern city like Atlanta was the cradle of commercial hillbilly recording. It was no accident that Ralph Peer of Okeh was in Atlanta in 1923, to be almost coerced into recording Fiddlin' John Carson on the first successful hillbilly disc. The exact places and circumstances may have been accidental, but the historical drama seems inevitable. Peer was looking for local talent to bolster the phonograph industry in the face of the looming competition of radio. He had already pioneered in the recording of Negro performers for the Negro trade. If he needed to be persuaded that the "pluperfect awful" performance of Carson would sell and that the "wool hat" audience would buy, he lost no time in being convinced and in following up

[5] "Wreck of the Southern Old 97" (Laws G2), Henry Whitter, Okeh 40015 (1923; released 1924).

the initial success. And the talent was ready and willing. The "Golden Age" of hillbilly music had begun.

The subsequent history of hillbilly music prior to 1941 cannot be neatly summarized nor really evaluated with any assurance. Even to sketch in its broad aspects is difficult. Too much of the information stems from the statements, activities, and opinions of recording and radio executives, and it is a proven fact that they were groping in the dark, did not know what they had, and were themselves operating under urban prejudices despite their financial stake in rural music. We do, however, have more information than we can summarize here.

After the success of hillbilly record sales, the recording industry began a large-scale search for regional talent, not only race (Negro) and hillbilly (white Anglo), but Cajun (Louisiana Acadian), Mexican, and other "ethnic" musics as well. They had discovered regional traditions and regional audiences, and now faced the problem of regional demand and sales. Consequently, they were torn between the necessity of satisfying these special demands and the hopes of finding an economical way of satisfying all regions with a single product. As we shall see, both aims were pursued until the second was almost completely successful, but we might question just how accurate the "regional" approach was as far as southern white music was concerned.

We have access to no regional sales figures for the period. We know that the recording companies did restrict the release of recordings by region and that apparently they did not exploit hillbilly recordings in the North (as they did in the South) by inviting the audience into a building, playing them recordings, asking which they liked, and selling them on the spot. We know there was a northern market for the music. The first successful radio barn dance program was established on WLS in Chicago in 1924 with a strong nucleus of Kentucky hill talent. All of the audience could not have been transplanted southerners or people from southern Indiana, Ohio, and Illinois. Much later, when certain types of hillbilly recordings were not available even from jobbers in the North except on special order, they were blaring from tavern juke boxes in the metropolitan North, and comparable records were selling in northern dime stores. Although other facts as well prevent our complete acceptance of the regional approach and the judgment of media executives based on it, we must admit that the early fare of WLS was "bland" compared with many of the southern recordings and that the few national hits in the 1920s were not strictly "southern." At any rate, we can establish that there was in hillbilly music an essence of wide rural appeal, even in the North where expressed urban opinion was contemptuous.

Early hillbilly music was strongly based in the country string band, frolic, and banjo-minstrel tradition, though the recording companies sampled almost everything available, even the Sacred Harp tradition (though not the oldest unaccompanied styles of secular singing). There was no stylistic uniformity, though to the outsider it seemed so. Instrumental styles ranged from simple to relatively complex, from self-taught guitar strums to somewhat complex banjo styles. Instruments had become available through urban contacts and mail order houses, but instrumental groups tended to be small. The fiddle played a lead role, although there were many solo performances with guitar or banjo.[6] The instruments used either were cast-offs from urban culture or were played in an unorthodox non-urban fashion. But we should note the criteria involved were not mystical; instruments were chosen that were available, portable, inexpensive, and relatively easy to adapt to traditional melodies and to each other. Because much early recording was done on location, there was little outside interference with instrumentation and style. Studio accompanists were added in exceptional cases, but it is notable that city imitators of the style, who sought and sometimes gained mass sales, cultivated the simplest elements in rural music and avoided anything suggesting urban refinement, although they seldom were able to avoid dynamics and "expressiveness." The "classic" approach, restrained and austere, was one of the most typical elements of hillbilly tradition represented on early recordings, which were largely from the Southeast. It perpetuated older tradition and reflected a continuing cultural value.

The cultural conservatism that reacts to changing conditions by adapting a selection of new materials into old patterns is demonstrated in the musical repertory, which was largely traditional. Tunes in older styles were simplified when characteristics of the new instruments demanded modification, but their essential structure remained, and older tunes were sometimes made the vehicles for texts borrowed from urban sources. No simple characterization can be made of the repertory, for it drew on many sources. It might be said that in some respects it corresponds to the polarization of the culture: orgiastic frolic tunes, low-down blues, and damn-fool ditties versus tragic ballads, lacrimose lyrics, and other-worldly sacred songs. But pervading the entire range is an attitude of seriousness, sincerity, and reality. This attitude survived and palliated the ultimate professionalism of the hillbilly musician. Songs had to be meaningful, in this sense real. I think this conclusion can be applied rather generally to songs retained from the older repertory and those borrowed from other sources. Largely missing from the hillbilly song bag are the older English and Scottish popular ballads, despite the contention that their themes are universal. Though the matter is difficult of proof and there are alternate explanations, I feel that the ballads rejected no longer had a ring of reality and "truth" to the singers and listeners of a culture in transition. This conclusion may seem ridiculous when one considers the preposterous plots of other ballads and the "unreal" and maudlin sentimentality of hillbilly standards. But if one can discard urban sensibilities and consider the hillbilly tradition and the responses of performers and audience, the conclusion cannot be rejected out of hand. Songs of wrecks, pathetic deaths, murdered girls, orphaned children, crumbling cabins, and weeping willows represented truth and reality—all the more perhaps because their attitudes as expressed in the language was foreign to the older tradition. The "hillbilly" culture was selecting and assimilating what it could, in ways least destructive of folk values. Thus, from nineteenth-century popular song it selected those with themes that did not in essence differ from its older songs. The lack of "austerity" in the texts was an acceptable novelty (though it was not far removed from the style of the English

[6] "Sal Let Me Chaw Your Rosin Some," Gid Tanner and His Skillet Lickers, Columbia 15267-D (1928).

"vulgar" ballad) and indeed served as a release from cultural tensions. The sentimentality of the texts, and many of the tunes, was overcome at first by the "objectivity" of performance style. We can observe how, with further acculturation, even this objectivity withers away.

The point can be further underlined by noting the attempts of the commercial recording industry to serve and exploit the musical tastes it had discovered. The industry executives sought to standardize their product and to develop new material for sale. They turned for material to urban composers with a folk background (for example, Carson J. Robison and Bob Miller) and folk composers whom they could commission (Andrew Jenkins). The most important productions were what they termed "tragedies" or "event" songs—largely factual, sentimental, and moralistic. Their success can be measured by record sales and by their occurrence in standard collections of folksong made since that time. For the performance of these songs and others with a greater background in folk tradition, the executives turned to urban performers with enough folk background to simulate what the executives felt to be the essence of rural performance ("Vernon Dalhart" [Marion Try Slaughter] and Frank Luther [Crow]). These recordings in the late 1920s generally sold more widely than the performances of authentic hillbillies. The songs and the performances may strike us as often tongue-in-cheek, but many of the songs found wide acceptance. The performance style did not; its real virtue was to convey the lyrics and music most intelligibly to various regions.[7] In point of fact, deliberate urban spoofs such as "They Cut Down the Old Pine Tree" also entered the hillbilly repertory, partially for reasons already outlined, but also—it must be added—because such spoofs are not alien to the in-group humor of the rural folk.

The problem of accommodating various regional styles was not solved successfully until recent years, but in 1927 Victor discovered almost simultaneously the Carter family and Jimmie Rodgers, rural performers whose performances appealed widely, at least in the South, and who stand for two interrelated streams of hillbilly tradition. Despite the fact that they shared material and utilized comparable sources and related professional techniques, the Carter family represents the domestic tradition of performance and song-making and warm, intimate family values (though A. P. and Sarah were divorced during most of their professional career);[8] while Rodgers represents the lone wanderer, the rounder, the "poor boy, long way from home" among the pitfalls of society.[9] Although Rodgers purveyed much sentimental, homey material and the Carter family drew on Negro tradition and performed blues, the distinction is valid. At the cost of oversimplification it can be said that the Carters epitomize the "country" tradition of the Southeast, while Rodgers at least prefigures the "western" tradition of the Southwest, now dominant in commercial country music. The distinction is relative, however, and the wide popularity of these artists is one of the reasons for the intermingling throughout the nation of the traditions they roughly represent.

Hillbilly music matured during the 1930s, in spite, or because, of the Depression. It effectively covered the nation with the help, if not the respect, of com-

---

[7] "Santa Barbara Earthquake" (Laws dG45), Vernon Dalhart, Columbia 15037-D (1925).

[8] "Poor Orphan Child," The Carter Family, Victor 20877 (August 1, 1927).

[9] "In the Jail House Now," Jimmie Rodgers, Victor 21245 (February 15, 1928).

mercial media. Hillbilly musicians were becoming thorough-going professionals, still capable of being exploited by the media but at the same time exploiting the media in their own ways. By and large the musicians were still oriented toward personal appearance, and they were anxious to use the commercial media for publicity. They recorded for flat fees and performed their radio shows for little or nothing in order to promote their appearances or to vend songbooks and merchandise on percentage. Media executives, on the other hand, were often slow to recognize a total tie-in of radio, recording, and personal appearances with merchandising. Though the totality was seldom achieved, varieties of the pattern were in operation, not just in the South but throughout the nation. If the music did not have a national audience, it had audiences everywhere in the nation. Recordings were available in dime stores nation-wide and from mail order houses; they sold profitably in the hardest of times. The music was aired on the radio in the early "rural" hours, sometimes at noon, and often on Saturday night "barn dances." Musicians performed at school houses, fairs, and lodge halls. After repeal of the Eighteenth Amendment, musicians and recordings were featured in working-class taverns even in northern cities—just as the music had appeared in illegal taverns earlier.

In various forms, hillbilly music was available everywhere. Who listened to it and supported it? In the South just about everybody with access to a radio, with an egg to trade for a record, or with fifty cents to see a performance. In the North? The extent to which the music appealed to transplanted southerners, to northern ruralites and to the northern working class is difficult if not impossible to determine. Hillbilly music in its widest sense had a broad appeal. The variety aired in the Northeast and in the Midwest during much of the thirties avoided many of the striking characteristics of southern performance styles. Its success indicates that there was a general audience in rural and working-class areas for the essence of hillbilly music, if not for its most distinctive styles. On the other hand, a good deal of the music from WLS and other Chicago stations was significantly "down home" and appealed in rural areas of the Midwest. Furthermore, many of the "hardest" southern performances were available from the border stations.

The programming of stations just outside the limits of the United States helps support the conjecture that commercial media in the United States were not reaching all significant segments of their audience. In 1930 the "goat-gland" specialist, Dr. John R. Brinkley, having lost his radio license in Kansas, launched the first of a number of radio stations just across the Mexican border, beamed to the United States on a wattage that blanketed the nation. Begun to publicize operations for sexual rejuvenation, the programs peddled reactionary politics, old time religion, hair dye, Peruna, mail-order tombstones, evergrowing plants, and pictures of J-E-S-U-S that glowed in the dark—all to the tune of a wide variety of hillbilly music. In the late thirties similar fare was available from CKLW, Windsor, Ontario—beamed to the Detroit hillbillies but audible as far south as Columbus, Ohio. It is worthy of note that despite their dependence on transcriptions, these stations stressed the "live" approach. XERA and other Mexican stations had live performers, but they often made use of transcriptions of full programs in the absence of the performers, rather than commercial recordings. When they did use commercial recordings, the announcers maintained the fiction that the artists were present. A nightly XERA program featured the performances of Bob and Joe (presumably derived from the Shelton Brothers), but on successive nights one might hear the recordings of Bill and Charlie Monroe, the Blue Sky Boys (Bill and Earl Bolick), the Callahan Brothers, or any other male duo whose records were available. CKLW normally used transcriptions by the Carter Family, Mainer's Mountaineers, and other performers to simulate live performances.

The music performed in the 1930s became less and less "traditional" in that the repertory of necessity expanded beyond the mountaineer's folk inheritance. But the repertory remained largely distinctive. Items of current urban song did appear, but sparingly. Only the rare items that seemed to fit were performed, and deliberate attempts to blend urban and rural traditions were not really successful. Northern radio stations did mix artists in programming, but their repertories were usually distinct. The new songs grew from the old—or at least on the pattern of the old, and they were normally the productions of the performers themselves. Such songs often entered tradition, the tradition of the professional hillbillies, who were learning from each other. But though they might monitor each others' programs and "cover" each others' records, a real "hit" technique had yet to develop. The new songs still dealt with the realities already outlined. There was on the one hand a more cynical, blues reaction to sexual relations and on the other a deepening of the nostalgic references to home, mother, and the farm. Current events were not neglected, and one can compile an impressive list of titles and recordings of topical and protest materials. These tended to be nonce productions and became "traditional" only through their discovery by urban intellectuals. But such songs, a distinct minority among the new productions, illustrate the realistic approach of hillbilly music. Along with tales of fires, floods, kidnappings, and bank robberies, the minstrels sang "The Old Age Pension Check," "Mean Old Sixty-Five Blues," and "Sales Tax on the Women." The repertory included a greater number of songs dealing more explicitly with sexual relationships, while preserving a large amount of traditional material, both "mountain" and "western."

We must note the relation of cowboy songs to the hillbilly repertory, style, and image. Cowboy songs were in the repertory of eastern hillbillies before the commercialization of the tradition. Ex-cowboys began recording in 1925. Yet the cowboy contribution, in addition to a relatively few traditional songs, was more image than actuality. Whatever was viable in the music of the cowboy was largely absorbed into hillbilly tradition by 1930. After this time, cowboy singers came under the spell of pop or hillbilly music, and whatever authentic cowboy culture remained now borrowed the hillbilly tradition. But the cowboy "myth" was as influential on hillbilly music as on American mass culture. Although cowboy and hillbilly music were and are often bracketed, there is a connotative difference. The cowboy's image was almost the reverse of the hillbilly's. Furthermore, the culture that gave birth to hillbilly music shared the general regard for the image of the cowboy as representing values that were being lost in the urbanization of America. After all, the hillbilly "uniform" is more humorous than romantic. So the hillbilly musician adopted the songs and the image of the cowboy; he composed ersatz cowboy songs, and assumed the ersatz dress of the movie cowboy. In style there was little to adopt.

The commercial media were spreading regional and individual styles so widely during the thirties that one can note a variety of tendencies among artists in all sections of the nation, but Southeast and Mideast developments tended to be more rooted in the so-called mountain tradition. Fiddle bands continued to flourish (though their documentation on phonograph recordings diminished) and their development was rather "straight-line": they became smoother and more integrated; when they became "hotter" it was largely through the influence of pop-jazz.[10] One of the outstanding developments was that of vocal duets, in which emphasis was often on a high tenor reminiscent of the style of older sacred music as well as the strident solo of older secular singing.[11] The emphasis on harmony stimulated the development of family units, often brother or husband-wife teams. More and more female artists became a part of the profession, though almost always as part of larger groups. Individual artists still roamed from radio station to radio station, and the hillbilly band was a standard unit; but the great "acts" of the period were the vocal duos, even when part of larger groups. The prominence of Bill and Charlie Monroe, Bill and Earl Bolick (The Blue Sky Boys), Jack and Jim Anglin, and Howard and Dorsey Dixon as well as the composition of larger bands demonstrate decreasing emphasis on fiddle and banjo, the triumph of the guitar as basic accompaniment instrument, and the emergence of mandolin or steel guitar as a lead instrument.[12] All these trends, as well as minor contradictions, can be observed in the rise to prominence of Roy Acuff. His band, which also illustrates the addition of a slapped bass or "doghouse," is not an example of the finest workmanship that developed in the traditional instrumental music of the Southeast. Nor did the vocal performances have the artistry within the tradition that can be remarked elsewhere. Rather, Roy Acuff and the Smoky Mountain Boys epitomize the southeastern tradition almost to the point of parody. The string band featured the unamplified wail of a steel guitar; banjo was restricted to frolic pieces or as background to performances that were actually humorous exaggerations of traditional performances; vocal solos and harmonies were high and strident. The entire performance was an immense and sincere wail of sorrow.[13] Acuff himself specialized in sentimental "heart songs," and his performance made "weepers" of whatever it touched, be the song from the older folk tradition, the nineteenth-century pop repertory, the gospel hymn books, the growing productions of hillbilly tunesmiths, or the increasing number of "blues" tunes.

The "blues" tradition—that is, the influence of Negro and Negro-based materials including jazz and genuine blues—was evident in hillbilly music from the moment it began to be documented. Southeastern performers were singing "white blues" and playing hot instrumentals in the 1920s. Jimmie Rodgers popularized both the songs and the style, so that there was no regional limitation to the style in the 1930s. But the tradition flourished most significantly in Louisiana, Texas, and Oklahoma. It was in this area, rather than in the hillbilly communities of the industrial North, that the greatest acculturation took place. Whereas in the Southeast the frolic pieces, the blues, and the sentimental songs coexisted in the repertory, usually with stylistic differences in performance, they tended to coalesce in southwestern tradition, dominated by a blues-jazz influence.

[10] "Let Her Go, God Bless Her," J. E. Mainer's Mountaineers, Bluebird 6104 (August 6, 1935).
[11] "I'm Thinking Tonight of the Old Folks," The Monroe Brothers (Charles and Bill), Bluebird 6773 (October 12, 1936).
[12] "Sales Tax on the Women," Dixon Brothers (Howard and Dorsey), Bluebird 6327 (1936).
[13] "Precious Jewel," Roy Acuff and the Smoky Mountain Boys, Okeh 05956 (April 1940).

There are a number of explanations for this acculturation, from the influence of the Louisiana blues and jazz traditions to the oil boom in Texas and Oklahoma. At country dances and in taverns or honky-tonks, the older Anglo country music met Cajun, blues, jazz, and even Mexican styles. The strength of the Anglo folk tradition had long been undermined by the growing heterogeneity of the population; there was not such a restrictive set of urban pop music values as obtained in the North; and there was a meeting of many traditions on a folk level. The southeastern white folk culture tended to reaffirm its values in the face of cultural change. The hillbilly ghettos in the North were continually reaching back to their heritage, but the folk of the Southwest became the leading urban hillbillies. Discounting the special influence of Cajun and Mexican traditions, we can perceive the pattern. The Southeast acculturated more slowly than the Southwest. The hillbilly tradition in the North (as illustrated in exposure and performance in the ghettos, but not on radio and recordings) accepted the southwestern trends, but it did not become creative until the newer music became influential in the Southeast.

Many southern string bands in the 1920s were essentially interested in playing music—any music—in the rather "hot" style they were developing. Clayton Mc-Michen, the talented fiddler of Atlanta, tried with no great success to record pop songs in hot string arrangements. Groups such as the Hack String Band of western Kentucky made no great hits with their instrumental rags. But in the Southwest the same kind of ideas came to fruition. Country bands in Texas began playing all kinds of tunes in styles strongly influenced by jazz rhythms. The small string ensembles developed into large aggregations fittingly called orchestras. They differed from their eastern counterparts not only in size but in instrumentation. A percussion-slapped bass, drums, and tenor banjo became prominent. The piano, rarely present in the East, was a staple in many bands. The extent to which the electrification of the steel guitar and later the "straight" guitar was necessary because of the competition of other instruments (or to be heard in the smaller ensembles in honky-tonks) is difficult to determine. At any rate, in the late thirties southwestern bands were not only hot but swinging. The hillbilly and jazz traditions had mingled. Jazz musicians sat in with the country string bands and facilitated the development of western swing. Prominent bands like Bob Wills' added horns—trumpets, trombones and saxophones. They played traditional breakdowns and pop tunes; and—most important—pseudocowboy or western numbers developed in the Southwest. The repertory ranged from low-down honky-tonk numbers, often with Mexican influence, to rather sophisticated urban songs. This was basically dance music, though the vocal refrains were not unimportant.[14] The tradition reached its apogee after World War II and its descent practically paralleled that of the big swing bands. The practicioners of western swing are now small combos playing their music in "western" clubs, but not a factor in big-time country-western music.

It was, paradoxically, the smaller groups of the Southwest that represent the basic stratum of current country-western music—or, one might say, some basic elements of western swing developed in another direction. Instead of following the route of the jazz ensemble and developing a predominantly dance form, the

[14] "Steel Guitar Rag," Bob Wills and His Texas Playboys, Okeh 03394 (September 30, 1936); "Bring It on Down to My House, Honey," Bob Wills and His Texas Playboys, Okeh 03492 (September 30, 1936).

other branch of southwestern tradition stuck more closely to the Jimmie Rodgers path. It emphasized a variety of "blues" vocal with mainly supporting instrumentation, developed from bluesy straight guitar to small honky-tonk combos, and of course eventually added the electrified steel guitar. At one extreme it was a white copy of the Negro "party blues" (for example, "She's Sellin' What She Used to Give Away"),[15] and at the other it was minor western swing. But what was most lasting in the tradition was the syncopated backing of lyrics expressing the problems of sexual and marital relationships in which the neon sign of the tavern was seldom absent. From rather pallid and derivative items like "Bear Cat Mama from Horner's Corners," the lyrics moved to the more significant problem of "When We Go Honky Tonkin'." Elements of this tradition were widespread in the late thirties, but reached a peak of development in the Southwest just at the outset of World War II, which facilitated the spread of this as well as other varieties of country music.

We have already seen that long before 1941 hillbilly music was a commonplace in both the rural and urban North. It was available on large stations and even on network shows—the WLS National Barn Dance, the WSM Grand Ole Opry, the WLW Boone County Jamboree, Gene Autry's Melody Ranch. But even when dressed in the sombrero and chaps of the cowboy, it had both a rural and low-class image. It was early morning and Saturday night music for the yokels. It was profitable, more profitable than the music industry generally recognized, but it did not appeal to the mass market to which the music industry pitched its product.

During World War II hillbilly made its largest single leap in mass appeal, and the music business recognized and exploited its new popularity. Certain internal disputes in the music industry facilitated the acceptance: the ASCAP dispute of 1940, which threw the media back on material in the public domain and on music under the control of licensing organizations more hospitable to country music eventually gave an economic boost to composers of country material; the American Federation of Musicians' recording ban of 1942–1944 promoted the fortunes of small hillbilly oriented labels that signed with the union. But these were relatively minor events that did little more than stimulate what now seems inevitable.

The significant reasons for the phenomenal growth of country music (for it soon outgrew the hillbilly title) involve population shifts, industrial and economic expansion, and the emotional temper of the war years. War industries shifted families from rural areas to the cities and from the Southeast and Southwest to the North and the West Coast. It put more money into the pockets of those with a taste for country music. Service in the armed forces tended to integrate (not without violence) boys from different areas with different musical tastes; country music was almost forced upon the serviceman, whether he liked it or not. He could not always silence a company radio tuned to the armed forces network; nor could he always silence the guitar of the boy on the next bunk. The training camps of the South and the Southwest exposed the recruit to a heavy dose of country music, on the radio and in the honky tonks. For example, one could stroll past a long succession of taverns in Biloxi, Mississippi, and often follow Ernest Tubb's "Try Me One More Time" verse by verse through the open doors.[16] One

[15] "She's Sellin' What She Used to Give Away," Buddy Jones, Decca 5613 (1938).
[16] "Try Me One More Time," Ernest Tubb, Decca 6093 (1942).

may well ask why, except for the location of training camps, the pattern was not reversed, why country music and its audience were not altered by exposure to urban music. One answer is, of course, that country music was to be affected tremendously. But the music and its listeners had already been long exposed to varieties of urban music, and country music was their answer, their bridge between folk and urban values. Finally, there were the temper and needs of the time.

Country music appealed to a wide range of simple and fundamental values. It was melodic and singable. Its lyrics dealt both directly and sentimentally with the problems of the time. The return to simplicity in song had already been shown by the national popularity of "You Are My Sunshine," which moved from country to pop in 1941. The draft and the war were treated directly and meaningfully in the country idiom, for example, "I'll Be Back in a Year, Little Darlin'." The country song writers could speak out with unabashed patriotism, though some of their efforts were awful by any standards. But the songs—old and new—dealt with love and separation, mother and home, drink and death. On the one hand, the music reinforced the fundamental values of all American society; on the other hand, segments of it were dealing with the gin mills, the B-girls, the broken romances and marriages under the stresses of urbanization in general and the war boom in particular. When pop music touched the same chords it had to go back to similar sources, for example, "Don't Sit Under the Apple Tree." Country musicians were reaching large segments of the populace, and country songs were spilling over into the pop repertory. Neither the country nor the pop professionals knew quite how to deal with the problem. Elton Britt's 1942 recording of "There's a Star-Spangled Banner Waving Somewhere" became such a national success that it made the radio "Hit Parade," and publisher Bob Miller threatened to sue if it was played again, for he felt its country style was being destroyed. But in 1943 the publishers of Al Dexter's "Pistol Packing Mama" sued the "Hit Parade" because their hit song was being ignored.

The decade following the end of World War II witnessed the development of country music into a significant segment of American mass music. A considerable part of the growth was in merchandizing—expanding radio coverage, better record distribution and promotion, and well-managed tours and personal appearances. The result was a considerable alteration in the character of the music and its producers and performers. Country music came under the aegis of the hit and star system. In 1941 *Billboard* began hesitantly to notice hillbilly music, first as "western," then as "folk," and finally in 1949 as "country and western." The recordings gained entry to the popularity charts, causing a shift in the emphasis at least of the country performers. They geared themselves more to the current, the immediate. One of the profitable aspects of hillbilly records had been the continued, if not enormous, sale of individual discs. Now the profits came in quick popularity, rapid sale, and "logging" of radio station plays. The performer needed new material, he needed to plug it, and he needed to identify himself with it. Instead of drawing on a deep and time-tested repertory, he tended to promote the current songs both on radio and at personal appearances. Performers without hits to promote were driven to cash in on the popularity of the performances of other artists. And of course the need for new material strained the capacities of the performers, so that they had to turn to the talents of others, and a Tin Pan Alley of country music grew rapidly.

The immediate postwar period was one of transition, in which older styles and materials had considerable influence. Regional styles were still in evidence; western swing was predominantly Southwest and West Coast, while southeastern string bands and vocal duos continued mountain traditional and tradition-based performances. But stylistic blending and innovation were proceeding rapidly. Ernest Tubb brought the southwestern music to the Grand Ole Opry stage in person, and electric guitars were adopted generally. Nonelectric bands like Johnnie (Wright) and Jack (Anglin) and The Tennessee Mountain Boys experimented with a Latin beat. Eddie Arnold, a Tennessee boy who had been a featured singer with the midwestern-styled Golden West Cowboys of Pee Wee King, rose to national prominence as a mellow-voiced singer of sentimental love songs, with the backing of a sweet-sliding electric steel guitar.[17] To observe Eddy Arnold and Ernest Tubb performing a Saturday afternoon show before an audience of screaming Nashville teenagers gave one an understanding both of the blending of styles and the development of a new audience.

Both points are well illustrated in the output of the new postwar label, King Records of Cincinnati. Its president, the late Sidney Nathan, seems to have deliberately set out to exploit the collision taking place between the old and the new, the East and the West. He developed "the King sound" by setting a performer of basically southeastern tradition against a studio background of southwestern style with a hot steel guitar and at times even clarinet and trumpet.[18] Or the performer would be given a new honky-tonk type song, sometimes composed by Nathan himself. Although Cajun and Anglo styles had been blending in the Southwest, it was Nathan who recognized the possibilities of "Jolie Blon" when Moon Mullican's band was using it as a "warm-up" number. Nathan turned it into the national sensation "New Pretty Blonde."[19] And Nathan, reversing the usual procedure, mated Mullican's Louisiana honky-tonk style with the maudlin "Sweeter Than the Flowers." The new and the old were also blended in the updating into a postwar hit of "Filipino Baby." As composed and recorded by Bill Cox before World War II, it recounted the romance of a "colored sailor" and a "black-faced" girl from the Caroline Islands. On (Lloyd) Cowboy Copas' King release, the "little sailor" returns from South Carolina to marry his "dark-faced Filipino baby." The King releases range between the extremes of the old-timey Mainer's Mountaineers to the near-jazz of Eddie Smith and the Chiefs, and they include many sacred songs in holiness styles. They indicate not only the range and interaction of postwar styles but the growing importance of the recording executive and the studio musician. No longer did the country musician unpack his song bag in the studio and perform as he did elsewhere. Material began to be "placed" with executives and performers. And the "sound" as well as the musician began to be programmed. So one cannot always assume identity between a recorded and a live performance (though the greatest difference was yet to come), just as one cannot judge com-

---

[17] "Bouquet of Roses," Eddy Arnold, RCA Victor 20–2806 (1948).
[18] "Rainbows at Midnight," Bill and Cliff Carlisle, King 535 (1946).
[19] "New Pretty Blonde," Moon Mullican and His Show Boys, King 578 (1947).

pletely the character of country-western music by the material that reached the top ten of *Billboard*'s popularity charts.

Once country-western music became established as a genre appealing to a national market, lines of distinction became even more tenuous. What is country-western becomes what is listed in that category of the charts, based on the categorization of recording companies and the decisions of disc jockeys. It is not altogether relevant for us to offer a differing categorization based on stylistic and content analysis when we are at the same time studying evolution and mutation in style and content. The artist is a better criterion, though after 1948 country and pop artists begin crossing chart lines, as does material. A socioeconomic analysis of the audience of all American music—which of course does not exist—might provide a better basis on which to categorize types of music as we are approaching them here. Otherwise we must accept the judgment and audience aim of the music industry. We can, of course, decide that the high position of Gene Autry's "Here Comes Santa Claus" on the charts reflects a certain specialized audience rather than anything we might want to categorize as urban hillbilly, but the issuance of country-western Christmas recordings in general is a significant development. The popularity chart may be used as indicative of major trends, as long as we remember that performances of somewhat different character also were available to the public and even made the top one hundred on the charts. We should not forget that musical forces significant to us are not represented. For example, the important genre of bluegrass never made the top ten of the *Billboard* charts, and nothing even derivative of it is represented before 1961.

In 1948 the chart situation is relatively clear. All artists are identifiably "country" or "western." Styles are almost all some form of honky-tonk, western swing, or smooth movie western. Songs are almost all artist-derived or from a small fraternity of tunesmiths like Fred Rose. There is a revival of an old item from the thirties yodeling tradition ("Chime Bells") and a genuinely traditional text ("Deck of Cards"). A ringer like "Buttons and Bows" by Gene Autry causes no consternation, but on the chart are two recordings of "Tennessee Waltz." Though neither ever attained the top position, "Tennessee Waltz" was to help make country-western music even less of a distinct genre when two years later it was recorded by Patti Page and became one of the best-selling songs in the history of American popular music. Country songs had "crossed the line" before, but "Tennessee Waltz" geared the industry to a far wider market.

Curiously enough, in the period between the height of popularity of "Tennessee Waltz" as a country-western release and its success in the broad field of popular music Hank Williams appeared as a summary of country-western trends and as the most important bridge to their broad popularity. And again curiously enough, Hank Williams was as country-based as they come, or rather he was a typical product of the forces of urbanization on the southeastern poor white. He reeked of the parched fields of Alabama, the dirty streets and dives of Montgomery. He embodied drunken Saturday nights in the tavern and soul-saving Sundays in the country church. It was all there in him, and it was all there in his music. He had the gospel, blues, and sentimental tradition from folk and professional sources. He had inhaled the postwar honky-tonk style with every breath, and miraculously he formed a band, the Drifting Cowboys, to complete the image. As the apogee of the honky-tonk style, he conquered the "core" country audience with older blues like "My Bucket's Got a Hole in It" and "Mind Your Own Business," but scored as well with the love-lorn "Wedding Bells." He presented—in fact he was—the dichotomy, the polarization of the urban hillbilly: he went "honky tonkin'," [20] but knew he was "Headed Down the Wrong Highway"; he cheated, was cheated on, cursed her "Cheatin' Heart," "Dreamed About Mama Last Night," [21] and looked forward to the land "Beyond the Sunset." Williams' popularity did not stop with what should have been his "normal" audience but apparently spilled over into general American culture, or at least his songs did. I say "apparently" because no breakdown can be made of the audience who accepted his performances. The extent to which Hank Williams' compositions are his own or those of Fred Rose is still argued. But in whatever division can be made, the spirit and essence of most of his songs are certainly his own, and he "sold" them so that they—rather than comparable country-western numbers—were taken up by pop artists. As far as Williams' message was concerned, the urban hillbilly audience was larger than one would have guessed. And henceforth country performers and composers could at least hope for a wider market.

The death of Hank Williams in 1953 was celebrated in a still-continuing series of "tribute" songs, the best of which, "Death of Hank Williams" by Jack Cardwell, was in the traditional "tragedy" pattern. The stage was set for another onslaught on the insularity of country-western music. Actually the appearance of "Goodnight Irene" on the charts in 1950 was an important portent of yet another influence, but its real force was not felt until much later. Blues and Negro music in general had long been a shaping force on the tradition embodied in country-western, but until 1954 the influence had come from the older country blues, jazz, and ragtime music. Now the newer rhythm and blues music exerted its influence. Rock-and-roll is demonstrably the fusion of country or country-oriented style with rhythm and blues. First recorded in the North, it erupted in Memphis in the form of rockabilly, with Elvis Presley and Carl Perkins. There is still argument whether or not early rock and roll is country-western music, but the argument is really futile in the face of the facts. Rock and roll grew away from country-western music but it left its mark. Early recordings of rock and roll made the country-western as well as the pop charts, and I can testify that a folk music collector can record "Blue Suede Shoes," "Raunchy," and "Bye Bye Love" in the field. Rock and roll affected both the style and attitude of everyone associated with country-western music. The last link in the country-urban chain had been forged. Country songs could make it in the pop world, and country musicians could also make it if they changed their styles.

As folk musicians had once raced to be exploited by commercial media, so many country-western performers now agreed to the necessary compromises in order to make the pop charts as performers. The fiddles and steel guitars that marked the honky-tonk sound began to disappear; drums, piano, choral, and lush violin backgrounds came in. The music was not all a bland, homogenized style—though this

[20] "Honky Tonkin'," Hank Williams, MGM 10171 (1946).
[21] "I Dreamed about Mama Last Night," Luke the Drifter (Hank Williams), MGM 11017.

trend was ever present—but it moved away from country, whether to rock or to pop. The cool, relaxed "Nashville" sound predominated.[22]

Country music was now moving toward pop faster than pop was moving toward country. That the movement was somewhat arrested is certainly due in part to two forces, one internal and the other external to the country-western industry, but which became temporarily joined: bluegrass music and the urban folk music "revival." Bluegrass music is a hybrid form developed basically from the southeastern styles of the 1930s, resisting the greatest impact of western swing and honky-tonk influences. The style grew within the Bluegrass Boys, a band of continually shifting personnel led by Bill Monroe, whose superb musicianship, dedication to his idea of music, and dominating personality were mainly responsible for the cocoon out of which bluegrass burst. During World War II, Bill Monroe's band was distinguished by its dedication to the older string-band tradition heavily influenced by the Jimmie Rodgers type of blues. It kept largely to a deep selection of the traditional repertory, which Monroe carefully taught his musicians. Then in 1945 his band evolved a complex ensemble style in which unelectrified instruments trade solo, countermelody and rhythm, and basic rhythmic and harmonic accompaniment. The most striking element was the prominence of the five-string banjo, which had almost disappeared from commercial hillbilly music, performed by Earl Scruggs in a three-finger style he had perfected from North Carolina folk tradition. The band featured vocal solos in the older high, tight, "objective" style, duets with the old high harmony, and gospel quartets.[23] Because of the wide and rapid touring of the Bluegrass Boys, as well as their Opry broadcasts, the style was well known before recordings of it were released. The style was new, yet old; modern, yet traditional. By 1953 it had spawned numerous bands in its exact image, and the Scruggs-style banjo was to become almost an epidemic. Bluegrass seemed to give southeastern tradition a new, if highly stylized, lease on life. In spite of its place at the grass roots, it would not have reached the stature it did had it not been for the urban folk music revival.

Just as country-western music in the fifties was attempting to shed the last of its rural and low-class trappings and become urban middle-class music, national taste turned back to the grass roots, to the folksy. The urban interest in folk music skipped over country-western, and at first even early hillbilly, to what was thought at least to be authentic folk. Such an approach was anathema to a burgeoning music market geared to the newly created rather than to the traditional songs in the public domain. Growing urban interest in folk music stressed participation, not consumption. The urban "folk musicians" assimilated the folk music to urban tastes and eventually saturated the very pop market country-western was seeking. The "revival" was of course much more complicated than this, but we are interested mainly in the reaction of the country music industry. One of the earliest efforts seems to have been the attempt to appeal to the image of the past that lay behind the revival by embodying it in new material, fake ballads. A real country musician, Jimmy Driftwood (James Morris), showed the way by setting new words to "The Eighth of January," creating "The Battle of New Orleans." In the

[22] "Four Walls," Jim Reeves, RCA Victor 447–0413 (1957).

[23] "Molly and Tenbrooks" (Laws H27), Bill Monroe and His Bluegrass Boys, Columbia 20612 (1945).

Nashville of a few years before, it is doubtful that he would have gotten a hearing, let alone have been granted an LP recording. Needless to say, Driftwood's country style was not promoted, but in 1959 "The Battle of New Orleans" became a hit for Johnny Horton, and Eddie Arnold put Driftwood's "Tennessee Stud" in the top ten the same year. "Johnny Reb," "Long Black Veil,"[24] "Sink the Bismarck," "Don't Take Your Guns to Town," and others followed.

The efforts of country-western music to capture the sound and image of the revival were not notably successful. Country-western recordings of folksongs popular in the revival were not top sellers ("500 Miles" was an exception). Nor did revival-tinged performances draw much play, though such techniques as modulation and stressing of flat sevenths became accepted techniques of arrangement. Country-western executives did try—even to the ridiculous lengths of "Bluegrass Hootenanny" albums, which were neither. Their efforts did not click with the old country audience, and the revival almost totally ignored country-western. Older performers were resurrected by the revival, and veterans still performing had to reach back to their roots before making the stage of the folk music night club or the folk music festival. Johnny Cash was the only leading performer to get a real hearing, with the exception of bluegrass musicians. Indeed bluegrass became the real "old-time" music to the urban intellectual as well as to the rural audience of the South. In turn bluegrass has shown the most revival influence in its recent material and style. It has been suggested that so little bluegrass is played by disc jockeys not only because of chart consciousness, but because they have been advised not to play the music under any circumstances, no matter how many requests they receive—a revenge for the attention given to bluegrass during the revival instead of to other forms of country-western.[25]

Yet the revival did turn country-western back toward its roots, which it had practically forgotten; the industry became more conscious of its history. Though the Country Music Association is a trade organization whose early efforts were directed against the onslaught of rock and roll, it eventually founded a Country Music Hall of Fame. Only recently has the Association come to realize that there was much country music before World War II, besides that of Jimmie Rodgers, but understanding is growing. This historical consciousness has been at least one of the factors that has made the industry more responsive to various segments of the buying public. The reissue of earlier recordings for a limited market—partially in response to "bootlegging"—is but one indication of the shift from the drive for a single, homogenized market. At least I believe I can detect the effects even in the top-selling recordings, for we must admit that promotion is a big part of popularity in the entertainment industry.

The music of recent years demonstrates a return to somewhat recent roots in a resurgence of the steel guitar and a form of southwestern honky-tonk. A new West Coast or "Bakersfield sound" has emerged, modifying honky-tonk with harder rock.[26] Basic audiences such as the truck-driving fraternity are being more successfully appealed to in songs like "Giddyup Go." Perhaps the death of the

[24] "Long Black Veil," Lefty Frizell, Columbia CL 2488 (1959).

[25] Bill Vernon, "Bluegrass Stands the Test," *The World of Country Music* (*Billboard*, Sec. 2), October 28, 1967, pp. 84–86.

[26] "We're Gonna Let the Good Times Roll," Buck Owens, Capitol ST 2283 (1967).

folk music revival and the emergence of folk rock and acid music have done much to point out that there is no longer one pop audience. Not that country-western has been driven back into an enclave—far from it. Country-pop is still strong, and performers and songs cross chart lines with great regularity. The line between genres is as hazy as ever. Not only has country-western inherited the twelve-string guitar from the urban revival, but all kinds of studio "noncountry" instruments are introduced at recording sessions, further removing the music from live performance.

I would, however, like to conclude by emphasizing one thematic element that may not unify recent country-western music but that is certainly a major thread in the fabric and directs us most particularly to an urban hillbilly audience. Sex, drink, and illicit love may or may not be the outstanding characteristics of urban society, but they are certainly so in a good percentage of country-western songs. The subjects were far from absent in early hillbilly music and in the folk music that preceded it. Folk and hillbilly music borrowed Paul Dresser's song of a repentant whore, "Tell Them That You Saw Me"; and hillbilly music produced the song about the fate of the wayward girl in "Unloved and Unclaimed." There is, of course, a difference in treatment in the more recent country-western approach, but I maintain that there is also an identity.

The earlier songs seem to be sharply divided in that there is one category of songs of drink and frolic and carnality, involving the performer and audience, and another category that laments, condemns, or moralizes from outside the situation. Both earlier categories, at least in general performance, are far from explicit in facing these situations, but the country-western approach seems to fuse the two and has become far more frank. Settings or referents in numerous songs are the barroom and tavern. To be sure, there are songs treating simply the convivial aspects of "Sam's Place" (1967), but there is usually a hint of problems, as in the rowdy and humorous "Don't Squeeze my Sharmon" (1967). More often the tavern is a lonely escape or a temptation and destroyer of explicit or assumed values. Women function in barroom scenes both as tempters and as the tempted and destroyed. The girl leaves the only one who ever loved her to go back to "The Wild Side of Life" (1952). The man may complain of being left within his "Four Walls" (1957), but his condemnation may be answered by the woman's pointing out that "It Wasn't God Who Made Honky Tonk Angels" (1952).[27]

The country-western lyrics face aspects of the current world of the urban hillbilly with directness unusual in popular song. And they are not "ballads" in the sense of narratives about the events. They are direct statements by the participants, with whom the listener identifies. The lyrics deal with the "real" world of current life and the "real" problems. The world and the life are accepted, but they are not approved of. Seldom, as in "City Lights" (1958), is the contrast between the rural and the urban scene made explicit, as it was in the older lyrics; but the contrast is implicit and sometimes suggested musically and symbolically. "The Wild Side of Life" and "It Wasn't God Who Made Honky Tonk Angels" are set to a tune that carries, among others, two well-known older texts: "I'm Thinking Tonight of My

[27] Kitty Wells, Decca 28232.

Blue Eyes" is a lament in the older tradition by a girl forsaken by her lover; "The Great Speckled Bird" is perhaps the most notable holiness-gospel song. Similar techniques may be observed in "Almost Persuaded" (1966), in which the narrator dances with a girl in a barroom and is "almost persuaded" to forget his marriage vows until he sees in her eyes the reflection of his wedding ring. Though the tune is only faintly reminiscent, the title is identical with that of a familiar gospel song.[28]

The lyrics may strike the "literary" critic as anything from ridiculous to maudlin, just as the wailing, melismatic honky-tonk vocal style will adversely affect the listener from another musical tradition, but both elements reflect a significant life style. And the lyrics manage, without violating language taboos, to give an amazingly accurate picture of at least a significant part of "The World of Country Music." The girl in the barroom who pleads, "Take Me to Your World" (1968), where love is not a four-letter word and she will not have to hear another dirty joke, may well become the matron who snarls, "Don't Come Home a-Drinkin' with Lovin' on Your Mind" (1966), only to be answered by her husband's reaction to "a worn-out wife like you." Whatever humor can be derived from the material resides in the embarrassing directness of its realism, not in its sentimentality and naiveté. The country-western text tends to face "The Cold Hard Facts of Life" (1967), the title of a song in which the man overhears a stranger in a liquor store announce that he is on his way to a party at the house of a woman whose husband is away. The husband proceeds unexpectedly to his home, sees the stranger's car in the driveway, commits murder, and faces the legal penalty.[29] Soap opera? Perhaps, but also tomorrow's headlines.

The recognition of marital problems and extramarital affairs has been a continuing and increasingly popular theme since the 1940s. "One Has My Name, the Other Has My Heart" (1948) was relatively reticent in its approach compared with later lyrics, though not as coy and moralistic as "Don't Rob Another Man's Castle" (1949). "Slipping Around" (1949)[30] is more direct, but full of guilty regret, while its sequel, "I'll Never Slip Around Again," shows how the later relationship of the guilty couple is poisoned. So "Back Street Affair" (1952) is answered by "(I'm) Paying for that Back Street Affair" (1953), this time from the viewpoint of the woman. Women have an increasing voice in songs of "The Stolen Moments" (1955) in the "Game of Triangles" (1966), whether as the aggressor in "If a Woman Answers" (1962) or the aggrieved in "The Home You're Tearin' Down" (1965). The wife may indeed appear not as a black or white morality character but as an ambiguous figure who complains of "The Evil on Your Mind" (1966) in such a way that the truth of her nagging suspicions is unconfirmed, particularly in the light of her account of her own opportunities, with the veiled threat of retaliation in kind.[31] The situation may be dramatized in a telephone conversation, with the "other woman" speaking openly of the relationship and the husband answering "Yes, Mr. Peters" (1965) for the benefit of his wife. The contrast with the older value system may again be musically im-

---

[28] David Houston, Epic 4–2257.
[29] Porter Wagoner, RCA Victor 447–0786.
[30] Floyd Tillman, Columbia 4–33058.
[31] Skeeter Davis, RCA Victor LSP 3667.

plied, as in "Come on Home" (1968), which echoes "Lord, I'm Coming Home."[32]

Explicit references to divorce, however, tend to trigger explicit moralizing. Only exceptionally, as in "Divorce Me C. O. D." (1946),[33] is the attitude at all flippant. While there are pleas for dissolution, for the woman to "Set Him Free" (1959), more often the idea of formal severance of the marriage bond makes explicit the conflict between moral and legal codes. So one is "Married by the Bible, Divorced by the Law" (1952),[34] and the woman asks, "Will Your Lawyer Talk to God?" (1962). Dramatizations can become quite sentimental, though "I'll Take the Dog" (1966) is unusual in its humor. Splitting up the material assets of the marriage, the couple fail to agree on custody of the canine, and are consequently reconciled.

That songs like this one and "Mama Spank" (1967) augur a more relaxed view of the problems is dubious, but certainly other songs indicate a more eman-cipated role for the female. As the woman's viewpoint tends to be more directly expressed, it becomes increasingly aggressive. The woman will react to infidelity in kind, singing "Your Good Girl's Gonna Go Bad" (1967) or taunting her husband with her knowledge of and intention to visit the fleshpots too, as in "Jackson" (1967), which takes probably the most cynical attitude toward marital sex problems expressed in country-western music. The woman is no longer the forlorn victim, and she will take direct steps to protect her "property," telling her rival, "You Ain't Woman Enough" (1966), and threatening to send her to "Fist City" (1968).[35] The man, on the other hand, may adopt the role earlier played by his spouse. He will plead desperately, "Ruby, Don't Take Your Love to Town" (1967). Reduced almost to abject self deception after hearing of the activities of a woman who looks like his wife, talks like his wife, and has the same name as his wife, he can whine, "Darling, Say It's Not You" (1968).

These themes do not represent the totality of even current country-western music. All songs do not deal with problems like "The Other Woman" (1965) or a bar-to-bar search for "Sweet Thang" (1966). Composers and singers may pre-sent pieces of almost surrealistic humor like "May the Bird of Paradise Fly up Your Nose" (1965); they may even insist that "It's Such a Pretty World Today" (1967). The fact that such songs are the more likely to move over into general popular acceptance merely emphasizes the sin-sex-booze patterns that are the staple commodities of country-western music. And the significance of the patterns in relation to the tensions of the urban hillbilly is perhaps the most striking ex-ample of the value of detailed study of country-western music as a barometer of certain aspects of American culture rather than merely a debased offspring of American folk music.

BIBLIOGRAPHICAL NOTE

Materials for the study of country-western music are vast but not easily accessible. Billy Charles Malone's "A History of Commercial Country Music in the United States, 1920–1964" (doctoral dissertation, The University of Texas, 1965) is a pioneer study significant for its dependence on

[32] Peggy Little, Dot 17068.
[33] Merle Travis, Capitol 290.
[34] Hank Snow, RCA Victor 20–4733.
[35] Loretta Lynn, Decca 32264.

published materials of the industry and interviews with selected performers and executives. It further provides references to information in popular and esoteric journals, which I shall not repeat. Malone's book has been published as *Country Music U.S.A.*, The American Folklore Society Memoir Series, Vol. 54 (Austin, 1968). Robert Shelton and Burt Goldblatt, *The Country Music Story* (Indianapolis, 1966) is an interesting and valuable pictorial record, but the text must be used with caution. An important group of articles appeared in the "Hillbilly Issue" of the JOURNAL OF AMERICAN FOLKLORE, 78 (1965), 195–286. Also of particular interest are Judith McCulloh "Hillbilly Records and Tune Transcriptions," *Western Folklore,* 25 (1967), 225–244; Judith McCulloh, "Some Child Ballads on Hillbilly Records," *Folklore and Society* (Hatboro, Pa., 1966), 107–129; Neil V. Rosenberg, "From Sound to Style: The Emergence of Bluegrass," JOURNAL OF AMERICAN FOLKLORE, 80 (1967), 143–150. The greatest single resource for original recordings, song folios, runs of rare journals, discographies, interviews with and memorabilia of artists and executives is The John Edwards Memorial Foundation, University of California, Los Angeles.

University of California
Los Angeles, California

Prepared Comments by Judith McCulloh

Before I learned that Professor Wilgus would be playing his demonstration tape, I had prepared a tape of my own, somewhat shorter, to illustrate the major country-music hybrids discussed in his paper. I find it instructive that two people working independently should have chosen precisely the same device as the most useful and necessary way of bringing the paper home to you. For it reflects directly one of the chief difficulties we have in studying traditional music, and not just its hybrid, urbanized, or commercialized aspects. Music is a sound system and is best presented as sound, rather than in word-pictures. There are occasions when descriptions and transcriptions are required and even more desirable than recordings, but this is not to say that graphic devices serve as direct translations of the music. Rather, they comment on and abstract from it. (For the moment I am using the word "music" in its narrow sense, of "sound *per se*," not in the larger sense, of music in its social or cultural setting. Professor Wilgus treats both aspects, both the ethno- and the musicology.)

We can write out song texts, and to a less satisfactory degree their melodies. We can indicate tempo, harmonic structure, instrumentation, and the like. We can attempt to describe melodic contour, patterns of ornamentation, vocal quality, the mood or spirit of the performance. It is when we try to communicate the style, the texture, or the sound of tradition as it blends all such features that we find ourselves with the least adequate professional vocabulary. One obvious solution is to present the music itself; thus we play tapes. We would not feel so impelled to supplement papers with recordings, perhaps, if folklorists were more familiar with the varied sounds of traditional music. I suspect, however, that many members of the American Folklore Society will respond to Professor Wilgus' paper as a good and impressive intellectual statement but that it will not hit home, because they have little or nothing in their experience to tie it to. They have not heard the music. I do not mean to suggest that all folklorists should immediately trade in their books for records, or that the American Folklore Society should stop publishing the JOURNAL and establish an LP series of current and reissued material—although these would both be valuable complementary projects. The point is that the extent and nature of our knowledge of American music reflects our exposure to it.

To supplement Professor Wilgus' historical survey we need intensive studies of the various musical hybrids he discusses. Mayne Smith and Neil Rosenberg have provided a good introduction to bluegrass. For other styles and substyles our best published sources are scattered articles, record reviews (notably those by D. K. Wilgus in the JOURNAL OF AMERICAN FOLKLORE and Ed Kahn in *Western Folklore*), and, increasingly, LP brochure and liner notes (such as Norm Cohen's description of *Early Rural String Bands* [RCA Victor LPV 552] and Chris Strachwitz and Bob Pinson's commentary on *Western Swing* [Old Timey OT 105]). The more we learn about each of these styles, too, the better we should understand the folk esthetic (or, more properly, esthetics) operative. Our questions progress easily from "How does it sound?" and "Why does it sound the way it does?" to "How should it sound? Why should it sound the way it does? What are the standards? What are the musical ideals?"

This might be an appropriate place to add a word of caution to my homily earlier on the virtues of listening to music: reissues of earlier recordings, like Cecil Sharp's *English Folk Songs from the Southern Appalachians,* may reflect the esthetic of the editor and only partially that of the folk. Thus for a time it seemed to the newcomer to the world of reissues that back in the twenties and thirties hillbilly musicians played square-dance music with a vengeance, with limited tolerance of waltzes and blues, and virtually no awareness of sacred material. It is much less difficult to evaluate current recordings against the current musical scene.

Awareness of these different folk and hybrid forms of American music also gives us new perspective on more traditional modes of study. It can suggest something about the history and the geographical spread of certain traditional songs. When I began putting together the tape meant to accompany Professor Wilgus' paper, I wanted to find recordings of the same song in all the major styles, on the theory that it might then be easier for the listener to hear the differences in treatment. For one piece, a lyric usually labeled "In the Pines" or "The Longest Train (I Ever Saw)," I have a discography of some sixty recordings, all but about five of which were issued commercially. From this list I chose an unaccompanied vocal performance representing early Kentucky tradition, a North Carolina string band recorded in Georgia in 1935, a close-harmony vocal duet with guitar and mandolin in the style of the thirties, a 1952 bluegrass treatment, a country-western version found recently in the local A&P store, and a folknik rendering from about 1963. A western swing example I could not find. So far as I know, only one item in the discography represents the Southwest tradition, but I do not yet have the recording.

Now, certain intriguing questions come to mind immediately. Did the song "In the Pines" not circulate beyond the Southeast until it entered bluegrass and folknik repertories? Or did it spread beyond the Southeast, without ever being recorded by any of the cowboy, western swing, or honky-tonk bands? If this was the situation, why wasn't it recorded? Was it coincidence or accident, or did someone perhaps feel it would not sell? We may extend the scope of the questions. Was there something about the styles—Southeast, Southwest—that permitted the crossover of some songs but precluded the acceptance of others? Was western swing, for instance, so geared to a dance beat that its practitioners did not pick up, or see fit to adapt a slow, nonemphatic piece like "In the Pines" to their esthetic? No doubt if we knew the distribution of many more songs and instrumental tunes among the various styles we could describe not only the character and boundaries of each style but also the nature and direction of musical acculturation, or the lack of it, from one style to another.

Finally, I would like to ask Professor Wilgus to speculate, if he would, on where he might draw the line on a causal relationship between the development of country-western music and the industrialization of the South, or the urbanization of the United States. Suppose we set up a kind of scale from one extreme of determinism to the other, with some of the steps along the way reading as follows: "Music, like language, changes naturally and by itself. Music changes when culture changes. Music changes because culture changes. Music changes to a particular form when culture changes in a particular way. Music changes to a particular form because culture changes in a particular way."

Would any of these statements obtain, with or without modification? Could we have had country music as we know it today without the industrialization and urbanization just mentioned? Is that urbanization both a necessary and a sufficient condition for the growth of country-western music? Is the development of that musical hybrid too complex, perhaps, for such simple-minded comment?

Urbana, Illinois

Discussion from the Floor

Wilgus:—If Mrs. McCulloh thinks I'm going to try to answer those questions, she is greatly mistaken. [Laughter] The questions are so good, there are no answers at this point. But if there are any questions from the audience we will try to field them.

George McMahon (Community Worker, Detroit Public School System):—I've an observation. I'm kind of fishing, I don't know quite how to express it. What you just said at the end about urbanization, change towards urbanization, does this mean a change in musical form? I noticed a real similarity—and I don't know quite how to say it because I don't know enough about music—a real similarity, perhaps not just technical, but I think it must be deeper than this (perhaps it's cognitive style or philosophical similarity or something) between soul music and a lot of what you played there.

Wilgus:—One similarity is that this music is always close to life and vitally reflects the life style. I would use "sincerity" in this case instead of "soul," since "soul" has a more restricted connotation. But there is also a development from an earlier life style partially reflected in the music, from a quality I call "objective." This is a high degree of restraint or control that one finds in older Appalachian culture. It begins to change, to become more "open" with the post–Civil War gospel music, toward a more expressive sound somewhat closer to what is now called soul music. Now, with the continued influence of urban styles, of Negro styles, there is a far less restrained sound. The tape I played gives some indication of this development. There is always more "soul" in the sense of sincerity in this music. It is meaningful, and the sound has a value. The value, however, and the esthetics change. Bluegrass music, which is sophisticated and highly technical, is now felt to be the real "old-timey" sound, while old-timers like me find that—well, it just ain't as good as the gravel-throated things we grew up on.

But still the sound reflects the life style. Of course country-western music tends toward a lesser reflection of the folk culture, and this is a partial answer to something Mrs. McCulloh said. That is, the music industry tends to exert more control over the sound. The industry has in the past tended to lag behind developments in country music. At one time the industry executives didn't really know quite what they were doing. If you think that the music industry was very smart in commercializing this music, you should read the record. They were far from knowledgeable about the music. It just got away from them, and at times they seemed heartily ashamed of it until it made so much money they had to establish a Country Music Memorial in Nashville. The Country Music Association hardly knew the history of its subject, and when they opened their facility they had little to go in it but Hank Williams' boots. They are now, with the cooperation of the John Edwards Memorial Foundation, building a large library of taped recordings.

The music does reflect more industry control, but its influence is not simple. Tennessee Ernie Ford was the favorite artist of many of my best Kentucky folk informants. They all loved him, but thank God they didn't sound like him.

Robert Tremain (Student, Wayne State University):—I noticed in recent country-western there's a great emphasis on breaking up the home. Is this really true or is it just picked up sort of randomly?

Wilgus:—No, it's a thread that runs through the lyrics. Because of the emphasis on the family in American folk culture, urban developments in family patterning have been a tremendous cultural shock. The folk attitude toward familial relationships is a survival of an earlier frontier approach, and much of the middle class still holds some of these values. Popular music of the past did not reflect the problems so directly as country-western music now does. I have no statistics at hand, but I would say that 50 percent of the hit country-western songs deal with one aspect or another of the sin-sex-booze-divorce pattern.

Arnold Pilling (Wayne State University):—I was hoping that I might hear at least an observation on your part concerning the role country music has played in the urban scene, not in the context of "The Folk" or the Appalachians, but in the context of the professional or nonprofessional political liberal. In this latter association, it seems to me that we have a different phenomenon than in the case of the use of country music by people from Appalachia. I was wondering to what extent there are materials available that deal with the use of country music in the context of liberal politics causes from the thirties onwards.

Wilgus:—There is information, but it reflects almost exactly the opposite of what you are saying. The music has been used for political purposes. Governor Jimmie Davis of Louisiana was and still is a prominent hillbilly singer. W. Lee "Pappy" O'Daniel was a flour peddler and sponsored Bob Wills' band. Then he turned politician with another band as support. His son Pat recently failed to make it using the same technique, but he was using the worst southwestern swing band I have ever heard. Generally the effective political employment of the music has been anything but liberal. When the urban intellectual got interested in American country music, he jumped clear back to "folk," then moved to bluegrass. Johnny Cash was, I think, the only country-western star that ever made it at all with the folk music "revival."

Whether it is true or not, I don't know, but I have heard that disc jockeys are told not to play bluegrass music as revenge, because bluegrass was noticed by intellectuals and country-western wasn't. Liberals have generally looked down on commercial country music, and I was indeed surprised at first by the "liberal" cast of the folk music revival. But the liberal approached Appalachian folk music through a misunderstanding of the Appalachian folk. I have been present at many so-called folk festivals and observed the "turned-on" kids using the music to illustrate ideas that would make the performers vomit. I recall the story of two bluegrass performers at an integrated student party.

One swallowed hard and tried to swing with it; the other "drank himself to death" in a corner (in fact, he really drank himself to death last year).

The "liberal" and "country" approaches have generally contrasted. Once in a while a "liberal" politician gets "converted," of course. LBJ was defeated by "Pappy" Lee O'Daniel, and that's when I think LBJ realized the value of country music. He now likes Cowboy Bob more than he used to.

Leslie Shepard (Gale Press, Detroit and London):—Most of us are trying to interpret the present topical music, and looking for Donovan's and Elvis Presley's place in what is occurring. How would you evaluate Elvis Presley, for example, in country-western music?

Wilgus:—Well, I'll try not to talk too long. Of course rock-and-roll is a combination of rhythm-and-blues and hillbilly. As usual, by accident the first recording was made in the wrong place—the North—but the music basically came out of Memphis. The owner of Sun records was quite astute in this matter. Elvis Presley's first Sun record was a very bad rendition of Bill Monroe's "Blue Moon of Kentucky," so he began to record things like Big Mama Thornton's songs. There then developed what I called rockabilly music. I believe I was the first to name it, though I cannot now locate the quotation. When rock and roll became popular, it was a great influence on country-western for a while, but it subsequently lessened. You can hear rock influences now, but as back-formation and reintroduction into the hybrid. Elvis Presley came right out of the meeting of country-western and rhythm-and-blues and was simply the most successful of a number of performers, such as Carl Perkins and Jerry Lee Lewis.

Edith Fowke (Toronto, Canada):—Where do the Beatles fit into this pattern?

Wilgus:—Into *this* pattern? They don't fit, directly, that is, except for the fact that they were at first imitating rhythm-and-blues. The main thing is that—like the Beatles and some others—country-western is now moving toward "studio sound," in which performances are produced that cannot be duplicated in personal appearances. Fortunately—to my mind—country-western is moving very slowly in that direction, but the tendency is there. And of course there are noncountry influences. For example a former colleague of mine, a musicologist on the faculty of a college sixty miles north of Nashville, used to make the journey regularly to play in the violin choir behind country-western performers.

Aili Johnson (Franklin, Michigan):—Would you comment very briefly on the *Sacred Harp* music? I have found only one record, an old Folkways recording.

Wilgus:—This music was actually recorded and released on so-called hillbilly records deriving from the Atlanta area. One of the more important was the Denson Quartet. The Denson family still continues to maintain the *Sacred Harp* tradition. The music was recorded and issued, but apparently it didn't sell well. I have no sales figures, but the practice ceased; and copies of the recordings are relatively scarce, indicating limited issue. They are a further example of the industry policy of that time—to record and test release almost any music the scouts found.

MORTON LEEDS

The Process of Cultural Stripping and Reintegration

The Rural Migrant in the City

WHAT HAPPENS IN THE MIGRATION to the city of people from the farm, the hill lands, and the small towns of the South is of critical importance to those of us who must deal with the cities of today. What follows may serve as a brief sketch of the movement to urban areas by the rural or small-town resident, who comes to seek a new life. A few rough indexes of the change process will be reviewed, as physical and social measures of what happens to family life when a move occurs. The picture is complicated, of course, by the problem of color, since moving is obviously not identical for the white and the Negro. For purposes of this analysis, however, they will be treated as a single group, since some universal elements are being sought.

In analyzing the problem of poverty and color, we discover the interesting fact that in absolute numbers there are more than twice as many poor whites as there are poor Negroes. This in part derives from the fact that whites outnumber Negroes nine to one. As measured by income levels, only 10 percent of white families had incomes below poverty levels in 1966, whereas 35 percent of the nonwhite families fell in this bracket. In absolute figures, this comes to 20.1 million whites, and 9.6 million nonwhites. Incidence of poverty, therefore, is three and a half times as great among Negroes.[1] The Negro problem is complicated by the social factor of caste discrimination—which combined with poverty, poor housing, poor education, and other forms of economic discrimination produces the tensions being seen in the cities today. Poverty is bad enough; but social discrimination makes it unbearable, particularly when television makes the discrimination obvious. The effect of TV as a social equalizing and disturbing force probably has not been correctly assessed as yet.

The drift to the great cities derives from the agricultural revolution, more than likely as great an agent of social change as any our society has experienced, but one that is further complicated by the roaring upsurge of our industrial capacity.

---

[1] Herman P. Miller and Dorothy K. Newman, *Social and Economic Conditions of Negroes in the United States* (Washington, D. C., 1967) 22, 25.

The problem we now face is not one of ability to produce enough for all, but rather how shall it be distributed equitably within the framework of a work-oriented society with not enough actual work for all. Fortunately, that problem is not our immediate concern. Rather, we are examining the social and cultural byproducts of the industrial change, as rural and small town residents enter the city and try to drop old ways for new.[2] This is not a new problem for us. It has been going on for more than a century as Europe's poor came here, assimilated into the culture, and raised their children to be middle-class Americans.[3] The difference this time is that we are trying to assimilate our own rural poor, who have a far stronger claim on the resources of the culture.

The driving force behind the move from rural to urban areas is largely economic, with some social pressures as well. A collapse of the small-farm economy has taken place during the past generation, in part triggered by large-scale industrial farming. City life has always served as a positive lure, but with the rapid development of industrialization, physical movement from the land has accelerated. For the rural poor, the city is a great, bright, noisy, exciting, and sinful place. Its rates of pay are far better, its facilities and services incomparably superior to that offered by the small, rural community or by farm life in general. The penalties and frustrations inherent in the process of a move into an urban society are always present in the back of the migrant's mind, but they tend to be subordinated when economic pressure becomes too great to bear.

The Movement From Rural Lower Class to Urban Lower Class

When the move occurs, it has its impact on all areas of social existence. The American rural family, based on the extended family, includes the nuclear parent-children group as well as the grandparents, unmarried siblings of the parents, and additional relatives, who may represent broken families or unmarried individuals. In the city this extended family may begin to break up, with the nuclear two-generation family tending to be the norm. Grandparents with sources of income, such as social security or old-age assistance payments, or unmarried mothers on relief can be prized for their economic contribution. In such instances, they may be a welcome addition to the nuclear group. The children are primarily occupied with school and spend much of their free time in the streets. For them the change in life style is almost as significant as it is for the men. Since the density of urban living produces a large group of peers with whom it is easy to identify, the norms of the children tend to separate from those of their parents, and their expectations rise rapidly, far outstripping those of the older generation.

The farm family works as a unit on the land. Farm duties are assigned to each

[2] Some of the better works on the subject include Nathan Glazer and D. P. Moynihan, *Beyond the Melting Pot* (Cambridge, Mass., 1963); M. M. Gordon, *Assimilation in American Life: The Role of Race, Religion and National Origins* (New York, 1964); John Gulich, C. E. Bowerman, and K. W. Bach, "Newcomer Enculturation in the City; Attitudes and Participation," in *Urban Growth Dynamics,* ed. F. S. Chapin, Jr., and S. F. Weis (New York, 1962), 315–358; Oscar Handlin, *The Uprooted,* (Boston, 1951); A. M. Rose and Leon Warshay, "The Adjustment of Migrants to Cities," *Social Forces,* 36 (1957), 72–76. Lee Taylor and A. R. Jones, Jr., *Rural Life and Urbanized Society* (New York, 1964).

[3] A surprising parallel to the current problems posed by the Southern migration to the cities appears in W. I. Thomas and Florian Znaniecki, *The Polish Peasant in Europe and America,* 2 vols. (New York, 1927).

physically capable member of the family, regardless of age or sex. Certain of the chores derive from physical limitations while others are traditionally assigned to certain types of individuals. The farm economy involves little cash and is tightly geared to the price of farm products, since the sale of these items is the chief cash income. There is a residual economic strength, however, for those living on the farm. Food can be raised directly; and where the talent, the land, and the weather are favorable, the family if nothing else is assured of food and shelter. For the share-cropper and the tenant farmer this is less true, of course, depending on individual circumstances, and for the migrant farm worker it does not apply at all. Upon the shift to the city everything changes rapidly. The sense of relatedness to the physical world is immediately severed. The men work when they can find employment. The women tend to work more regularly, finding employment in the more menial and poorer paying jobs—as domestics, laundry workers, and unskilled factory workers, for example. For the children there is little opportunity to work, except running itinerant errands and doing the small jobs that no adult would accept.

Farm food is usually home-grown and frequently adequate. For those living on the small farm especially, only certain types of foods have to be obtained from the grocery. Certain favorite foods tend to be repeatedly used on farms, particularly where the economic level is low. The city offers a much broader variety, but also a necessary reliance on canned and partially prepared foods. Quality is only fair in the poorer areas; although fresh vegetables and familiar farm foods are sought after, they are not always available. The price differential between the rural area and the city can be quite great, especially when price and quality gouging occurs.

The dialects of the southern farm or rural area vary locally. There is a very strong reliance on parochial, esoteric, and regional speech. Whole groups of consonants may vanish from the speech, so that it becomes almost unrecognizable to those in the North or Far West. The change in language usage on arrival in the city tends to be less drastic than changes involving other factors, because the family normally will follow other relatives to a given city. Since the immediate environment is parochial and protective, it is some time before language begins to change. When it does, it appears in the form of accretion and agglomeration on the rural linguistic base, although loss of regional accent does take place upon further acculturation. For the young, change can sometimes be very dramatic when peer-group contacts produce specialized in-group language forms. In school the child is subjected to stereotyped middle-class linguistic presentations that are assimilated with various degrees of effectiveness. For the child well-integrated into family life, school language becomes a second language that is used first in school and then in later life. For the ambitious, bright, or perceptive child, however, school language becomes a vehicle for leaving the family environment when this becomes desirable.

In rural areas work clothes are the daily norm, with the stress on cleanliness and durability rather than style, cut, color, or match. A special set of clothes is kept for Sunday, church, or holiday observance. Upon the family's moving to the city, the clothing pattern does not change very much, except that there is less reliance on jeans and more on cheap imitations of middle-class daily clothes.

Farm and rural life is monotonous with continuous work, particularly during the growing season, and long stretches of inactivity during cold weather. Special occasions include weekly dances, mainly on Saturday night, church picnics on Sunday afternoons, ritual holiday events, periodic fairs around the harvest time, plus some hunting and fishing in season. Alcohol, though used covertly, is overtly frowned upon. In the city this pattern changes—on Friday and Saturday nights there are parties, T.V. is the daily staple, and mass spectator events occur frequently. Holidays become less important. Alcohol is heavily used as a social catalyst, with less disapproval expressed over its use.

Rural education is inadequate, tends to be extremely short—generally for eight or fewer years—with the school year shorter than in the city because of the nature of farming and farm duties. In a thin population, several grades may be grouped simultaneously. Equipment and facilities tend to be inadequate, and there is not too much variety. The lower class urban school has some of the deficiencies of rural education, plus some additional ones.[4] Density is high instead of low, producing highly fractionized age groups. Peer group identification becomes very strong, and there is a weakening of interage relationships. Facilities and equipment are not particularly good. Classes tend to be much larger, with poor student discipline. Academic standards, however, tend to be somewhat more demanding than in rural areas, and schooling tends to be longer, without the special demands of family chores on the land.

The Penalties of Movement to the City

The family and the individuals composing it can move in several directions: either laterally, remaining in the lower class without major change; downward, with collapse of the family and the shattering of its social and economic role; or upward into the lower middle-class by dint of great effort and good fortune. Lateral movement essentially involves a treadmill status, producing no major forward movement. This can occur where the family slowly begins to perceive urban norms and expands its wants slowly, as it expands its earning ability, but never enough to accrue capital or skills that would permit its members to move ahead in a class sense. Such a family within a few years develops a real sense of frustration and in some ways is worse off than the rural family without aspirations. City life becomes an exhausting dead-end, and such families truly lead lives of quiet desperation. Their one source of strength is the knowledge that they are not at the bottom of the social heap. The future is dim in general, but they do have their self-respect and integrity as a family, and they can cling to these for whatever they are worth. Their children, at least, may break out of the mold, and in many cases they do.

For many families, migration to the city is destructive. Previously, the man was the center of the family, and around his daily farm work the fears and aspirations of his wife and children could revolve. Though poor, they at least drew upon a centuries-long heritage of male dominance and relatedness to the land that supported them. The family's structure was supported and rarely challenged. The city provides a different setting. The man frequently cannot find work, or what work he can find is part-time, unskilled, undemanding, and demeaning. The work, in a

---

[4] For the social and educational tragedies that can take place in urban lower-class schools see Jonathan Kozol, *Death at an Early Age* (Boston, 1967).

sense, demands only part of the man and thereby makes him less of a whole man. A vast job hierarchy looms over the unskilled man, and he is at the bottom of the structure. Worst of all, he is without education and committed to remain at the bottom for most of his job life. Where skills, intelligence, adaptability, emotional make-up, or physical handicap stand in the way, the picture is even bleaker, since the man begins with further hazards to adequate employment.

But the demands of the city are relentless. The children are trying to go to school and need city clothes. Television, that most subversive of technical developments, offers a fairy box of the unattainable. To help meet these pressures the wife goes to work, and still further family problems arise. Her earnings may be steadier than her husband's, despite the menial character of her work. But the children may be neglected most of the day, and slowly the family pattern is reshaped. In some families the man breaks away, and the fatherless household appears.[5] Temporary husbands, illegitimacy, and the attendant train of full family disorganization are thereby set into motion. Squalor, poverty, illness, and unemployment reinforce each other, and the disruptive cycle is in full operation.

Economic problems, then, are central to social disorganization and represent much of the difference between the lower-class working family and the disorganized slum family. Steady work and a regular source of income, in effect, mark the difference between the two groups. Welfare for the disorganized family is not only a holding action but frequently a future disorganizing force, since the essential thrust of current welfare programs is maintenance of the *status quo*. As a result, many families continue the cycle of disorganization through several generations.

The disorganized family gets food when it can, at levels that match the income. Food tends to be starchy and fatty, cheap and inadequate, a pale echo of the poor farmer's fare that at least could count on the standard staples of corn, hominy, fowl, and eggs. While there is famine much of the time, the sudden arrival of a check, a visiting relative, or a temporary break of good fortune, is the cause for feasting and a temporary abundance of the good edibles of life. On such occasions the extended family or guests may be invited to share one's fortune.

The slum language demonstrates the qualities of a genuine subculture. Slang predominates; there are a great many local references that derive from the community's character, industry, and immediate qualities. Colloquial forms are heavily used. The choice of words is concrete and extremely picturesque. Since the written forms are subordinated or absent, vernacular forms tend to take over. Speech, therefore, can evolve fairly rapidly, breaking out of the written mold. The slum culture is largely unrecorded; therefore, language becomes the mirror of a rapid evolution. This is one of the areas where the slum has a great deal to contribute to the upper levels of the society. Interpersonal relationships become important, and forms of verbal jousting and personal contending take on a structurally ritualized but verbally more creative content. This is especially true of male-female interactions, where one wishes to take advantage of or predominate over the other. At times, they resemble the parlor games of another leisure class, the upper class.

Clothing in the slums consists of hand-me-downs, the tired, worn clothes that may have been brought from the farm, were made available by more affluent rela-

---

[5] A highly personal example is shown in Dick Gregory's *Nigger* (New York, 1964).

tives, or were bought in second-hand stores. Sometimes, in moments of temporary affluence, there will be an expensive purchase of special shoes or a hat, standing as a kind of wild waving in the wind of human aspiration.

Recreation at this level takes on a special quality. Banter and street play become quite important. It is as if the challenge of everyday living has proved overwhelming and there has been a regression to childish norms and standards. The man whose role is shattered will very often engage in adolescent behavior or street corner play, messing or fooling around, deriving personal advantage through ability to show off or demonstrate his importance. This is highly ritualized behavior that provides many secondary gains. Saturday night remains important for formal recreation, although many recreation events may go on for days at a time depending upon new resources and assets and the influx of new personnel. Activity at this level interweaves with the marginal or illegal sector and becomes in part an economic standby for the slum dweller, while serving as recreation for the middle-class or lower-class person. This would include the numbers game, crap games, card playing, and race betting, since they may have economic overtones. The same events, then, can have different meanings for different classes. The participants, too, may feed off the illegal activities as suppliers of refreshments or as procurers and pimps. Successful members of such groups, of course, may have an opportunity for upward mobility, enabling them to break out of the slum.

The slum school can become a kind of babysitting service that in part serves to keep the children off the street. Teachers, schools, books, libraries, and equipment tend to be inadequate for the problems at hand, and the picture of hopelessness is tragic, since the school in our society represents the key to the future. A hopeless school means a hopeless younger generation, and a custodial school represents the illusion of progress. The education that comes through interpersonal peer group experience becomes transcendent and represents far more powerful norms than those of a discredited school system. When schooling is rejected, the teacher is seen as a model of failure, and the school experience is seen as something to be ridden through like a storm. For some children with fully disorganized families, however, school can be a refuge, if only because the child experiences less direct anger, frustrations, and aggression and more of a sense of searching for unknown answers than at home.

The Rewards of Movement to the City

For the farm family that maintains its sense of coherence—with strong parental guidance, a fortunate choice in economic skills, good ties to an ongoing business or industry, special personal characteristics, or just good fortune—the rewards of the city can be very great. The family trudges in the footsteps of those who have followed the American Dream. They dream the dreams of the past century, bearing special burdens but also winning the benefits that others have carved before them. The various socioeconomic cushions—such as unemployment insurance, social security benefits, medicare, and similar benefits—may help the family in its long march. A bright child can become the focus of the family's dreams. A hardworking mother can keep her fist in the dike of economic troubles and keep a family going through many vicissitudes. Family birth planning helps keep family needs under control, and church attendance does the same for personal aspirations, giving a sense of relatedness to the universe at large. Two generations under one roof become the norm. The family dreams of moving out of the slum neighborhood, and successively into better and better areas. Television serves as the constant spur, and the parents become quite choosy about a child's friends. Eventually, ownership of a car and of a home becomes the seal of the ascent into the middle class.

An interesting conflict comes into play with the choice of foods since attachment to early dietary fare is one of the most persistent of cultural traits. The grandparents most of all, but the parents too, may continue their interest in lower-class food, while the children express a yearning for the newer, processed, more expensive foods now available in great variety. With the shift from one neighborhood to another better one, lower-class foods become less available, and the more standard American foods become the norm. The parents may have a desire for the foods of the farm, the fresh satisfying foods that become less and less available. In time, of course, the family tends to complete the change and to depend heavily upon frozen or prepared foods that require little or no cooking.

Again there is a conflict of generations as the children become accustomed to two languages. Those that adapt to middle-class norms have the greatest opportunities for advancement. They are the ones who can quickly adapt to and take on the protective coloration of urban middle-class vocabulary and pronunciation. They learn to read and write earlier and are subjected to a variety of verbal and intellectual stimulants. They step into the broad stream of the written English language and begin to assimilate another part of its cultural heritage. A dual vision proceeds for some time, however, since these children continue to transact with strong parents. The verbal limitations of the parents, whose norms are still those of the farm, gradually become obvious to the children. Sometimes loyalty is strained, but for the successful family the ties of affection override embarrassment at parental inadequacies.

At this stage clothing becomes a badge of change itself, and the tremendous stress Americans place on the formal presentation of self begins to show. The power of the adaptive dream goes into successful generations of clothing changes, so that the family slides more and more into ideal type patterns. Clothing becomes an expression of success. Clothing can conceal past origins too, as well as inadequate living arrangements, since the bulk of contacts with significant others take place outside the home. Clothing improvement is commensurate with, if not ahead of, the family's income. It becomes a mirror in which the family can interpret its increasing success. Clothing is changed more frequently to fit the special activity; specific clothes for sports and recreation, for gardening, for partying, or for special events are worn in imitation of the more affluent upper class.

The excitement of the slum, with its disorganized and haphazard daily and weekly events, slowly gives way to the more routinized life of the middle class. Television can be watched after homework has been done. The football game becomes a reward for personal diligence, and the Saturday night party becomes more restrained and decorous. Refreshments are more expensive, the more esoteric sports come to be followed or imitated, and special hobbies are taken up after the latest fashions. The children may be taught dancing, where previously they learned it from each other, and art lessons are encouraged to bring out creativity.

Education becomes the means of salvation; children are seen as extensions of parental dreams about what might have been as well as what might be. Children are pushed, prodded, lured, and intimidated into absorbing as much education as their minds will tolerate. Such attendance becomes a criterion by which the child is judged, and the rewards of affection and love are doled out generously to those who follow middle-class norms. Pressure for success is high; children are encouraged to go on to college wherever possible or to take specialized schooling that will prepare them for a proper class career. Schools are better, in better neighborhoods, and the accomplishments of the children reflect this. The rural child slides in beside his city cousins and, if he is adaptable, assimilates into the urban landscape.

Research Needs

There are a number of questions that we would like to see answered by anthropologists, ethnologists, sociologists, and psychologists. To what extent, for example, are capitalistic acquisitiveness and emergence from slum life related? How important, for instance, were Jewish tendencies toward business enterprise in the 1930s and 1940s to the resultant broad acceptance of the Jew in middle-class American life during the 1950s and 1960s? What does this mean for the Puerto Rican, who seems to be following in the footsteps of the Jew? Turning the question around, what kind of penalty, if any, is being levied against the Negro for the absence of such acquisitiveness? That is to say, is the Protestant ethic a significant barrier to the emergence of a Negro middle class in America? A puzzling question, a corollary to this one, would be, why are Catholic Puerto Ricans oriented toward small capitalism, while Protestant Negroes are not?

One of the factors in slum family failure is related to the male role in the family. How do we reinforce the male role in the slum family? The most obvious answers, of course, involve successful employment and disrupting the patterns of discrimination. Above and beyond this, however, it should be possible to understand more about family dynamics and how they can be used to reinforce father images and husband roles. Should the Negro, for instance, try harder to attain the medical professional role, at the top of the social heap? To what extent can Big Brother movements provide transitional role models for the fatherless child?

We need longitudinal studies of the ghetto family with follow-ups every decade or so. These can follow the patterns of Oscar Lewis, or other styles as well. Such studies could be very useful in revealing the dynamics of break-out from the ghetto, as well as increasing understanding about further entrenchment into the ghetto system. The dynamics and the gestalt of the ghetto family as a functioning or malfunctioning support system need to be explored in great detail. Certainly the positive factors exposed by successful break-out should be understood and where uncovered should be publicized. Some of the resultant findings could be extremely useful for helping families break out of successive generational patterns of slum living.

What is the relation between creativity and ethnicity? How much creativeness derives from the fact that one is different from the majority group, from a need to justify one's differences or to rationalize or interpret the differences? How many books like *Native Son* or *Invisible Man* would have remained unwritten in the absence of racial prejudice? How much of the protest literature of the 1930s produced by Jewish authors would have been aborted in a more congenial atmosphere? The neutral climate regarding Jews in the 1960s suggests some of the answers, but they are not definitive. This problem is a real one because creativity represents a wellspring from which many of a society's greatest achievements are derived. Social and ethnic differences demand a heavy price, but one that may produce significant fruit.

Margaret Mead has suggested that the upwardly mobile family can be helped to keep together as a cultural unit if all members of the family share in the education process. Can this be used as a technique for narrowing the intergenerational gap between slum parents and children? What are the essential ethnic characteristics that help us distinguish a subcultural group? Is it language? Food? Dress? Religious practices? Family organization? A combination of these? How can we help retain the most meaningful aspects of ethnic differences in subgroups without disrupting the larger society? What elements are meaningful and satisfying, providing differences but not disruption? What are the minimal differences that can be tolerated or encouraged?

Can a community be transferred to different locations and still retain the social and cultural ties that mark it as unique? This has special meaning not only for the southern rural and small-town migrants but also for local urban relocation programs that may inadvertently damage a cultural community. What are the differences in urban assimilation between the rural Negro and the white? What are the handicaps and the advantages for membership in each ethnic group? What are the rates of change, the sources of insecurity? A series of comparative studies, analyzing similar components, could be very useful in understanding the assimilation of these two quite different groups.

Washington, D.C.

Prepared Comments by Lawrence E. Gary

It is of critical importance for policy makers, professionals, social scientists, and others to have adequate information about the life styles of people who migrate from the rural areas of the South to our big urban centers. Given the explosive nature of the urban crisis, it is imperative for us to develop functional and realistic programs to assist these people in adjusting to our urban culture. But in order to do this, we must acquire meaningful knowledge about their heritage within the context of an urban environment. A symposium of this nature is long overdue.

In his paper Mr. Leeds tries to identify indexes of some of the basic social and physical adjustments that families experience as they move from rural situations to urban settings. Although the paper provides us with some new insight and raises some crucial research questions, it has some serious shortcomings particularly as it relates to black people. Basically, the paper lacks a clear conceptual frame of reference. Given the title, one would expect a cultural analysis of the migration process; however, his report reminds one of a typical sociological analysis. It seems that within this sociological perspective, Mr. Leeds vacillated between two conceptual orientations: the structural-functional and social process models. Both of these perspectives are static, and this is reflected in his paper in that he failed to show the constant and dynamic interaction between rural people and their city relatives. In the black community there is an intimate relationship between the recent migrants and their "down-home" rural relatives. There is a communication system providing information about resources, opportunities, and problems of city life to the prospective migrants. These recent migrants make regular trips to their hometowns so that they can see relatives and exchange resources and information about the urban culture. This suggests that the socializing process begins long before the prospective migrants move to the city. Although Leeds gave some consideration to these issues, for the most part he stereotyped rural migrants; and this stereotyping seems to be based on old sociological writings and assumptions rather than on the behavioral findings.

My main criticism of this paper is that Mr. Leeds failed to recognize a definitive, viable black culture. In order to identify general characteristics of the migration process, it seems logical to group all migratory populations. This may be a valid reason for grouping white and black migrants. But at the same time, one has to be careful to distinguish meaningful cultural differences between groups. At this point one can see conceptual and methodological contradictions throughout this paper. First, Mr. Leeds admits that the adjustment processes for black and white migrants are not identical; then he proceeds to group them. But at the end of his report, he raises some research questions, centered around the idea that the assimilation process is quite different for the two groups. If this is a significant research question, why combine the two groups? The effect of grouping black and white migrants is to denigrate black culture; such effect eliminates the use of characteristics of black culture as inputs for the study of the migratory process.

By not approaching the migrants from a cultural perspective, Leeds continues to make grave errors, especially in his discussion of research questions, clothing, and family structure. Many of his research questions reflect a negative orientation, with emphasis on pathology, deviancy, and social disorganization. Also, many of these questions seem to be geared toward social stability rather than social justice. If Mr. Leeds had employed a cultural analysis, he may not have made so many value judgments. He implies that middle-class white values are "good" and lower-class values are "bad." The concept of cultural relativity should have been applied in the discussion of many of these issues and problems. Moreover, he fails to show how many cultural norms and ways (songs, dancing, language, dress, foods, and so forth) of the black community have been transferred into the white community. His discussion of clothing is extremely weak in content. For example, he implies that lower-class blacks buy clothes that are cheap imitations of middle-class daily clothes. I would argue that the reverse is true; that is, today many middle-class white males are imitating lower-class black males in their clothing patterns. Moreover, it is very difficult to differentiate between social classes in the black community on the basis of clothing, especially men.

Leeds' treatment of the black family is inadequate in that it is full of the typical sociological stereotypes. In fact, his proposed research needs on the slum family do not raise any new empirical, conceptual, or methodological questions. First, one must recognize the fact that the black family is developing; it has never been developed. Therefore, the implication that it is breaking down is questionable. Moreover, since black people have managed to survive in a hostile society, there must be some strengths within their particular familial institution. Secondly, one must learn more about the actual behavioral performance of the different actors in the white family before comparing the two racial groups. In suggesting the necessity for more adequate male role models in the black family, one needs to learn more about the functional significance of this concept in the white family. The following behavioral research questions might be relevant: (1) To what extent does the ordinary male match the ideal male role in any family? (2) What percentage of the time is the white professional male or father absent or present in his home? (3) Do the traditional role models make sense in a society where the line of demarcation between masculine and feminine behavior is thin? (4) Are there several male role models that can be carried out equally in different family structures? (5) Can we identify within our society the various sources for a positive male identity? These research questions suggest that we do not know very much about the functional significance of role models in the family.

In conclusion, the intellectual must not be content to rest upon stereotypes or "ideal types" to explain variance. He must, rather, seek the most precise measurements of the culturally distinct characteristics that act as important intervening variables on what he wishes to measure. Mr. Leeds has made a contribution in that he approached the migrants from an urbanizing process perspective, but his paper would have been more meaningful if he had separated black and white migrants instead of emphasizing class differentiation. To try to generalize about two different populations, especially after admitting their uniqueness, is likely to obscure meaningful differences. If one combines the two migrant groups, I would argue that a basic variable influencing the rural migrants' adjustment to the urban culture is the extent to which they have been exposed to it through previous socialization. In this context a strong cultural identity and the significance of the church become important intervening variables, at least for black people. Unfortunately, Mr. Leeds does not discuss the role of the church in the adjustment process. It has always been a crucial socializing institution in the black community. In fact, in Chicago the governmental policy of not building churches in the public housing field has been, to some extent, responsible for the destruction of this institution. Therefore, the policy makers as well as intellectuals must be aware of the functional significance of black cultural institutions. If we are to have a pluralistic society, we must recognize cultural differences, and we must not confuse them with deviance.

University of Michigan
Ann Arbor, Michigan

Reply to Prepared Comments by Morton Leeds

In his comments Mr. Gary objects to sociological analysis, but this is precisely what my presentation intended. He further objects to role theory and ideal types. These have been and remain, despite Mr. Gary, legitimate techniques of study and analysis. He assumes that cultural analysis is the only means of studying a group in movement. But his cultural relativism breaks down in the intellectual sphere, when it comes to other disciplines. At that point, he insists that only one yardstick may possibly be used—his!

His criticism of the clothing discussion is amusing, in light of the opposite criticism I sustained recently at a Brookings industry presentation. There the businessmen insisted that I had underestimated the extraordinarily rapid assumption of white middle-class norms by groups of newly-employed lower-class black men. Both criticisms may have some validity, but numbers by far weigh more heavily on the side of upward middle-class identification by the majority of blacks.

The initial suggestion of black-white differences acknowledges their existence, but my subsequent discussion attempts to study the constants of the urban process. I am not satisfied that good studies exist analyzing the differences and have therefore stressed the need for additional study of the area. This final call is still legitimate.

Mr. Gary's last comment implies a cultural imperialism charge, but this is a charge based on Mr. Gary's historical, cultural, and legal ignorance. The "governmental policy of not building churches in the public housing field" is rooted in the basic structure of our society, since government may not subsidize the building of churches. Is Mr. Gary perhaps suggesting that, for the black community alone, it should? With which denominations would he care to begin?

NOTES ON THE CONTRIBUTORS

ROGER D. ABRAHAMS. Dr. Abrahams, folklorist and Afro-Americanist, was born in Philadelphia on June 12, 1933. He received his B.A. with honors from Swarthmore College in 1955, his M.A. with honors from Columbia University in 1959, and his Ph.D. in literature and folklore from the University of Pennsylvania in 1961. He has done folklore and ethnographic field work in Philadelphia and on four islands in the British West Indies. Professor Abrahams has taught at the University of Texas at Austin since 1960; he has been a visiting professor at Indiana University and Carleton College and has lectured in many colleges and universities across the country and abroad. He is author of *Deep Down in the Jungle: Negro Narrative Folklore from the Streets of Philadelphia, Positively Black*, and *Jump Rope Rhymes: A Dictionary*, as well as many other books, articles, and reviews. Professor Abrahams is active in the American Folklore Society and has served on its Executive Board since 1968. He has also been a member of the Social Science Research Council's Committee on Afro-American Societies and Cultures since 1968.

LINDA DÉGH. Presently a professor of folklore at Indiana University, Folklore Institute, Dr. Dégh is also founder and editor of *Indiana Folklore*, and an associate editor of both the *Journal of the Folklore Institute* and the *Uralic and Altaic Series Publication*. She is a member of the International Society of Folk Narrative Research and the Société Internationale d'Ethnographie et de Folklore. In 1963 she was awarded the Pitré Prize, and during 1970–1971 was a Guggenheim Fellow. Dr. Dégh has written several books including *Folktales of Hungary* (1965, 1969), *Folktales and Society* (1969), and *East European Folk Narrative Studies*. She is currently working on a book that is concerned with the culture and folklore of the Calumet Hungarians. Research interests include folk narrative genres, performers and performance, urban and regional ethnic folklore in Europe and in the United States.

RICHARD M. DORSON. Professor of history and folklore and director of the Folklore Institute at Indiana University, Richard Dorson was born in New York City in 1916. He received three degrees from Harvard, taking his doctorate in the history of American civilization in 1943. His sixteenth and latest book is *American Folklore and the Historian* (1971), and he is also general editor of the *Folktales of the World* series. He has directed thirty Ph.D.'s in folklore, and his students now teach folklore at many universities.

LAWRENCE E. GARY. Dr. Gary, an assistant professor of social work at the University of Michigan, completed his undergraduate work at Tuskegee Institute and did graduate work at the University of Michigan, where he received his Ph.D. degree. He has developed and taught several courses on the Afro-American experience in the New World. Also, he has worked on problems of Black Americans with child guidance clinics, universities, settlement houses, and teachers' organizations. His current research interests center on the impact of social policies on the black community and on black voluntary associations, especially the church and the theatre.

MORTON LEEDS. Dr. Leeds is presently the director of Plans, Programs and Evaluation Staff, Renewal and Housing Management, Department of Housing and Urban Development, Washington, D.C. He holds his doctorate in political science from the New School for Social Research in New York City. He is the editor of *The Proceedings of the Washington Colloquium on Science and Society*, Vol. 2, and is the author and editor of three other books on aging and the community. His article in this volume arose in part from a series of presentations in which he discussed the causes of the urban crisis with buisnessmen at the Brookings Institution, students in various universities in Washington, D.C., participants in the Foreign Service Institution, and vistors to HUD. The views Dr. Leeds expresses in his article are his own and do not necessarily reflect those of the Department of Housing and Urban Development.

HUBERT G. LOCKE. Director of Religious Affairs, faculty associate of the Center for Urban Studies, adjunct professor of Urban Education and, during the academic year 1969–1970, Franklin Memorial Professor of Human Relations at Wayne State University in Detroit, Hubert G. Locke is also a consultant on urban affairs for a number of national agencies and foundations. He holds honorary degrees from the Payne Theological Seminary and the University of Akron and has written *The Detroit Riot of 1967* and *The Care and Feeding of White Liberals*.

JUDITH McCULLOH. Dr. McCulloh holds degrees from Ohio Wesleyan University, The Ohio State University (English), and Indiana University (Folklore). She provided a new Foreword to Ira Ford's *Traditional Music of America* (reprinted, 1965); edited LPs of Illinois and cowboy music; has written articles on hillbilly music; and has transcribed southern white music (commercial and field recordings), Negro work songs, and cowboy songs for various publications. Dr. McCulloh's interests also include Finnish traditional fiddling, melodic identification and classification, and archiving.

LEONARD W. MOSS. Leonard Moss is presently professor of anthropology at Wayne State University and was formerly chairman of the then joint Department of Sociology and Anthropology. A University of Michigan graduate who drifted away from sociology into anthropology, he has completed three Fulbright-years doing field work in Italy. His publications include work in the fields of archaeology, linguistics, folklore, cultural anthropology, and history. He serves on the summer faculty of Trinity College (Hartford), Rome Campus. He was recently decorated by the Italian government, being granted the Knighthood of the Order of Merit.

MARION PEARSALL. Subsequent to her training in traditional anthropological specialties at the universities of New Mexico and California (Berkeley), Marion Pearsall has devoted most of her career to research and teaching in the American South. Her publications include studies of American Indian groups, rural Appalachian neighborhoods, small Southern towns, the sociology of health professions, and problems involved in introducing modern medicine to folk and ethnic populations. She is currently a professor of behavioral science and anthropology at the University of Kentucky. Since 1965, she has also been editor of *Human Organization*, the official journal of the Society for Applied Anthropology.

ELLEN J. STEKERT. Organizer of the symposium on "The Urban Experience and Folk Tradition" at Wayne State University in 1968, Dr. Stekert has taught at that university for seven years. Her interests are depth collecting, the utilization of psychological tools in the collection and analysis of folklore materials, and the process by which folklore is transmitted. She has done research and collecting in folksong, folk religion, folk medicine, and urban folklore. Presently an associated editor of the *Journal of American Folklore* and an executive board member of the American Folklore Society, she is associate professor of English at Wayne State University, where she is also the director of the Folklore Archive. Her field work has been in the Southern Appalachian Mountains, upper New York State, Michigan, and the urban centers of Detroit and New York City.

D. K. WILGUS. Professor of English and Anglo-American folksong and chairman of the Folklore and Mythology Group at the University of California at Los Angeles, Professor Wilgus was one of the first American folklorists to investigate the relationships between hillbilly music and American folk music. He is the author of *Anglo-American Folksong Scholarship since 1898* and other books and articles on American folklore. He has done extensive fieldwork in the United States and Ireland, established the Western Kentucky Folklore Archive, founded and edited the *Kentucky Folklore Record*, has been for many years record review editor of the JOURNAL OF AMERICAN FOLKLORE, and is currently editor of *Western Folklore*.

A PRELIMINARY BIBLIOGRAPHY
OF URBAN FOLKLORE MATERIALS

Richard A. Reuss and
Ellen J. Stekert

As consciously recognized phenomena, urban folklore studies are a relatively new feature in folklore activity, having developed in substantial number only in the past decade.[1] However, traditions in and of the city environment long have been collected and studied by scholars under other names, most frequently with reference to investigations of the lore of immigrants, rural peoples transplanted to the urban milieu, certain industrial and professional occupations, and special subcultures primarily identified with urban contexts, such as college students and the military.

The purpose of this bibliography is to provide a working guide to various types of urban folklore literature available to the scholar as of March, 1971. It makes no pretense of being exhaustive even insofar as the standard folklore publications go, though we have tried to cover the more current periodical and monograph material as thoroughly as possible. We also have culled references to relevant articles from such journals as the *American Journal of Sociology* and *Human Organization*, which are listed below, but we would note that these indeed represent only a small sampling of the useful social science literature. It is our contention that urban folklore cannot be meaningfully comprehended or assessed, either from a humanistic or a cultural perspective, unless some attention is given to the social organization, structure, and functional operation of the many groups comprising contemporary urban society. Regrettably, folklorists have been slow not only in turning their attention to the study of tradition in an urban context but also in grasping the importance of mastering the knowledge of a culture as well as its lore. Consequently one must turn to the adjacent social science disciplines for much of the needed data.

This bibliography therefore is a *potpourri* of sound analytical studies, descriptive essays and impressionistic reminiscences, folk narrative and song collections with traditional type, motif, and other classification numbers, selected relevant anthropological and sociological works, theoretical and historical writings on urban folklore and culture problems, monographs and brief notes, and so on. The arrangement of the items cited is arbitrary and utilitarian in character; in ordering the material presented we are aware of the conceptual difficulties inherent in organizing such a mass of diverse data. In the

---

[1] While it is not possible here to give a history of urban folklore study in the United States or elsewhere, we think it worth mentioning the names of three individuals who must be considered "pioneers" in the study of urban traditions in our own country. B. A. Botkin's books, *Sidewalks of America* (1954) and *New York City* (1956), while popular anthologies with limited academic apparatus, did call attention to the many varieties of city lore. Richard M. Dorson's "Modern Folklore" in *American Folklore* (1959) was also influential, positing the notion that urban centers indeed were a rich source of indigenous traditions. Roger D. Abraham's *Deep Down in the Jungle . . .* (1964) was the first book-length academic study of a body of urban (nonimmigrant) folklore to integrate literary and cultural methodology.

interests of expediency, we have limited ourselves principally to a listing of materials from American folklore publications though we have seen fit to include some discussion of urban traditions in foreign periodicals and books. We likewise have not ventured very far from academic sources in compiling our bibliography, for the gamut of popular discussion and raw collections available in the mass media is endless and undoubtedly would prove a morass from which this survey might never be extricated. Similarly, our annotations—where they exist at all—are of the utmost brevity and solely descriptive. We trust that the interested reader will take the trouble to evaluate and criticize specific readings himself as research requires.

We cannot conclude without a word of thanks to the many students and colleagues who contributed to this bibliography by providing references to additional sources or by calling attention to material overlooked, especially in publications off the beaten track. We especially appreciate the efforts of Barbara Kirschenblatt-Gimblett and Roger D. Abrahams in this regard. It is our hope that this preliminary list soon may be supplemented by a much more extensive survey of new and valuable publications pertaining to the study of urban folklore.

Wayne State University
Detroit, Michigan

ABBREVIATIONS USED

AA	*American Anthropologist*	JAF	*Journal of American Folklore*
AJS	*American Journal of Sociology*	JPC	*Journal of Popular Culture*
AS	*American Speech*	KFR	*Kentucky Folklore Record*
ASR	*American Sociological Review*	KSFQ	*Keystone Folklore Quarterly*
CFQ	*California Folklore Quarterly* (now *Western Folklore*)	MF	*Midwest Folklore*
		NYFQ	*New York Folklore Quarterly*
EM	*Ethnomusicology*	SFQ	*Southern Folklore Quarterly*
FF	*Folklore Forum*	TFSB	*Tennessee Folklore Society Bulletin*
HF	*Hoosier Folklore*		
IF	*Indiana Folklore*	WF	*Western Folklore*

I. Bibliography

Haywood, Charles. *A Bibliography of North American Folklore and Folksong.* 2d rev. ed. New York, 1961. Scattered references to urban lore.

II. Theoretical, Conceptual, and Historical Problems Relevant to the General Study of Urban Folklore.

Abu-Lughod, Janet. "Urban-Rural Differences as a Function of the Demographic Transition." *AJS*, 69 (1964), 476–490.

Aurbach, Herbert A. "An Empirical Study in the Application of the Folk-Urban Typology to the Classification of Social Systems." Ph.D. dissertation, University of Kentucky, 1960.

Axelrod, Morris. "Urban Structure and Social Participation." *ASR*, 21 (1956), 13–18.

Beers, H. W., and Heslin, C. "The Urban Status of Rural Migrants." In *Urban Adjust-*

ments of Rural Migrants: A Study of 297 Families in Lexington, Ky., 1942. Kentucky Agricultural Experiment Station Bulletin 487. Lexington, 1946.

Bell, Wendell. "Urban Neighborhoods and Informal Social Relations." AJS, 62 (1956–1957), 391–398.

Benton, Michael P., ed. The Social Anthropology of Complex Societies. New York, 1966.

Cox, Harvey. The Secular City: Secularization and Urbanization in Theological Perspective. New York, 1965.

de Caro, Frank A. "Urban Folklore in the Nineteenth Century." FF, 1 (1968), [10–11].

Dorson, Richard M. "Is There a Folk in the City?" JAF (special issue), 83:328 (1970), 185–216. Prepared comments by Linda Dégh and Leonard W. Moss, pp. 217–224, and reply by Dorson, pp. 224–225.

Fishwick, Marshall. "Folklore, Fakelore and Poplore." Saturday Review, 50 (August 26, 1967), 20–21.

"The Folklore Scene" column, NYFQ, frequently contains items of a miscellaneous character relevant to urban folklore.

Foster, George M. "What Is Folk Culture?" AA, 55 (1953), 159–173.

Jackson, George Pullen. "Revolution in Pittsburgh." TFSB, 12 (1946), 1–6. Dealing with the mishandling of folk materials in urban schools.

James, Thelma. "Report on Wayne University Archives." MF, 5 (1955), 62–64.

Kahl, Joseph. "Some Social Concomitants of Industrialization and Urbanization." Human Organization, 18 (1959), 53–74.

Komarovsky, Mirra. "The Voluntary Associations of Urban Dwellers." ASR, 11 (1946), 686–698.

Leeds, Morton. "The Process of Cultural Stripping and Reintegration: The Rural Migrant in the City." JAF (special issue), 83:328 (1970), 259–267. Prepared comments by Lawrence E. Gary, pp. 268–270, and reply by Leeds, p. 270.

Miner, Horace. "The Folk-Urban Continuum." ASR, 17 (1952), 529–537.

Munch, Peter A. "A Study of Cultural Change: Rural-Urban Conflicts in Norway." Studia Norvegica, 3 (1956), 1–104.

Paredes, Américo. "Introduction" to "The Urban Experience and Folk Tradition." JAF (special issue), 83:328 (1970).

Redfield, Robert. "The Folk Society." AJS, 52 (1947), 293–308.

Seeger, Charles. "Folk Music in the Schools of a Highly Industrialized Society." Journal of the International Folk Music Council, 5 (1953), 40–44.

———. "The Folkness of the Non-Folk vs. the Non-Folkness of the Folk." In Folklore and Society, edited by Bruce Jackson, pp. 1–9. Hatboro, Pa., 1966.

Stekert, Ellen J. "Foreword" to "The Urban Experience and Folk Tradition." JAF (special issue), 83:328 (1970).

Vidich, Arthur J., and Bensman, Joseph. Small Town in Mass Society. Garden City, N.Y., 1960.

Wirth, Louis. "Urbanism as a Way of Life." AJS, 44 (1958), 1–24.

Wright, George O. "Projection and Displacement: A Cross-cultural Study of Folktale Aggression." Journal of Abnormal and Social Psychology, 49 (1954), 523–528. On the displacement of groups.

III. Genre

Folksongs

Anderson, E. N., Jr. "The Folksongs of the Hong Kong Boat People." *JAF*, 80 (1967), 285–296.

Belz, Carl I. "Popular Music and Folk Tradition." *JAF*, 80 (1967), 130–142.

Cantrick, Robert P. "The Blind Men and the Elephant: Scholars on Popular Music." *EM*, 9 (1965), 100–114.

Cohen, Norman. "Tin Pan Alley's Contribution to Folk Music." *WF*, 29 (1970), 9–20.

———. "The Skillet Lickers: A Study of a Hillbilly String Band and Its Repertoire." *JAF* (Hillbilly issue), 78 (1965), 229–244.

Cray, Ed. *The Erotic Muse*. New York 1969.

Denisoff, R. Serge. "The Proletarian Renascence: The Folkness of the Ideological Folk." *JAF*, 82 (1969), 51–65.

———. "The Religious Roots of the American Song of Persuasion." *WF*, 29 (1970), 175–184.

———. "Rock Folk Music, Protest, or Commercialism?" *JPC*, 3 (1969), 214–230.

———. "Songs of Persuasion: A Sociological Analysis of Urban Propaganda Songs." *JAF*, 79 (1966), 581–588.

———. " 'Take It Easy but Take It': The Almanac Singers." *JAF*, 83 (1970), 21–32.

Downey, James C. "Revivalism, the Gospel Songs, and Social Reform." *EM*, 9 (1965), 115–125.

Evanson, Jacob A. "Folk Songs of an Industrial City" (Pittsburgh). In *Pennsylvania Songs and Legends*, edited by George Korson, pp. 423–466. Philadelphia, Pa., 1949.

———. "Pittsburgh-Region Folksongs for Pittsburgh Children." *KSFQ*, 5 (1960), 30–40.

Faier, Billy. "Folk Singing Styles and the Phonograph Record." *Folk Music*, 1 (June, 1964), 24–29, 31.

Goldstein, Kenneth S. "The Ballad Scholar and the Long-Playing Record." In *Folklore and Society*, edited by Bruce Jackson, pp. 35–44. Hatboro, Pa., 1966.

Green, Archie. "Hillbilly Music: Source and Symbol." *JAF* (Hillbilly issue), 78 (1965), 204–228.

Greenway, John. *American Folksongs of Protest*. Philadelphia, Pa., 1953.

———. "Jimmie Rodgers—a Folksong Catalyst." *JAF*, 70 (1957), 231–234.

Gronow, Pekka. "International Trends in Popular Music." *EM*, 13 (1969), 313–316.

Hall, James A. "Concepts of Liberty in American Broadside Ballads 1850–1870: A Study of the Mind of American Mass Culture." *JPC*, 2 (1968), 252–277.

Kahn, Ed. "Hillbilly Music: Source and Resource." *JAF* (Hillbilly issue), 78 (1965), 257–266.

Laufe, Abe. "Sing Along Songs." *KSFQ*, 10 (1965), 35–42.

Letich, Bonnie. "Saturday Night and Sunday Morning: Honky-Tonk and Gospel Meeting in Country Music." *Folklore Annual No. 2 of the University Folklore Association*, pp. 67–71. Austin, Texas, 1970.

Malone, Bill C. *Country Music, U.S.A.* Austin, Texas, 1968.

McCulloh, Judith. "Some Child Ballads on Hillbilly Records." In *Folklore and Society*, edited by Bruce Jackson, pp. 107–129. Hatboro, Pa., 1966.

Merriam, Alan P., and Garner, Fradley H. "Jazz—the Word." *EM*, 12 (1968), 373–396.

Morgan, Sandi. "Antiwar Protest Songs: Folklore in a Modern Age." *Folklore Annual No. 2* of the University Folklore Association, pp. 73–80. Austin, Texas, 1970.

Nettl, Bruno. "Preliminary Remarks on Urban Folk Music in Detroit." *WF*, 16 (1957), 37–42.

Rhodes, Willard. "Folk Music, Old and New." In *Folklore and Society*, edited by Bruce Jackson, pp. 11–20. Hatboro, Pa., 1966.

Rosenberg, Neil V. "From Sound to Style: The Emergence of Bluegrass." *JAF*, 80 (1967), 143–150.

Smith, L. Mayne. "An Introduction to Bluegrass." *JAF* (Hillbilly issue), 78 (1965), 245–256.

Stearns, Marshall and Jean. "Vernacular Dance in Musical Comedy: Harlem Takes the Lead." *NYFQ*, 22 (1966), 251–260.

Stekert, Ellen J. "Cents and Nonsense in the Urban Folksong Movement: 1930–1966." In *Folklore and Society*, edited by Bruce Jackson, pp. 153–168. Hatboro, Pa., 1966.

Tallmadge, William H. "The Responsorial and Antiphonal Practice in Gospel Song." *EM*, 12 (1968), 219–238.

Truzzi, Marcello. "The 100% American Songbag: Conservative Folksongs." *WF*, 28 (1969), 27–40.

Upadhyaya, Hari S. "Collection of Folksongs from and the Life History of a Bhojpuri Folksinger of India." *TFSB*, 34 (1968), 87–92.

Vega, Carlos. "Mesomusic: An Essay on the Music of the Masses." *EM*, 10 (1966), 1–17.

Wilgus, D. K. "Country-Western Music and the Urban Hillbilly." *JAF* (special issue), 83:328 (1970), 157–179. Prepared comments by Judith McCulloh, pp. 180–182.

———. "The Hillbilly Movement." In *Our Living Traditions*, edited by Tristram P. Coffin, pp. 263–271. New York, 1968.

———. "An Introduction to the Study of Hillbilly Music." *JAF* (Hillbilly issue), 78 (1965), 195–203.

———. "The Rationalistic Approach." In *Folksong and Folksong Scholarship*, edited by Roger D. Abrahams, pp. 29–38. Dallas, Texas, 1964. Reprinted from *A Good Tale and a Bonnie Tune*, Texas Folklore Society Publication XXXII. In part a discussion of the importance of considering commercial and popular source materials in the study of folksong.

Tales and Legends

Barnes, Daniel R. "Some Functional Horror Stories on the Kansas University Campus." *SFQ*, 30 (1966), 305–312.

Beardsley, Richard K., and Hankey, Rosalie. "More on the 'Vanishing Hitchhiker.'" *CFQ*, 2 (1943), 13–26.

———. "The Vanishing Hitchhiker." *CFQ*, 1 (1942), 305–335.

Bennett, John. *The Doctor to the Devil* (Grotesque Legends and Folk Tales of Old Charleston). New York, 1946.

———. "Folk Tales from Old Charleston." *Yale Review*, 32 (1943), 721–740.

Burgess, Don. "Russian Astronauts First to Land on Moon." *WF*, 29 (1970), 192–193.

Byrd, James W. "'Traveling Anecdotes' and War." *TFSB*, 34 (1968), 50–51.

Carter, Albert H. "Some Folk Tales of the Big City." *Arkansas Folklore*, 4 (August 15, 1953), 4–6.

Clarke, Kenneth. "The Fatal Hairdo and the Emperor's New Clothes Revisited." *WF*, 23 (1964), 249–252. "Analysis" of an urban legend satirizing structural and psychological folklore approaches.

Cohen, Bernard, and Ehrenpreis, Irvin. "Tales from Indiana University Students." *HF*, 6 (1947), 57–65.

Cord, Xenia E. "Department Store Snakes." *IF*, 2 (1969), 110–114.

Dégh, Linda, and Others. "Folk Legends of Indiana." *IF* (special issue), 1 (1968), 9–109. See also *IF*, 2 (1969), 3–74, for many individual urban legend studies.

Edgerton, William B. "The Ghost in Search of Help for a Dying Man." *JFI*, 5 (1968), 31–41.

Gallant, Samuel, and Shapiro, Irwin. "Two Urban Folk Tales." *NYFQ*, 4 (1946), 276–278.

Girdler, Lew. "The Legend of the Second Blue Book." *WF*, 29 (1970), 111–113.

Hartika, H. D. "Tales Collected from Indiana University Students." *HF*, 5 (1946), 71–82.

Hawes, Bess Lomax. "La Llorona in Juvenile Hall." *WF*, 27 (1968), 153–170.

Hermann, H. M. "Folk Humorist from Brooklyn." *The New York Times Magazine*, December 17, 1950, pp. 114ff.

Howard, James. "Tales of Nieman-Marcus." *Folk Travelers*, Texas Folklore Publications XXV, pp. 160–170. Austin and Dallas, 1953.

Jagendorf, Moritz. "Tales of New York City." *NYFQ*, 21 (1965), 194–206.

Jones, Louis. "Hitchhiking Ghosts in New York." *CFQ*, 3 (1944), 284–292.

"McCartney's Lyle-Wake." *FF*, 2 (1969), 167–168.

Miller, William Marion. "A Modern Atrocity Story." *JAF*, 58 (1945), 156–157. World War II Japanese atrocity tale.

———. "Another Phantom Hitchhiker Story." *HF*, 5 (1946), 40–41.

Mitchell, Carol A. "The White House." *IF*, 2 (1969), 97–109. Fort Wayne place legend.

Neely, Charles. "Ghost Stories in Egypt." In *Tales and Songs of Southern Illinois*. McNasha, Wisc., 1938.

O'Bryant, Joan. "Two Versions of 'The Shipman's Tale' from Urban Oral Tradition." *WF*, 24 (1965), 101–103.

Parochetti, Joann S. "Scary Stories from Purdue." *KSFQ*, 10 (1965), 49–57.

Peckham, Howard H. "Folklore of the Homefront." *HF*, 6 (1947), 101–102.

Reaver, J. Russell. "Embalmed Alive: A Developing Urban Ghost Tale." *NYFQ*, 8 (1952), 217–220.

Reuss, Richard A. "More Current Folk Tales." *Australian Tradition*, no. 20 (August, 1969), 28–29. (See also Bill Scott, "Current Folk Tales.")

Ridley, Florence H. "A Tale Told Too Often." *WF*, 26 (1967), 153–156. Ancient and current versions of the "Sir Hugh" mutilation story.

Schnapper, M. B. "Tall Tale Teller from Paducah." *The New York Times Magazine*, November 18, 1951, p. 22.

Scott, Bill. "Current Folk Tales." *Australian Tradition*, no. 19 (March, 1969), 3–4. Urban legends in Australia.

Wilson, William A. "Mormon Legends of the Three Nephites Collected at Indiana University." *IF*, 2 (1969), 3–35.

Woodward, Robert H. "The Stolen Grandma." *Northwest Folklore*, 1 (1965), 20.

Humor (Jokes and Rhymes)

Abrahams, Roger D. "Ghastly Commands: The Cruel Joke Revisited." *MF*, 11 (1961), 235–246.

———, and Wukasch, Charles. "Political Folklore of East Germany." *TFSB*, 33 (1967), 7–10.

Adams, Cindy. ". . . And Then There's the One about the Joke Collector." *TV Guide*, October 25, 1969, pp. 16–18. About Leo Fechtner, great humor collector.

Attebery, Louie. "Governor Jokes." *SFQ*, 33 (1969), 350–351.

Barrick, Mac E. "Racial Riddles and the Polack Joke." *KSFQ*, 15 (1970), 3–15.

———. "The Shaggy Elephant Riddle." *SFQ*, 28 (1964), 266–290.

———. "You Can Tell a Joke with Vigah if It's about a Niggah." *KSFQ*, 9 (1964), 166–168.

Brunvand, Jan Harold. "Classification for Shaggy Dog Stories." *JAF*, 76 (1963), 42–68.

Burns, Tom. "Involving the Introductory Student of Folklore in the Functional Analysis of the Material He Collects." *Perspectives on Folklore and Education,* Folklore Forum Bibliographic and Special Series no. 2 (May, 1969), 13–27. Includes modern jokelore.

"Campus Joke Books." *Newsweek*, March 30, 1959, pp. 96–97.

Clements, William M. *The Types of the Polack Joke.* Folklore Forum Bibliographic and Special Series no. 3 (November, 1969).

Crane, Maurice. "Bop Jokes." *JAF*, 73 (1960), 249.

Cray, Ed. "The Rabbi Trickster." *JAF*, 77 (1964), 331–345.

Cross, Paulette. "Jokes and Black Consciousness." *Folklore Forum*, 2 (1969), 149–161.

Dempsey, John. "Why Automation Is a Laughing Matter." *Fact* (September–October, 1966), pp. 17–19. Psychological analysis of computer jokes.

Dorson, Richard M. "Jewish American Dialect Stories on Tape." In *Studies in Biblical and Jewish Folklore*, edited by Raphael Patai and others, pp. 111–177. Bloomington, Indiana, 1960.

———. "More Jewish Dialect Stories." *MF*, 10 (1960), 133–146.

Dundes, Alan. "Here I Sit—a Study of American Latrinalia." *Kroeber Anthropological Society Papers*, no. 34 (Spring, 1966).

———, and Abrahams, Roger D. "On Elephantasy and Elephanticide." *The Psychoanalytic Review*, 56 (1969), 225–241.

———. "The Passing of the President in Oral Tradition." *TFSB*, 30 (1964), 127–128.

Jason, Heda. "The Jewish Joke: The Problem of Definition." *SFQ*, 31 (1967), 48–54.

Johnson, Jerah. "Professor Einstein and the Chorus Girl." *JAF*, 73 (1960), 248.

LaBarre, Weston. "The Psychotherapy of Drinking Songs." *Psychiatry*, 2 (1939), 203–212. About limericks.

[Legman, G.]. *The Limerick*. Paris, 1953. Reprinted in two paperback volumes by Greenleaf Publications.

————. *The Rationale of the Dirty Joke*, Part I. New York, 1968. Part II is forthcoming.

Middleton, R., and Moland, J. "Humor in Negro and White Subcultures: A Study of Jokes among University Students." *ASR*, 24 (1959), 61–69.

Monteiro, George. "Parodies of Scripture, Prayers, and Hymns." *JAF*, 77 (1964), 45–62.

Partridge, Eric. *The "Shaggy Dog" Story: Its Origins, Development, and Nature*. London and New York, 1953.

Porter, Kenneth W. "Humor, Blasphemy, and Criticism in the Grace before Meat." *NYFQ*, 21 (1965), 3–18.

————. "More Examples of Humor, Blasphemy, and Criticism in the Grace before Meat." *NYFQ*, 24 (1968), 64–66.

Rourke, Constance. *American Humor*. New York, 1931.

Schmaier, Maurice D. "The Doll Joke Pattern in Contemporary American Oral Humor." *MF*, 13 (1963), 205–216.

Sutton-Smith, Brian. " 'Shut Up and Keep Diggin': The Cruel Joke Series." *MF*, 10 (1960), 11–22.

Varisco, Raymond. "Campaign Jokes—Goldwater and Johnson." *TFSB*, 31 (1965), 108–112.

Walker, G. "The Way Those Joke Cycles Start." *The New York Times Magazine*, October 26, 1958, pp. 32ff.

Welsch, Roger L. "American Numskull Tales: The Polack Joke." *WF*, 26 (1967), 183–186.

Folk Heroes and Characters

Asbury, Herbert. "The Noble Experiment of Izzie and Moe." In *The Aspirin Age*, edited by Isabel Leighton, pp. 34–50. New York, 1949.

Bernstein, A. A. "Queen of the Bowery." *NYFQ*, 23 (1967), 196–201.

Dorson, Richard M. "Mose the Far-Famed and World-Renowned." *American Literature*, 15 (1943), 288–300.

Hoffman, Daniel G. *Paul Bunyan: Last of the Frontier Demi-Gods*. Philadelphia, 1952.

Thomas, W. Stephen. "Folklore Figures of Rochester, N.Y." *NYFQ*, 10 (1954), 9–17.

Beliefs

Barrett, Linda K. and Vogt, Evon S. "The Urban American Dowser." *JAF*, 82 (1969), 195–213.

Beckwith, Martha. "Signs and Superstitions Collected from American College Girls." *JAF*, 30 (1923), 1–15.

Buckley, Tom. "The Signs are Right for Astrology." *The New York Times Magazine*, December 15, 1968, pp. 30–31, 133–139, 142, 144–146.

Davidson, Levette J. "Superstitions Collected in Denver, Colorado." *WF*, 13 (1954), 184–189.

deLavigne, Jeanne. *Ghost Stories of Old New Orleans.* New York, 1964.

Del Bourgo, Fanya. (as told to B. A. Botkin). "Love in the City." *NYFQ*, 21 (1965), 165–178. Additional comments by B. A. Botkin, pp. 231–233. Mores and customs of New York City at the turn of the century regarding youngsters' learning about sex.

Herzfeld, Ella G. "Superstitions of the Tenement-House Mother." *Charities*, 14 (1905), 983–986.

Holbrook, Stewart. *The Golden Age of Quackery.* New York, 1959.

Jones, Louis. "The Ghosts of New York. An Analytical Study." *JAF*, 57 (1944), 237–254.

————. *Things That Go Bump in the Night.* Austin and New York, 1959.

Passin, Herbert and Bennett, John W. "Changing Agricultural Magic in Southern Illinois: A Systematic Analysis of Folk-Urban Transition." In *The Study of Folklore*, edited by Alan Dundes, pp. 314–328. Englewood Cliffs, N.J., 1965.

Stekert, Ellen J. "Focus for Conflict: Southern Mountain Medical Beliefs in Detroit." *JAF* (special issue), 83:328 (1970), 115–147. Prepared comments by Marion Pearsall, pp. 148–152, and reply by Stekert, pp. 152–155.

Sutton, Thomas C. and Marilyn. "Science Fiction as Mythology." *WF*, 28 (1969), 230–237.

Tallant, Robert. *Voodoo in New Orleans.* New York, 1946.

Wine, Martin L. "Superstitions Collected in Chicago" *MF*, 7 (1957), 149–158.

Customs, Rites, and Ceremonies

Anderson, John Q. "For the Ugliest Man: An Example of Folk Humor." *SFQ*, 28 (1964), 199–209.

Bosmajian, Haig A. "The Use of the Symbol 'Unknown' in Nazi Persuasion." *Folklore*, 77 (1966), 116–122.

Friedman, Albert B. "The Scatological Rites of Burglars." *WF*, 27 (1968), 171–179.

Glah, Robert A. "The Philadelphia Mummers: A New Year Pageant." *NYFQ*, 8 (1952), 291–300.

Herald, Childe. "Freud and Football." In *Reader in Comparative Religion*, edited by William A. Lessa and Evon Z. Vogt, pp. 250–252. New York, 1965. Football as ceremony and ritual.

Mitford, Jessica. *The American Way of Death.* New York, 1963.

Mook, Maurice. "Halloween in Central Pennsylvania." *KSFQ*, 14 (1969), 124–129.

Talley, Jeannine E. "Ritual Defecation and Defilement" *WF*, 29 (1970), 193–194.

Warner, Lloyd W. "An American Sacred Ceremony." In *Reader in Comparative Religion*, edited by William A. Lessa and Evon Z. Vogt, pp. 216–226. New York, 1965. About Memorial Day celebrations. Reprinted from Warner's book *American Life*, 1953.

Welch, Charles E., Jr. "The 'Blackface' Controversy in the Philadelphia Mummers Parade: The Trial of a Tradition." *KSFQ*, 9 (1964), 154–165.

————. " 'Common Nuisance'—the Evolution of the Philadelphia Mummers Parade." *KSFQ*, 8 (1963), 95–106.

————. "Oh, Dem Golden Slippers: The Philadelphia Mummers Parade." *JAF*, 79 (1966), 523–536.

Winkler, Carol and Louis. "Thousands of Years of Halloween." *NYFQ*, 26 (1970), 204–215.

Proverbs and Speech

Ainsworth, Catherine Harris. "Black and White and Said All Over." *SFQ*, 26 (1962), 263–295.

Babbitt, E. H. "The English of Lower Classes in New York and Vicinity." *Dialect Notes*, 1 (1890–1896), 457–464.

Baldwin, L. Karen. "A Sampling of Housewives' Proverbs and Proverbial Phrases from Levittown, Pa." *KSFQ*, 10 (1965), 127–148.

Bauman, Richard, "The Turtles: An American Riddling Institution." *WF*, 29 (1970), 21–25.

Botkin, B. A. "The Spiels of New York." *NYFQ*, 9 (1953), 165–175.

Brunvand, Jan Harold. "Some Thoughts on the Ethnic-Regional Riddle Joke." *IF*, 3 (1970), 128–142.

Legman, Gershon. "The Limerick: A History in Brief." In *The Horn Book: Studies in Erotic Folklore and Bibliography*, pp. 427–453. New York, 1964.

Loomis, C. Grant. "American Limerick Traditions." *WF*, 22 (1963), 153–158.

McKelvie, Donald. "Proverbial Elements in the Oral Tradition of an English Urban Industrial Region." *JFI*, 2 (1965), 244–261.

Pinkowski, Edward. "Philadelphia Street Cries." *KSFQ*, 5 (1960), 10–12.

Rea, J. "Seeing the Elephant." *WF*, 28 (1969), 21–26. Proverb history.

Rennick, Robert M. "The Brooklyn Public Library's Baby-Naming Service." *NYFQ*, 24 (1968), 212–220.

———. "The Folklore of Curious and Unusual Names." *NYFQ*, 22 (1966), 5–14.

———. "The Inadvertent Changing of Non-English Names by Newcomers to America: A Brief Historical Survey and Popular Presentation of Cases." *NYFQ*, 26 (1970), 263–282.

———. "Successive Name-Changing: A Popular Theme in Onomastic Folklore and Literature." *NYFQ*, 25 (1969), 119–128.

Stimson, Anna K. "Cries of Defiance and Derision and Rhythmic Chants of West Side New York, 1893–1903." *JAF*, 58 (1945), 124–129.

Uysal, Ahmet E. "Street Cries in Turkey." *JAF*, 81 (1968), 193–215.

Very, Francis, "Parody and Nickname among American Youth." *JAF*, 75 (1962), 262–263.

Weiner, Meryl. "The Riddle Repertoire of a Massachusetts Elementary School." *FF*, 3 (1970), 7–38.

Winslow, David. "Folklore in the Chester Commonplace Book." *SFQ*, 30 (1966), 236–248.

Wylie, Jim. "What They Are Saying." *Esquire* (July, 1965), pp. 44–45. Modern hip language, folkspeech, especially teenage.

Miscellaneous Genres

Davidson, Levette J. "Some Current Folk Gestures and Sign Language." *American Speech*, 25 (1950), 3–9.

Dundes, Alan. "Some Minor Genres of American Folklore." *SFQ*, 31 (1967), 20–36.

———, and Georges, Robert. "Some Minor Genres of Obscene Folklore." *JAF*, 75 (1962), 221–226.

McNeil, W. K. "From Advice to Laments: New York Autograph Album Verse, 1820–1850." *NYFQ*, 25 (1969), 175–194.

————. "From Advice to Laments Once Again: New York Autograph Album Verse, 1850–1900." *NYFQ*, 26 (1970), 163–203.

Walter, Marie-Louis. "Folk Art in the New York Subway." *NYFQ*, 14 (1958), 268–270.

IV. Miscellaneous Lore Organized by Cities

Asbury, Herbert. *The Barbary Coast*. New York, 1933. Description of life and history of notorious section of San Francisco. Some coverage of underworld lore, Chinese customs, etc.

Bleakney, F. Eileen. "Folklore from Ottawa and Vicinity." *JAF*, 31 (1918), 158–169.

Botkin, B. A. "Living Lore of the New York City Writers' Project." *NYFQ*, 2 (1946), 252–263.

————. *New York City Folklore*. New York, 1956.

————. *Sidewalks of America*. Indianapolis, 1954.

Celoria, Frances. "A Preliminary Survey of London Folklore." *JFI*, 2 (1965), 262–265.

Dorson, Richard M. *American Folklore*. Chicago, 1959.

————. "Folklore at a Milwaukee Wedding." *HF*, 6 (1947), 1–13.

Edwards, G. D. "Items of American Folklore Collected in Boston." *JAF*, 12 (1899), 97–107.

Huddleston, Eugene L. "Depictions of New York in Early American Poetry." *NYFQ*, 24 (1968), 275–293.

Korson, George. *Pennsylvania Songs and Legends*, pp. 423–466. Philadelphia, 1949.

Rowles, Catharine Bryant. "Lore and Legends from Johnstown." *NYFQ*, 21 (1965), 109–118.

Schwartz, Tony. "I Record the Sounds of Life around Us." *Sing Out!* 8:3 (1959), 27–29.

————. *New York 19*. Folkways Record FD 5558.

————. *Sounds of My City*. Folkways Record FC 7341.

Singer, Milton. "The Great Tradition in a Metropolitan Center: Madras." *JAF*, 71 (1958), 347–388.

Still, Bayrd. "The Personality of New York City." *NYFQ*, 14 (1958), 83–92.

V. Immigrant Group Lore

General and Theoretical

Dégh, Linda. "Approaches to Folklore Research among Immigrant Groups." *JAF*, 79 (1966), 551–556.

Dorson, Richard M. "Ethnohistory and Ethnic Folklore." *Ethnohistory*, 8 (1961), 12–30.

Erdely, Stephen. "Research on Traditional Music of Nationality Groups in Cleveland and Vicinity." *EM*, 12 (1968), 245–250.

Handlin, Oscar. *The Uprooted*. Boston, 1951.

————. *Children of the Uprooted*. New York, 1966, 1968.

Haugen, Einar. *Bilingualism in the Americas: A Bibliography and Research Guide*. Publication of the American Dialect Society, no. 26. University, Alabama, 1956.

Köngäs, Elli Kaija. "Immigrant Folklore: Survival of Living Tradition." *MF*, 10 (1960), 117–127.

Harris, Pauline Beatrice. *Spanish and Mexican Folklore as Represented in Two Families in the Detroit Area.* M.A. Thesis, Wayne University, 1949.

Hauptmann, O. H. "Spanish Folklore from Tampa, Florida (IV) Superstitions." *SFQ*, 2:1 (1938), 11–31.

Schinhan, Jan Philip. "Spanish Folklore from Tampa, Florida (VI) Folksongs." *SFQ*, 3 (1939), 129–163.

Zeehandlaar, F. J. "La fiesta de los angeles." *Arrowhead Magazine*, 1 (February, 1906).

Miscellaneous Northern and Western European

Flom, George T. "English Elements in Norse Dialects of Utica, Wisconsin." *Dialect Notes II* (part 4), 257–268.

Hare, Maud Cuney. "Portuguese Folk Songs from Provincetown." *Musical Quarterly*, 14 (1928), 35–53.

Köngäs, Elli Kaija. "Nicknames of Finnish Apartment Houses in Brooklyn, N.Y." *JAF*, 77 (1964), 80–81.

Lang, Henry R. "The Portuguese Element in New England." *JAF*, 5 (1892), 9–15.

Rogers, W. Stuart. "Irish Lore Collected in Schenectady." *NYFQ*, 8 (1952), 20–30.

Miscellaneous Central and Eastern European

Balys, Jonas. "Lithuanian Ghost Stories from Pittsburgh, Pennsylvania." *MF*, 2 (1952), 47–52.

Bonos, Arlene Helen. "Romany Rye of Philadelphia." *AA*, 44 (1942), 251–274. Lore among four gypsy tribes of Philadelphia.

Borcherdt, Donn. "Armenian Folk Songs and Dances in the Fresno and Los Angeles Areas." *WF*, 19 (1959), 1–12.

Cincura, Andrew. "Slovak and Ruthenian Easter Eggs in America: The Impact of Culture Contact on Immigrant Art and Custom." *JPC*, 4 (1970), 155–193. Cleveland.

Dégh, Linda. "Two Old World Narrators in Urban Setting." In *Kontakte und Grenzen: Probleme der Volks-, Kultur- und Sozialforschung.* Festschrift für Gerhard Heilfurth zum 60. Geburtstag Herausgegeben von seinen Mitarbeitern. Göttingen, Germany, 1969. In English.

Edwards, G. D. "Items of Armenian Folklore Collected in Boston." *JAF*, 12 (1899), 97–107.

Erdely, Stephen. "Folksinging of the American Hungarian in Cleveland." *EM*, 8 (1964), 14–27.

Halpert, Herbert. "Hungarian Lying-Contest Tales About America." *NYFQ*, 1 (1945), 236–237.

Hoogasian, Susie and Gardner, Emelyn E., eds. "Armenian Tales Collected in Detroit." *JAF*, 57 (1944), 161–180.

Hoogasian-Villa, Susie. *100 Armenian Tales and Their Folkloristic Relevance.* Detroit, 1966. Foreword by Thelma James.

Lakowski, Cornelius J. "Polish Tales of the Supernatural Collected in Albany, N.Y." *NYFQ*, 10 (1954), 165–175.

Logan, Edgar. "The Strange Ones." *Human Relations Review*, 6 (1966), 10–11. Detroit gypsy population beliefs and culture.

Montgomery, Margaret. "Slovenian Folklore in Indianapolis." *HF*, 6 (1947), 121–132.

Nettl, Bruno and Moravcik, Ivo. "Czech and Slovak Songs Collected in Detroit." *MF*, 5 (1955), 37–49.

Pawlowska, Harriet M. *Merrily We Sing: 105 Polish Folksongs.* Detroit, 1961.

Pirkova-Jakobson, Svatava. "The Folk-Narratives of the Slavic Emigrants in America: A Study in Acculturation with Two Examples." *IV International Congress for Folk-Narrative Research in Athens: Lectures and Reports,* ed. Georgios A. Megas, pp. 185–190. Athens, 1965.

————. "Functional Study of Czecho-Slovakian Folksong." Folklore Institute of America *Annual Report, 1946.* 4 pp. mimeo. Subsections on "Study of Czech folksong in New York," etc.

————. "Harvest Festivals among Czechs and Slovaks in America." *JAF*, 69 (1956), 266–280.

Tilney, Philip V. R. "The Immigrant Macedonian Wedding." *IF*, 3 (1970), 3–34.

Ware, Helen. "The American-Hungarian Folk-Song." *Musical Quarterly*, 2 (1916), 434–441.

"Wayne University Project to Record Polish Culture." *Michigan History*, 26 (1942), 407–408.

Asia (China and Japan)

Asbury, Herbert. "Chinese in Boston." *JAF*, 5 (1892), 321–324.

"Cantonese Riddles in San Francisco." *WF*, 6 (1947), 68–72.

Genthe, Arnold. *Pictures of Old Chinatown.* New York, 1909.

Hoffman, Charles. "Japanese Folk Songs in New York City." *JAF*, 59 (1946), 325–326. No texts—discussion of records.

Hoy, William J. "Chinatown Devises Its Own Street Names." *CFQ*, 2 (1943), 71–75.

Kawamoto, Fumi. "Folk Beliefs among Japanese in the Los Angeles Area." *WF*, 21 (1962), 13–26.

Opler, Marvin K. "Japanese Folk Beliefs and Practices, Tule Lake, California." *JAF*, 63 (1950), 385–397.

Wang, Joseph. "The Bill Collector: A Chinese Ghost Tale from New York City." *NYFQ*, 1 (1945), 231–232.

Wood, Willard. "A New Year's Celebration in China Town." *Sunset* 2:1 (May, 1903), 59.

Other

Naff, Alixa. "Belief in the Evil Eye among the Christian Syrian-Lebanese in America." *JAF*, 78 (1965), 46–51.

Pelly, Francine. "Gypsy Folktales from Philadelphia." *KSFQ*, 13 (1968), 83–102.

Wilson, Howard Barnett. "Syrian Tales from Boston." *JAF*, 16 (1903), 133–147.

VI. Negro

Abrahams, Roger D. "The 'Catch' in Negro Philadelphia." *KSFQ*, 8 (1963), 107–111.

————. *Deep Down in the Jungle . . .* Hatboro, 1964. Revised edition, Chicago, 1970.

————. "The Negro Stereotype: Negro Folklore and the Riots." *JAF* (special issue),

83 (1970), 229–249. Prepared comments by Hubert Locke, pp. 250–251, and reply by Abrahams, pp. 252–253.

———. "Playing the Dozens." *JAF*, 75 (1962), 209–219.

———. *Positively Black*. Englewood Cliffs, N.J., 1970.

———. "Some Riddles from the Negro of Philadelphia." *KSFQ*, 7 (1962), 10–17.

———. "The Toast: A Neglected Form of Folk Narrative." In *Folklore In Action*, edited by Horace P. Beck, pp. 1–11. Philadelphia, 1962.

Anderson, John Q. "The New Orleans Voodoo Ritual Dance and Its Twentieth-Century Survivals." *SFQ*, 24 (1960), 135–143.

Ayoub, Millicent R., and Barnett, Stephen A. "Ritualized Verbal Insult in White High School Culture." *JAF*, 78 (1965), 337–344.

Barnett, Stephen A. Reply to Bruce Jackson's "White Dozens and Bad Sociology." *JAF*, 80 (1967), 89–90 (below).

Beynon, Erdmann Doane. "The Voodoo Cult among Negro Migrants in Detroit." *AJS*, 43 (1938), 894–907.

Cole, Johnnetta. "Culture: Negro, Black, and Nigger." *The Black Scholar*, 1:10 (June, 1970), 40–44.

Cray, Ed. "An Acculturation Continuum for Negro Folksong in the United States." *EM*, 5 (1961), 10–15.

Dollard, John. "Dozens: Dialect of Insults." *American Imago*, 1 (1939), 155–164.

Dorson, Richard M. "The Career of 'John Henry.' " *WF*, 24 (1965), 155–164.

Dresser, Norine. "The Metamorphosis of the Humor of the Black Man." *NYFQ*, 24 (1970), 216–228.

Fauset, A. H. "Tales and Riddles Collected in Philadelphia." *JAF*, 41 (1928), 529–538.

Ferris, William R., Jr. "Racial Repertoires among Blues Performers." *EM*, 14 (1970), 439–449.

Haywood, Charles. "Negro Minstrelsy and Shakespearean Burlesque." In *Folklore and Society*, edited by Bruce Jackson, pp. 77–92. Hatboro, Pa., 1966.

Holyknecht, K. J. "Some Negro Song Variants from Louisville." *JAF*, 41 (1928), 558–578.

Jackson, Bruce. "What Happened to Jody?" *JAF*, 80 (1967), 387–396.

———. "White Dozens and Bad Sociology." *JAF*, 79 (1966), 374–377. Comment on Ayoub' and Barnett's "Ritualized Verbal Insult in White High School Culture" (above).

Keil, Charles, *The Urban Blues*. Chicago, 1965.

Kmen, Henry A. "Old Corn Meal: A Forgotten Urban Negro Folksinger." *JAF*, 75 (1962), 29–34.

Kornfield, Barry. "Reverend Gary Davis: Folksinger of the Streets." *Sing Out!* 9:4 (1960), 4–5.

Labov, William; Cohen, Paul; Robins, Clarence; and Lewis, John. *A Study of the Non-Standard English of Negro and Puerto Rican Speakers in New York City*. 2 vols. Cooperative Research Project no. 3288. New York, 1968.

Lee, C. "Negro Lore From Baltimore." *JAF*, 5 (1892), 110–112

Longini, Muriel Davis. "Folksongs of Chicago Negroes." *JAF*, 52 (1939), 96–111.

Major, Clarence. *Dictionary of Afro-American Slang*. New York, 1970.

Morgan, Kathryn L. "Caddy Buffers: Legends of a Middle Class Negro Family in Philadelphia." *KSFQ*, 11 (1966), 67–88.

Mullen, Patrick B. "A Negro Street Performer: Tradition and Innovation." *WF*, 29 (1970), 91–103.

Peterson, Clara Gottschalk. *Creole Songs from New Orleans in the Negro Dialect.* New Orleans, La., 1902.

Powdermaker, Hortense. "The Channeling of Negro Aggression by the Cultural Process." *AJS*, 48 (1948), 750–758.

Stearns, Marshall and Jean. "Frontiers of Humor: American Vernacular Dance." *SFQ*, 30 (1966), 227–235. Negro vaudeville and nightclub traditions.

Suthern, Orrin Clayton, II. "Minstrelsy and Popular Culture." *JPC*, 4 (1971), 658–673.

Szwed, John F. "Musical Adaptation among Afro-Americans." *JAF*, 82 (1969), 112–121.

———. "Negro Music: Urban Renewal." In *Our Living Traditions*, edited by Tristram Coffin, pp. 272–281. New York, 1968.

Winslow, David J. "Bishop E. E. Everett and Some Aspects of Occultism and Folk Religion in Negro Philadelphia." *KSFQ*, 14 (1969), 59–80.

VII. Occupational Lore

Labor and Industrial

Boatright, Mody C. *Folklore of the Oil Industry.* Dallas, 1963.

———. *Gib Morgan: Minstrel of the Oil Fields.* Dallas, 1958.

———, and William Owen. *Tales from the Derrick Floor.* New York, 1970.

Fowke, Edith. "Labor and Industrial Protest Songs in Canada." *JAF*, 82 (1969), 34–50.

Graves, Bernie. "Breaking Out: An Apprenticeship System Among Pipeline Construction Workers." *Human Organization*, 17 (1958), 9–13.

Green, Archie. "American Labor Lore: Its Meaning and Uses." *Industrial Relations*, 4 (1965), 51–68.

———. "John Neuhaus: Wobbly Folklorist." *JAF*, 73 (1960), 189–217.

———. "The Workers in the Dawn: Labor Lore." In *Our Living Traditions*, edited by Tristram Coffin, pp. 251–262. New York, 1968.

Hand, Wayland D. "American Occupational and Industrial Folklore: the Miner." In *Kontakte und Grenzen: Probleme der Volks- Kulture- und Sozialforschung*, edited by Hans Foltin, pp. 453–460. Gottingen, Germany, 1969.

Harding, Charles. "The Social Anthropology of American Industry." *AA*, 57 (1955), 1218–1231.

Hobsbaw, E. J. "Ritual in Social Movements." In *Primitive Rebels.* New York, 1963.

Jansen, William Hugh. "Lore of the Tankbuilders." *Hoosier Folklore Bulletin*, 3 (1944), 27–29.

Kornhauser, Arthur William. *Mental Health of the Industrial Worker: A Detroit Study.* New York, 1965.

Korson, George. *Coal Dust on the Fiddle.* Philadelphia, Pa., 1943.

———. *Minstrels of the Mine Patch.* Philadelphia, 1938.

McKelvie, Donald. "Aspects of Oral Tradition and Belief in an Industrial Region." *Folk Life*, 1 (1963), 77–94.

Smith, A. W. "Some Folklore Elements in Movements of Social Protest." *Folklore*, 77 (1966), 241–252.

Weiner, Harvey. "Folklore in the Los Angeles Garment Industry." *WF*, 23 (1964), 17–21.

Miscellaneous Urban Occupations

Allen, Lee. "The Superstitions of Baseball Players." *NYFQ*, 20 (1964), 98–109.

Bennett, John Michael. "Folk Speech and Legends of the Trade of House-Painting." *SFQ*, 33 (1969), 313–316.

Charpenel, Mauricio. "Calling Cards for an Old Profession." *Folklore Annual No. 1* of the University Folklore Association, pp. 16–19. Austin, Texas 1969.

Freud, Ralph. "George Spelvin Says the Tag: Folklore of the Theatre." *WF*, 13 (1954), 245–250.

Gross, Dan. "Folklore of the Theatre." *WF*, 20 (1961), 257–263.

Loomis, C. Grant. "Sign Language of Truck Drivers." *WF*, 5 (1956), 205–206.

Niederhoffer, Arthur. *Behind the Shield: The Police in Urban Society*. New York, 1967.

Phillips, George L. "Street-Cries of American Chimney-Sweepers." *NYFQ*, 8 (1952), 191–198.

Sanderson, Stewart. "The Folklore of the Motor-Car." *Folklore*, 80 (1969), 241–252.

Truzzi, Marcello. "The American Circus as a Source for Folklore." *SFQ*, 30 (1966), 289–300.

Whittlesay, Wes. "The Ritual of the Surgical Scrub." *NYFQ*, 20 (1964), 122–125.

Wilson, David. "Post Office Vocabulary." *KSFQ*, 7 (1962), 14.

Wilson, Gordon, and Clarke, Kenneth. "Folklore in Certain Professions: The English Teacher and Folklore." *TFSB*, 36 (1970), 25–28.

————, and Jesse Funk. "Folklore in Certain Professions: The Physician and Folklore." *TFSB*, 35 (1969), 1–5.

————, and Addie Suggs Hilliard. "Folklore in Certain Professions: The Shakespeare Teacher and Folklore, or Shakespeare's Nature at Mammoth Cave." *TFSB*, 33 (1967), 98–108.

Winslow, David J. "Occupational Superstitions of Negro Prostitutes in an Upstate New York City." *NYFQ*, 24 (1968), 294–301.

VIII. Other Urban Subcultures

Children

Abrahams, Roger D. *Jump-Rope Rhymes: A Dictionary*. Austin, Texas, 1969.

————. "Some Jump-Rope Rhymes from South Philadelphia." *KSFQ*, 8 (1963), 3–15.

————. "Some Jump-Rope Rhymes from Texas." *SFQ*, 27 (1963), 196–213.

Ashton, J. W. "Marble-Playing in Lewiston Fifty Years Ago." *Northeast Folklore*, 3 (1960), 24–27.

Atkinson, Robert M. "Songs Little Girls Sing: An Orderly Invitation to Violence." *Northwest Folklore*, 2 (1967), 2–7.

Berkovits, Rochelle. "Secret Languages of Schoolchildren." *NYFQ*, 26 (1970), 127–152.

Castagna, Barbara. "Some Rhymes, Games and Songs from Children in the New Rochelle Area." *NYFQ*, 25 (1969), 221–237.

Cray, Ed. "Jump-Rope Rhymes from Los Angeles." *WF*, 29 (1970), 119–127.

Culin, Stewart. "Street Games of Boys in Brooklyn." *JAF*, 4 (1891), 221–237.

Jablow, Alta, and Withers, Carl. "Social Sense and Verbal Nonsense in Urban Children's Folklore." *NYFQ*, 21 (1965), 243–257.

Jones, Michael Owen. "Chinese Jumprope." *SFQ*, 30 (1966), 256–263.

Krueger, John R. "Parodies in the Folklore of a Third Grader." *SFQ*, 32 (1968), 66–68.

Mills, Dorothy, and Bishop, Morris. "Songs of Innocence." *The New Yorker*, 13, no. 39 (1937), 32–42. Texts transcribed by Charles Seeger.

Opie, Iona and Peter. *The Lore and Language of Schoolchildren*. Oxford, England, 1960.

Philip, Andrew. "The Street Songs of Glasgow." *Tradition* (London), 1 (1966), 11–17.

Schwartz, Tony. *1, 2, 3 and a Zing, Zing, Zing*. Folkways Record FC 7003.

Silverstein, Arthur B. "Variations on Stickball." *NYFQ*, 21 (1965), 179–183.

Sutton-Smith, Brian, and Rosenberg, B. G. "Sixty Years of Historical Change in the Game Preferences of American Children." *JAF*, 74 (1961), 17–46.

Walker, Barbara K. "Folklore in the Schools Collected by Seventh Graders." *NYFQ*, 4 (1946), 228–236.

Williams, T. "A Game of Children in Philadelphia." *JAF*, 12 (1899), 292.

Winslow, David J. "Children's Derogatory Epithets." *JAF*, 82 (1969), 255–263.

———. "Children's Picture Books and the Popularization of Folklore." *KSFQ*, 14 (1969), 142–157.

Withers, Carl. "Current Events in New York City Children's Folklore." *NYFQ*, 3 (1947), 213–222.

College and High School

Ames, Karl. "Teaching Folklore in Urban High School." *NYFQ*, 21 (1965), 206–212.

Dorson, Richard M. "The Folklore of Colleges." *American Mercury*, 68 (1949), 671–677.

Gillespie, Angus K., and others. "Teaching and Collecting Folklore at a Boy's Prep School: Field Work Example from 'The Academy'—Pennsylvania." *KSFQ*, 15 (1970), entire special issue.

Huguenin, Charles A. "A Prayer for Examinations." *NYFQ*, 18 (1961), 145–148.

———. "Burial of Calculus at Syracuse." *NYFQ*, 17 (1961), 256–262.

Mook, Maurice A. "Quaker Campus Lore." *NYFQ*, 17 (1961), 243–252.

Reuss, Richard A. "An Annotated Collection of Songs from the American College Student Oral Tradition." M.A. thesis, Indiana University, Bloomington, 1965.

Reynolds, Neil B. "Lore from Union and Princeton." *NYFQ*, 17 (1961), 253–255.

"Scatological Lore on Campus." *JAF*, 75 (1962), 260–262.

Sherman, Constance. "Oberlin Lore." *NYFQ*, 18 (1962), 28–34.

Taylor, Archer. "Pedro, Pedro!" *WF*, 6 (1947), 228–231. College cheer or call.

Tillson, William. "Purdue Classroom Recollection." *NYFQ*, 18 (1962), 55–57.

Toelken, J. Barre. "The Folklore of Academe." In *The Study of American Folklore*, edited by Jan Brunvand, pp. 317–337. New York, 1968.

Drug Cultures and Lore

Bradley, Haldeen. "Riding the White Horse." *SFQ*, 25 (1961), 167–177.

Casey, John J., Jr., and Preble, Edward W. "Taking Care of Business—the Heroin User's Life on the Street." *International Journal of the Addictions*, 4 (1969), 1–23.

Feldman, Harvey. "Ideological Supports to Becoming and Remaining a Heroin Addict." *Journal of Health and Social Behavior*, 9 (1968), 131–139.

Finestone, Harold. "Cats, Kicks and Color." *Social Problems* 5 (1957), 3–13.

Mitchell, Eve. "Folklore of Marijuana Smoking." *SFQ*, 34 (1970), 127–130.

Spitzmiller, Olive. "The Head Community as Deviant Subculture." *Folklore Annual No. 1* of the University Folklore Association, pp. 1–11. Austin, Texas, 1969.

Miscellaneous Subcultures

Becker, Howard S. *Outsiders: Studies in the Sociology of Deviance*. London, 1963.

Carey, George C. "A Collection of Airborne Cadence Chants." *JAF*, 78 (1965), 52–61.

Fife, Austin and Alta. *Saints of Sage and Saddle*. Bloomington, Ind., 1956. Mormon lore.

Jackson, Bruce. "Folk Ingenuity behind Bars." *NYFQ*, 22 (1966), 243–250.

———. "Prison Folklore." *JAF*, 78 (1965), 317–329.

Thorpe, Peter. "Buying the Farm: Notes on the Folklore of the Modern Military Aviator." *Northwest Folklore*, 2 (1969), 11–17.

Underwood, Agnes. "Folklore from GI Joe." *NYFQ*, 3 (1947), 285–297.

IX. Folklore and Modern Mass Media

Brewster, Paul G. "Witchdoctor Advertising: Folklore in the Modern Advertisement." *NYFQ*, 14 (1958), 140–144.

Burns, Tom. "Folklore and Mass Communication: Television." *FF*, 2 (1969), 90–106.

Carpenter, Richard. "Ritual, Aesthetics, and TV." *JPC*, 3 (1969), 251–259.

Craigie, Carter W. "Folklore on Television." *Perspectives on Folklore and Education*, Folklore Forum, Bibliographical and Special Series no. 2 (1969), 28–31.

DuBose, Robert W., Jr. "Updating the Cowboy." *SFQ*, 26 (1962), 187–197.

Dundes, Alan. "Folklore and Advertising." *NYFQ*, 19 (1963), 143–151.

Hoffmann, Frank A. "Prologomena to a Study of Traditional Elements in the Erotic Film." *JAF*, 78 (1965), 148–153.

Linick, Anthony. "Magic and Identity in Television." *JPC*, 3 (1969), 644–655.

Mason, Julian. "Some Uses of Folklore in Advertising." *TFSB*, 20 (1954), 58–61.

McLuhan, Herbert Marshall. *The Gutenberg Galaxy*. Toronto, 1962.

———. *The Mechanical Bride*. New York, 1951.

———. *The Medium Is the Massage*. New York, 1967.

———. *Understanding Media*. New York, 1964.

Rosenberg, Neil V. "Some Comments on Folklore in the Mass Media." *FF*, 3 (1970), 39–41.

Steiger, Brad. *Beyond Unseen Boundaries*. New York, 1967.

Taylor, Mark. "Television Is Ruining Our Folktales." *Library Journal*, 84 (1959), 3822–3884.

INDEX

tinguished from Negroes', 75–76, 88–89, 91, 94; as distinct minority group, 76

migrants, rural: effects on, of urban experience, 49–50, 95–127 *passim*, 165–173. SEE ALSO Appalachia, people of; Appalachia, region of; migration to urban centers; rural tradition

migration to urban centers: from Appalachia, 95; reasons for, 165–166; effects of, 165–173; effect of, on family unit, 166–167, 168–169; and employment, 167, 168–169; effect of, on language dialects, 167, 169, 171; and clothing patterns, 167, 169, 171; and food, 167–171; and social activities, 168, 170, 171; and changes in education, 168, 170, 172. SEE ALSO Appalachia, people of; Appalachian medicine, attitudes and practices of; migrants, rural; rural tradition

Mihajlovich, Draža: as Serbian folk hero, 32, 46

Milio, Nancy: on folk medicine, 105; medical program of, 124

Miller, Bob: composes hillbilly music, 144; as song publisher, 150

minority groups: folk tradition of, 21–52, 55–57, 65–85, 95–127. SEE ALSO Appalachia, people of; Croatians; Greeks; Hungarians; Mexican-Americans; Negroes; Puerto Ricans; Serbians

Monroe, Bill: 146, 147, 154, 164

Monroe, Charlie: 146, 147

Moreland, "Peg": as itinerant balladeer, 140

Morris, James: 154

Moss, Leonard: 15

mother church issue: effect of, on Serbians, 32

mountains, Appalachian. SEE Appalachia, people of; Appalachia, region of

mountain songs. SEE hillbilly music

Muhammed Ali: as "cat," 84

Mullican, Moon: 151

music: of Negroes, 27, 44, 140, 142, 144, 147; of Serbians, 31, 32, 35, 44; of Croatians, 36; of Mexicans, 39; of Puerto Ricans, 42. SEE ALSO bluegrass music; country-western music; folk music; gospel music; hillbilly music; rock-and-roll music

music, commercial. SEE industry, entertainment

"musty": connotations of, in Negro folktales, 72

Nashville, Tenn.: country-western music in, 151, 154

"Nashville sound": in country-western music, 154

Nastich, Bishop Varnava: as Serbian folk hero, 33–35, 47, 48

Nathan, Sidney: and recording company, 151

nationalism: Serbian, in Indiana, 33–35, 47–48

Negroes: as subjects of urban folklore studies, 11; study of, in Indiana, 24–31; folktales of, 24–27, 69–85; and religion, 27–29, 44; influences of, in music, 27, 44, 140, 142, 144, 147; stereotyped, as slaves, 66; self-image of, 66, 69–70, 73–76, 84, 87; as distinct minority group, 75–76, 77; situation of, distinguished from Mexican-Americans', 75–76, 88–89, 91,

94; and the American Dream, 76, 79; and self-destruction, 84, 87; concept of "soul," 92; use of urban facilities, 98; and urban tensions, 165; poverty among, 165. SEE ALSO folktales, Negro; riots, Negro

New Mexico: Negro and Mexican-American activity in, compared, 75–76

Nicosia, John B.: as mayor of East Chicago, 22; mentioned, 42

North Uist: folklore studies in, 16, 21–22; tradition of, 22

Obilich, Miloš: as Serbian folk hero, 32

O'Daniel, Pat: 163

O'Daniel, W. Lee "Pappy": 163, 164

"Old Marster": mentioned, 24, 25; in Negro folktales, 70–71

oral culture: in Indiana, 45

Page, Patti: mentioned, 152

paramythia: among Greeks, in Indiana, 39, 43

Paris, Edmond: book by, mentioned, 32

Passmore, William: 23, 26

pathos: in Negro folklore, 88

Pavelich, Ante: Serbian folktale about, 32, 33

Pearsall, Marion: on Appalachia, 96, 113, 125; mentioned, 15, 16

Peer, Ralph: records hillbilly music, 141

Perkins, Carl: 153, 164

personal history: narratives of, among ethnic groups in Indiana, 44–45, 57; as genre, 45

Picou, Thomas: on newspaper coverage of Negroes, 26

Pinson, Bob: on western music, 160

plena songs: among Puerto Ricans, in Indiana, 42

pluralism, cultural. SEE cultural pluralism

Powell, Adam Clayton: as "cat," 84

preacher, the: in Negro folklore, 73, 86–87, 89

Presley, Elvis: and country-western music, 164; mentioned, 153

proverbs: Negro, in Indiana, 24, 25

Puerto Ricans: conflicts with Mexican-Americans, in Indiana, 40–41, 48; study of, in Indiana, 41–43; Voodoo tradition of, 42–43

"Pushin' Days": as example of Negro aggression, 70, 86, 89

racism: as topic of folklore study, 63–64

Radcliffe-Brown, A. R.: 16

Radich, Stepan: assassination of, 36

radio: and hillbilly music, 141, 142, 145–146, 149; border stations, 145–146. SEE ALSO country-western music; hillbilly music; industry, entertainment

Reed, Blind Alfred: as itinerant balladeer, 140

"Region," the (Indiana): folklore study in, 22–52. SEE ALSO East Chicago, Ind.; Gary, Ind.

religion: in Negro folk tradition, 27–31, 44; Serbian, in Indiana, 32–35, 47

revolution, agricultural: and migration to urban centers, 165–166

riots, Negro: message of, 65–66; motives of,